IMAGES
of America
OAK HILL

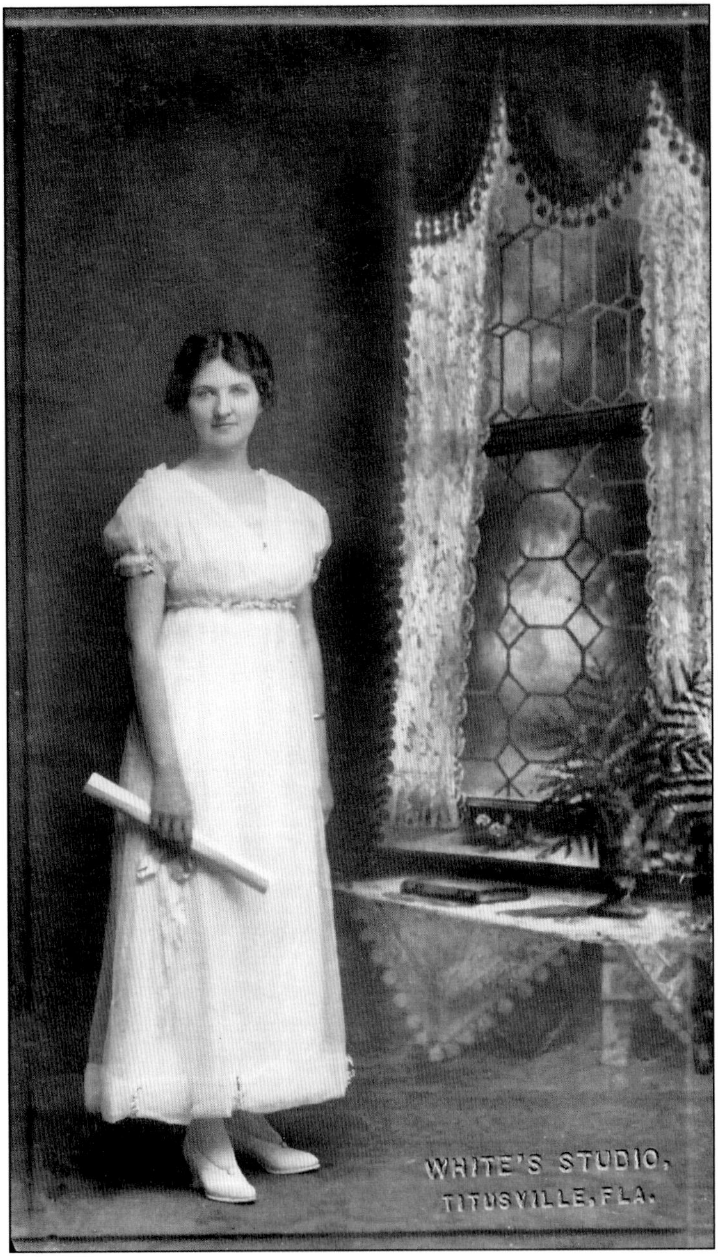

After her high school graduation in Titusville in 1915, Mary Mosby Baldwin married Van Buren Baldwin, and they moved to Oak Hill. They joined her brother, Leonard Mosby, in working at his general store. This is where the author's story begins, with her grandmother Mary's passion to contribute to the community and the photographs she left behind. (Courtesy of the author's collection.)

ON THE COVER: A successful day of Oak Hill fishing along the Indian River was shared in 1909 by (standing, from left to right) Josephine Haughton, Louisa Haughton, C. Williams, and Charles Ebenbeck. Eliza Ebenbeck is seated with one-year-old Kenneth Haughton. Charles Ebenbeck was justice of the peace at this time. (Courtesy of Hazel Haughton Wilkinson.)

IMAGES
of America

OAK HILL

Dana Thompson

ARCADIA
PUBLISHING

ISBN 978-0-7385-6859-1

Published by Arcadia Publishing
Charleston SC, Chicago IL, Portsmouth NH, San Francisco CA

Printed in the United States of America

Library of Congress Control Number: 2008936274

For all general information contact Arcadia Publishing at:
Telephone 843-853-2070
Fax 843-853-0044
E-mail sales@arcadiapublishing.com
For customer service and orders:
Toll-Free 1-888-313-2665

Visit us on the Internet at www.arcadiapublishing.com

To my family, who have invested their lives in making this community a better place, and to my grandchildren . . . the hope of the future.

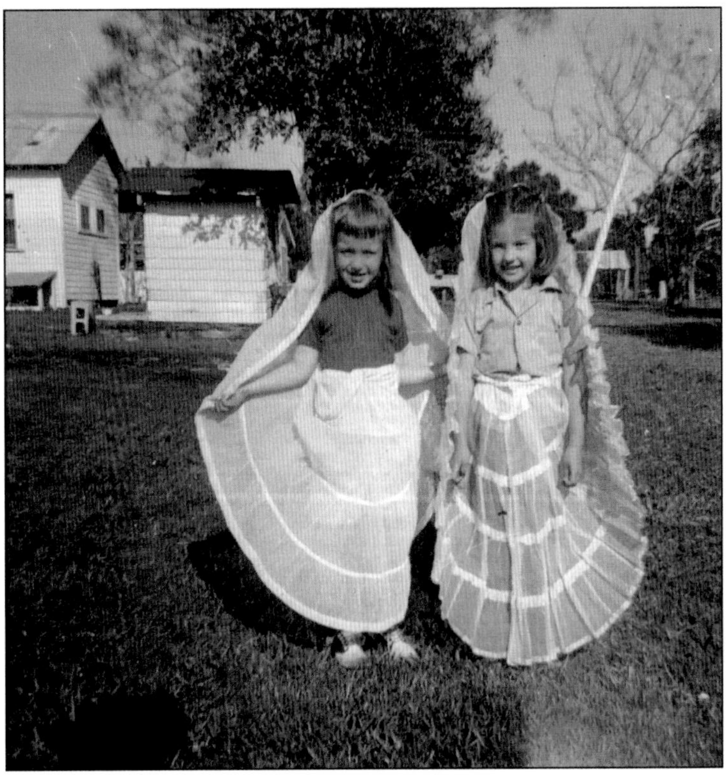

Welcome to a community where most families agree this is the best place on earth to enjoy a wonderful childhood. At least, Jennifer Goodrich Bonamo (left) and Becky Bellamy Ferguson (right) thought so. (Courtesy of Ida Goodrich.)

Contents

ACKNOWLEDGMENTS

The author is especially grateful to Ida Goodrich, wife of the longtime mayor Clarence Goodrich, for her photographs, constant encouragement, and investment in this project. It would not have happened without her and her sister, Marie Goodrich. Many thanks to the local historian, Betty Bellamy, who shared her many years of dedicated research and collection of photographs. The work done by Mary Dewees in 1984 also served as inspiration, as well as Joanne Sikes, Kathy Bittle, and the former local historical preservation board. Since many local families have lived here for four or more generations and are very proud of their heritage and home, this compilation of photographs, postcards, and memories of Oak Hill has been a community project. The author wishes to acknowledge the contributions of the following: Euda Mary Alderman, Sally Bayles, Edith Beauchamp, Cathy Berse, Kathy Bittle, Dot Burch, Edward Clark, Bill Dyall, Sally Gillespie, Johnnie Mae Golding, Jim Goodrich, Vernon Goodrich, Marie Griesse, Jo Ann Hilldale, Ida Haverly, Harlen Hutchins, Dorothy Lee Hutchinson, Frances Johnson, Lennon Guy Jordan Jr., Kathleen Laramie, Mary Ann Lopez, Bill McGee, Bill Mead, Dot Moore, Mary Ann Moffett, Patty Nelson, Martha Parks, Nikole Payne, Marion Porta, Johanna Riddle, Juanita Robinson, Marjorie Shine, Ann Simmons, Eddie Smith, Jan Spurgeon, Shirley Sullivan, Jean and Jimmie Vann, Richard Wheeler, and Hazel Wilkinson. Finally, to my husband, Mike, thank you for your love and encouragement, not just in this project, but in everything. Unless otherwise specified, the photographs are from the author's collection. All author proceeds from the sale of this book will go to the Community Trust, Inc., which will continue to tell the story of Oak Hill with pride.

INTRODUCTION

First documented on the 1564 map drawn by French explorer Jacque LeMoyne, Oak Hill has long played a part in the story of Florida. A walk along the high riverbanks reveals a glimpse of Oak Hill's history as the shell mounds emerge in the background. The Timucuan natives, who called this area home 2,000 years ago, created these mounds. The abundance of shellfish, mostly clams and oysters, and fish made this an ideal area for a permanent settlement.

Although many such mounds and middens were made along the Volusia County coastline, most of them were destroyed at the dawn of the 20th century by the demand for shell to make roads. In 1880, Lord Hatton Turnor built a house on and around the coastal mounds in Oak Hill. Fortunately, in the early 1900s, Wesley Snyder purchased the Turnor house and refused to give in to the economic pressure to sell the shell for roads, thus preserving an important part of the area's past. These ancient middens are also a reminder to visitors of the lure and serenity of coastal Florida during the golden age of tourism.

In the 1850s, the Swift brothers, William, Rodolphus, and Obed, of Massachusetts identified the old twisted oak trees along this same riverfront area as their "point of entry" to the live oak forests. It is believed that the name of the town originated with these seasonal loggers who arrived in the fall to cut timber for Northern shipbuilding.

Life in this rural southeast Volusia County community has always been simple, sustained by the bountiful waters of the Indian River and Atlantic Ocean, and supported by land rich in timber and well suited for farming. The treasures of a diverse ecosystem of a lagoon, marshland, cypress hammock, and pine forest drew those first Florida pioneers who settled in Oak Hill following the Civil War. The local cemetery has 11 Civil War veteran burials—five Union and six Confederate. Many settlers harvested the natural resources of timber, turpentine, and salt, while others worked as beekeepers, citrus growers, or fishermen.

The center of the settlement gradually shifted from the river when the railroad came through in the late 19th century. Early settlers like the Andersons, Sauls, and Howeses donated land to the railroad company so it would pass through the town. They were willing to invest in the progress of the area and understood what additional transportation could mean to those who lived and worked in Oak Hill. Corrals were soon built close to the railroad tracks so cattle could be sent by railcar. Citrus grove owners took advantage of moving individual and company fruit by rail, expanding the market. Soon fish, turtle, and shellfish were being shipped to fine restaurants as far north as New York. The first store, owned by William Howes, moved from the shores of the Indian River to the west closer to the new railroad.

The passage of the 18th Amendment in 1919 brought a new kind of business to the town. The unique location of the beach ridge and lagoon provided easy access for the distribution of illegal liquor being smuggled by boats from the Bahamas. This colorful period of Oak Hill's past is filled with amazing stories shared only on the back porch by best friends.

By 1924, the Dixie Highway was paved, bringing more businesses, buildings, and activity to the town. Automobile gas stations, garages, grocery stores, cafés, a citrus packinghouse, and even a hotel were built along newly constructed U.S. Highway 1. By this time, there were churches, schools, a community center, and the beginning of a city government. The Florida State Legislature granted a city charter to Oak Hill in 1927, establishing a mayor-commission form of government. However, the country was in a depression, and a petition was filed in 1930 to deactivate the government until further notice. The fight to reactivate in 1962 was led by J. U. Gillespie and his son, William Gillespie. The city election was held, and Clarence Goodrich Jr. became mayor in 1963 and remained in that position for the next 27 years. Mayor Goodrich worked diligently to move the city forward while maintaining the uniqueness and charm of the place where he was born and lived his entire life.

Since 1907, when early pioneer families established the Village Improvement Association, there has been a community spirit of helpfulness and concern for others by most residents. Social gatherings were frequently held, usually involving music, food, dancing, and baseball games. The Woodmen of the World Hall was built in 1911 for civic and town meetings. Concerned for the education of the local children, the people established their own school board and built a schoolhouse.

Families grew, and most generations that followed remained in the area, many on the land claimed by their forefathers. Four and five generations later, families continue fishing the waters that were familiar to their great-grandfathers. Some have replanted citrus groves on family land. A few still have beehives as a hobby. Life is still simple, for the most part, enriched by the natural beauty and pristine environment that drew Oak Hill's first inhabitants to the area. The lagoon, known both as the Mosquito Lagoon and Indian River Lagoon, is a unique geological feature of the area. Considered to be the most diverse estuary in North America, the lagoon supports more than 3,000 species of animal and plant life, including dolphins, sea turtles, and more than 100 species of birds. The "rules of the river" have changed, and many local commercial fishermen are now fishing guides. State legislators passed a net ban in the 1990s, and local nets were hung up for the last time in 1995, ending commercial fishing in Oak Hill. The state offered a new program for commercial fishermen and provided training in clam farming.

Weather was another crucial factor in area economics for those people who were citrus growers. Hard freezes over several decades ended citrus as a thriving industry. However, today most residents enjoy living where their ancestors put down their roots and gladly commute north or south to earn their livelihood. The city leaders of Oak Hill continue to work toward improving economic, environmental, and cultural areas while preserving the richness of its history and heritage. Most citizens embrace positive, planned changes that are necessary but continue to value their heritage, understanding that the struggles and hard work of good families is what built this community.

One

Earliest Inhabitants

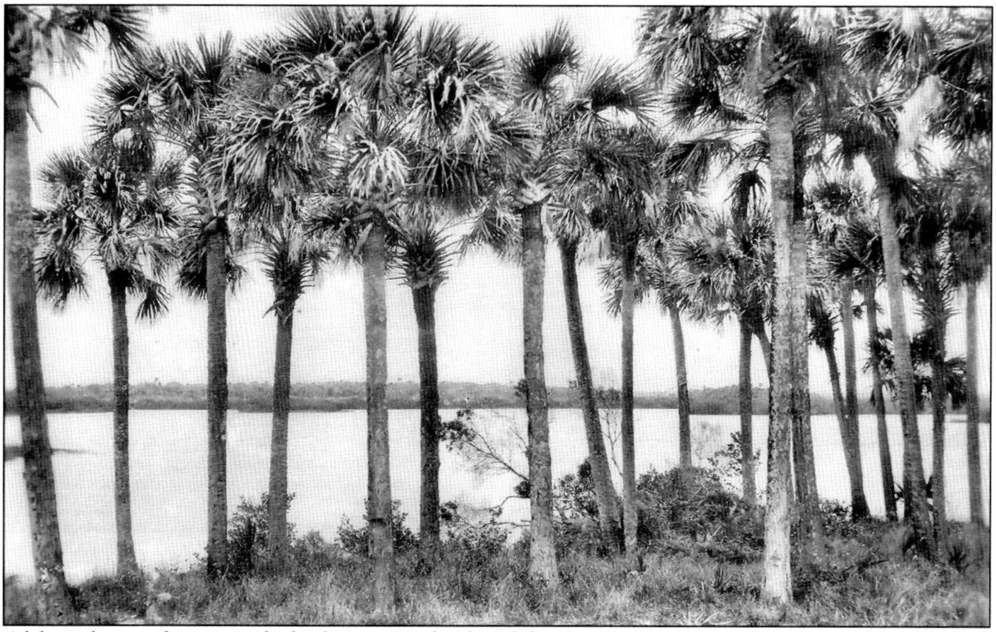

Although time has passed, the beauty and gifts of the river remain. It continues to provide food, transportation, recreation, and hope brought by each new sunrise. Locals and tourists alike enjoy climbing high on a hill to catch the beauty and river breezes, often unaware of the stories that remain hidden in the piles of oysters and clam shells that lie beneath the grass-covered mounds. In 1990, archaeologists learned a great deal about the tribe of early natives that lived along the Oak Hill river shore from 2000 BC until the Europeans arrived in the 1500s.

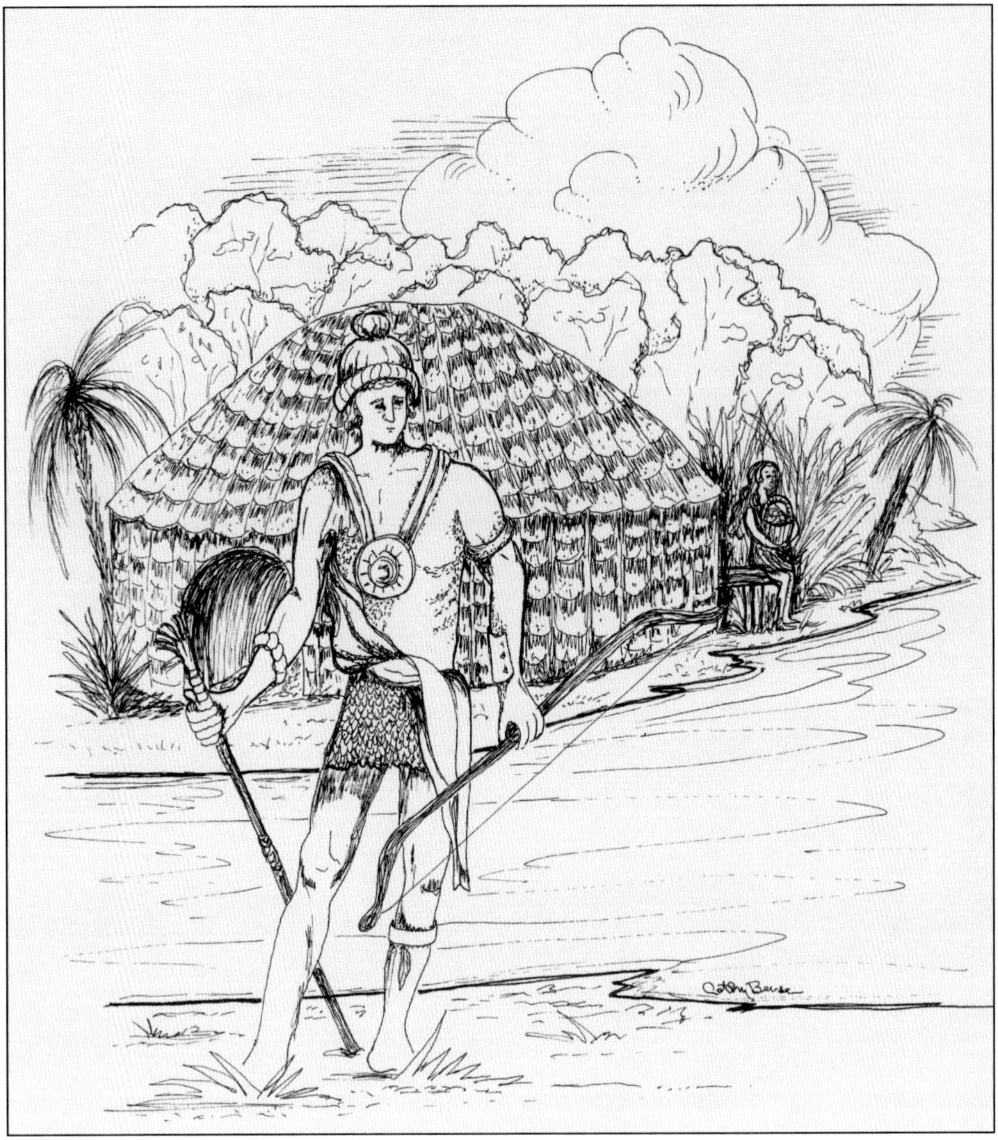

These Timucuans, as the tribe was called, harvested food from the river, discarding oyster and clam shells, and the remains from trout, shark, and bass. Over time, this life pattern created an 18-foot-high mound, 340 by 740 feet across, and with 17 layers. Inside some of these layers, archaeologists also found dried berries, charcoal, ash, ceramics, and shards of pottery. It is believed the Timucuans established a permanent village in this area because food was plentiful from the lagoon and nearby forest, which provided meat boiled in broths. Plants, roots, nuts, and berries were also used to prepare their food. Dugout canoes took them to deeper waters, and traps, nets, and spears were used to catch fish. When illustrator Jacques LeMoyne came to Florida as part of the French Expedition, he left the only visual record of this now-extinct civilization. Prior to 1900, many such mounds existed along the river shore, but Henry Flagler needed shell for roads and fill on the railroad as he pushed south. Most of the mounds were destroyed, sold by the railroad car loads. In 1918, it is recorded that 2,000 railroad cars of shell were removed from area mounds. Local artist Cathy Berse provided her impression of Timucuan life in Oak Hill about 1,200 years ago.

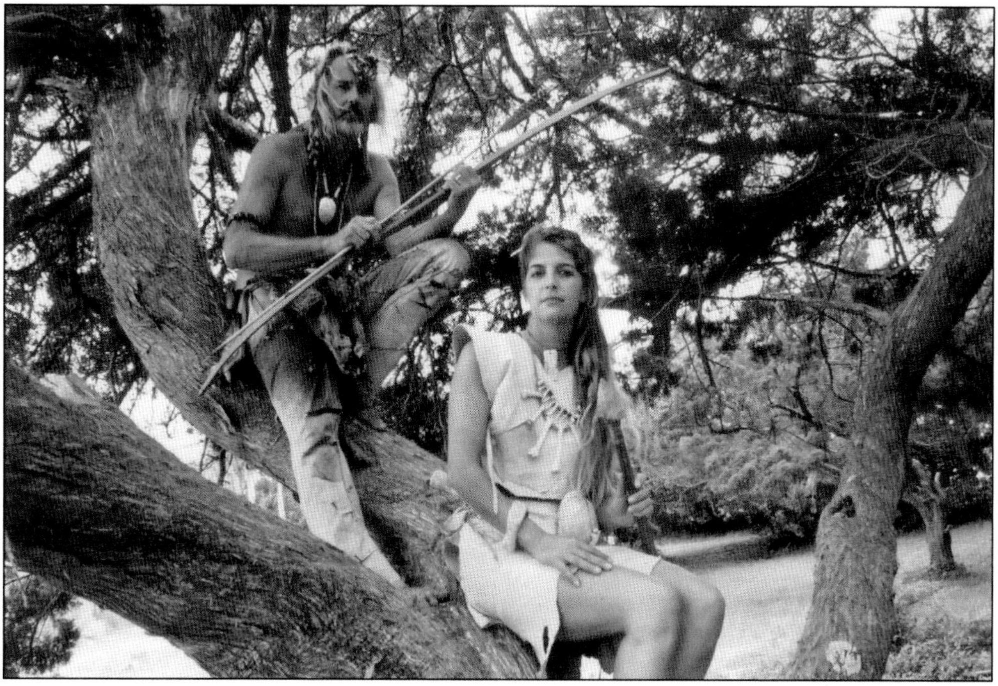

Native Timucuan reenactors Reese Moore and Andrea Kirlinger remind visitors today of the importance of hunting for small game such as deer and birds. They used bows, arrows, and spears, much like those Reese is holding.

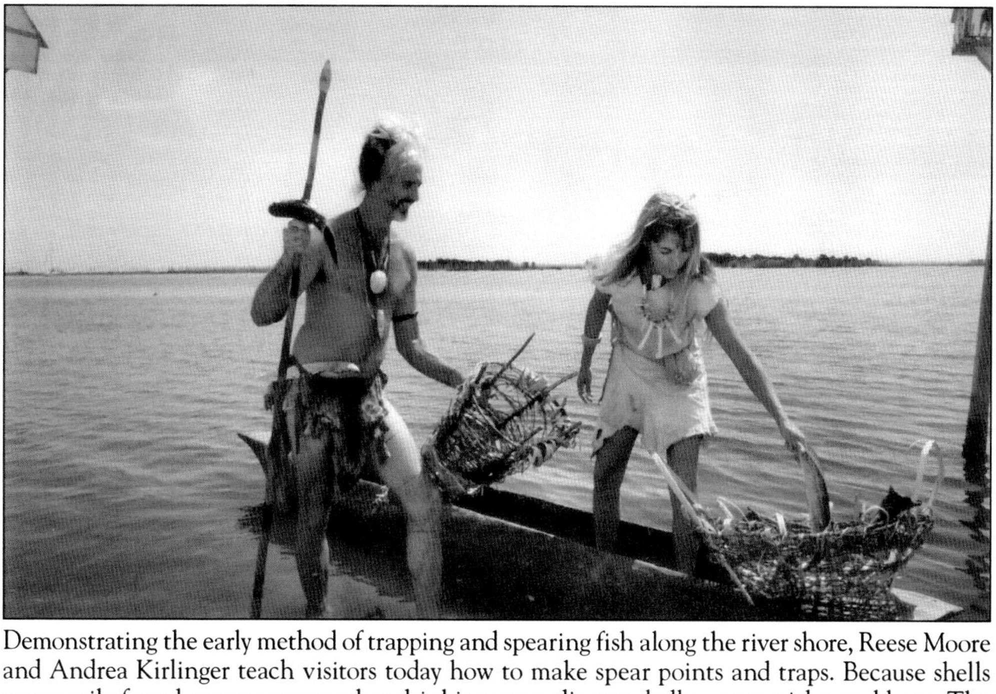

Demonstrating the early method of trapping and spearing fish along the river shore, Reese Moore and Andrea Kirlinger teach visitors today how to make spear points and traps. Because shells were easily found, many were used as drinking cups, dippers, ladles, axes, picks, and hoes. The Timucuans made a shell hoe from the whelk, a large sea snail that builds a hard shell from the calcium carbonate extracted from seawater.

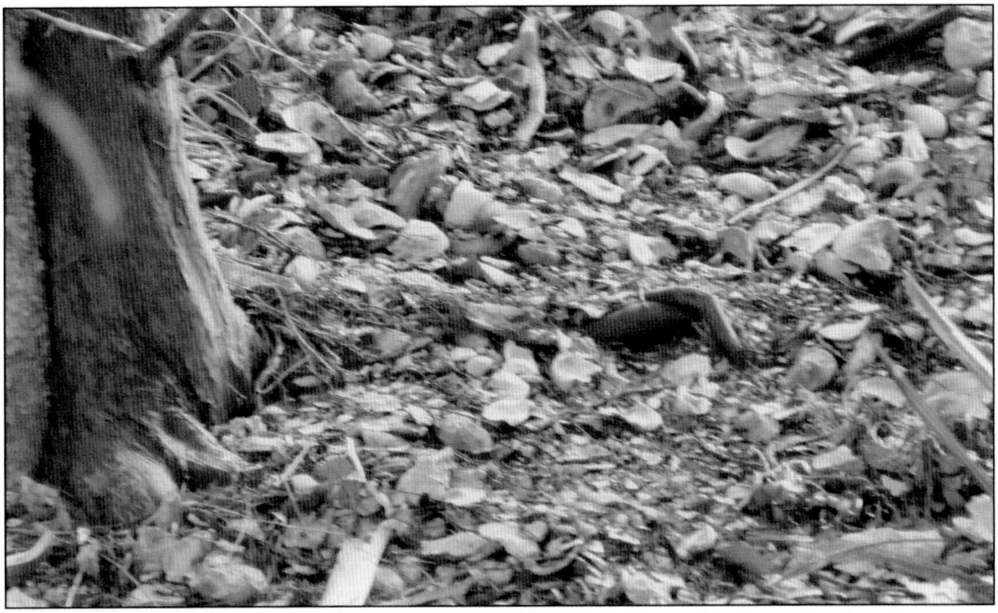

The ancient midden remains, with piles of oyster and clam shell eaten by those who have long gone before us. In 1917, Amos W. Butler wrote in a paper he presented to Congress on his observations of shell mounds of the eastern coast of Florida, "The Oak Hill Mound, perhaps the largest in area in the entire territory, has been purchased by the county for road purposes. . . . they should by all means be preserved." A debt of gratitude is owed to Wesley Snyder, who refused to sell the shell for road building at the beginning of the 20th century, according to his granddaughter, Marion Snyder Porta.

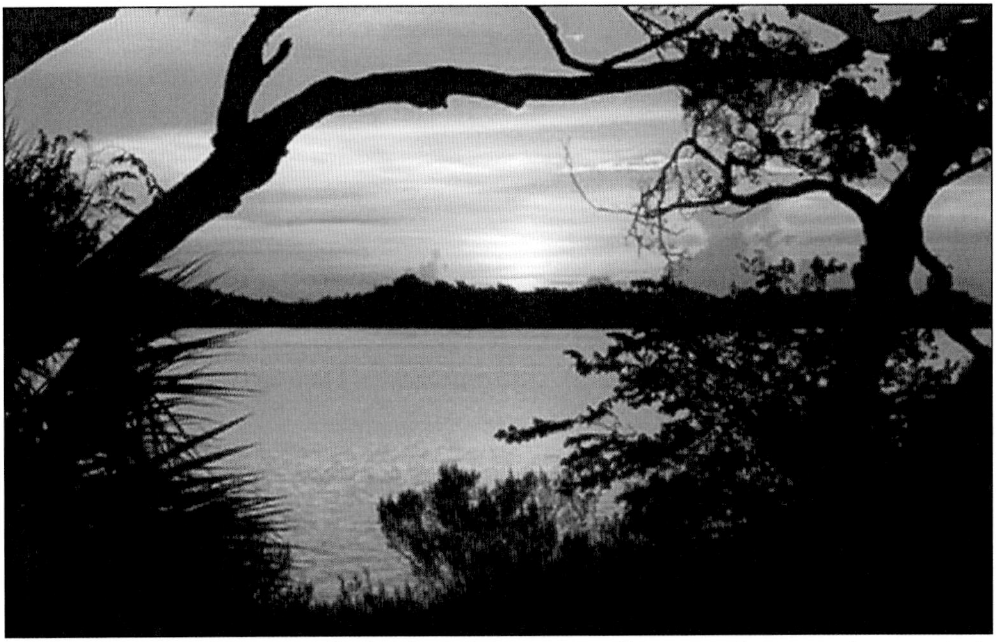

This view remains for present-day locals and tourists to reflect on its beauty and to creatively imagine all that happened on this mound in the past. It has become a place for many people to escape, relax, and refresh before reentering their busy world with all its demands.

Two

Tied to the River and Land

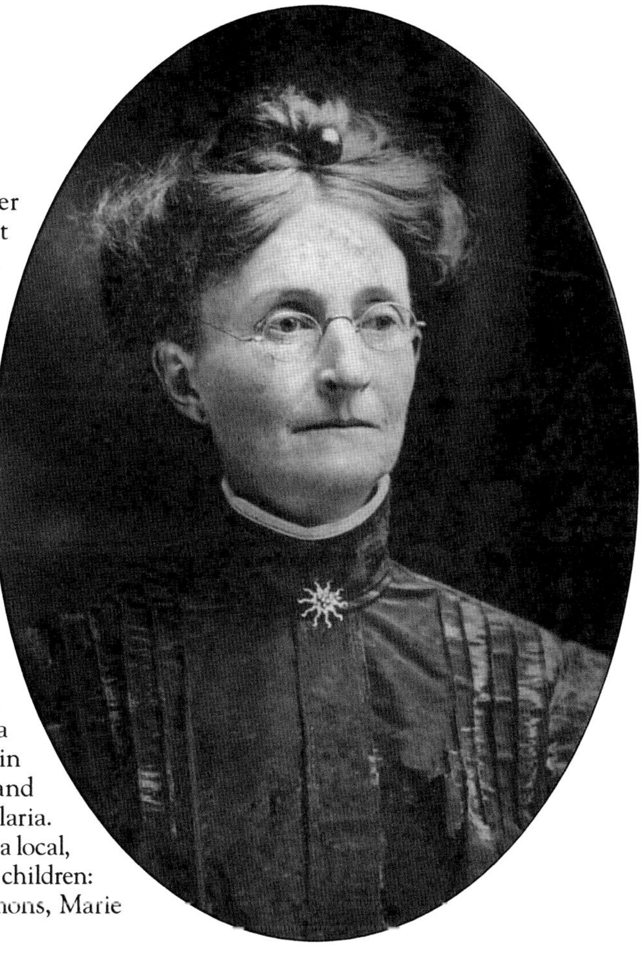

New Yorkers Dr. Henry Guller and his first wife, Anna, bought 40 acres of land in Oak Hill in 1890. They developed extensive orange groves here, coming from Mount Dora, where they had been homesteaders in the 1880s. He was an osteopath and former Methodist minister. Two years after his wife's death, Dr. Guller married Ida Daniel Henry, a widow from Tennessee (pictured here), in 1910. She came to Oak Hill with her youngest daughter, Ida Elizabeth Henry, age 14. The new Mrs. Guller was a former elementary school teacher and taught piano lessons. She owned one of the first cars in Volusia County. Their early experiences in the area included a hurricane and young Ida's serious illness with malaria. Her daughter Ida Elizabeth married a local, Harry Simmons, and they had four children: Lillian (Papouleas), Arthur Simmons, Marie (Goodrich), and Ida (Goodrich).

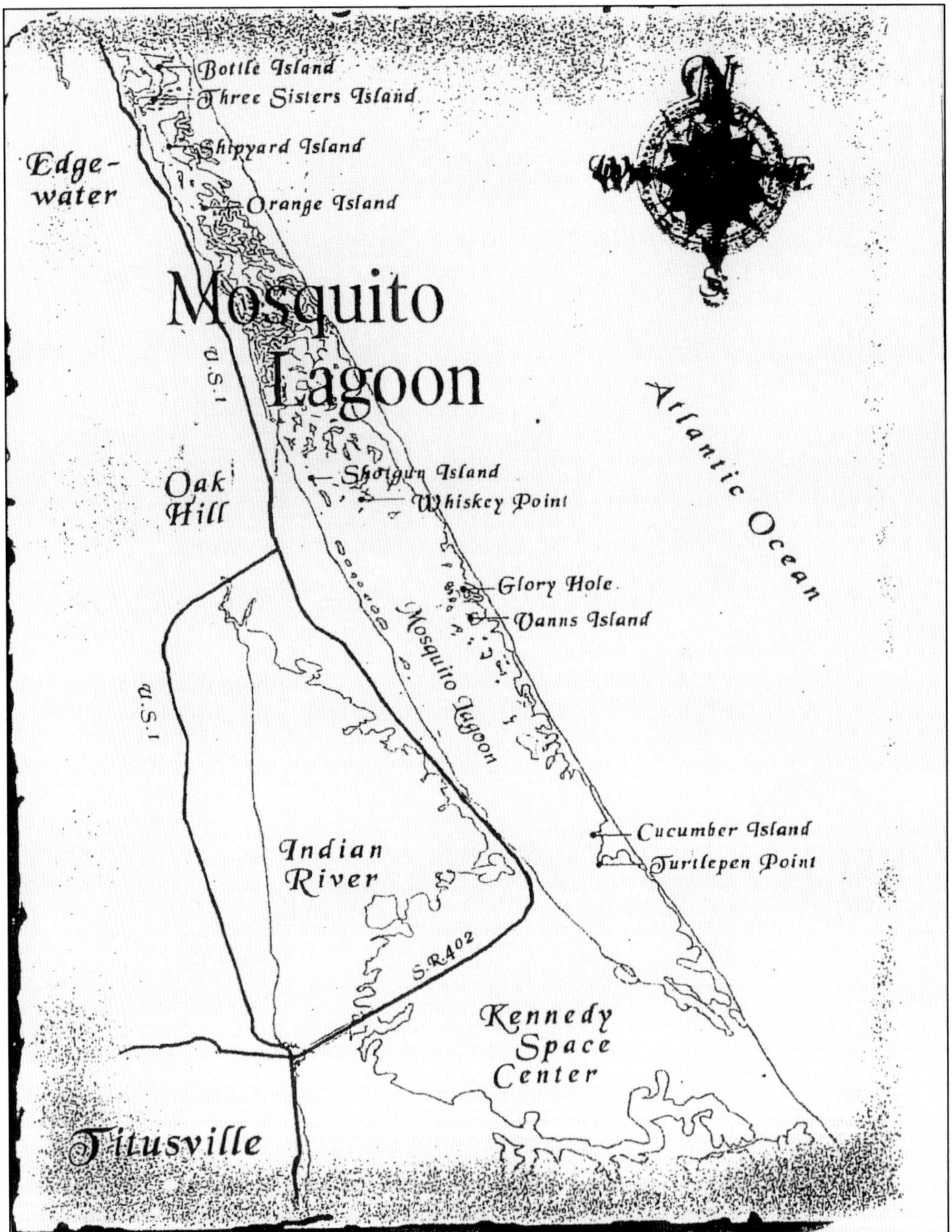

This map of Mosquito Lagoon will be helpful as the story of Oak Hill unfolds. Adolphus and Elonza Swift set up a successful logging business in the Oak Hill area. Having obtained a government contract to cut cedar and live oaks needed for shipbuilding, they entered the Ponce Inlet and came south. They approached a high stand of live oaks along the shore dotted with shell mounds. They used this landmark as their point of entry, calling it Live Oak Hill. Lumber crews began cutting the huge trees and floated them north to the inlet, where they were loaded on sailing vessels just off shore. Note Vann's Island on the map, where John Darling Vann and Hannah Vann settled in 1850. (Courtesy of the *Daytona Beach News-Journal.*)

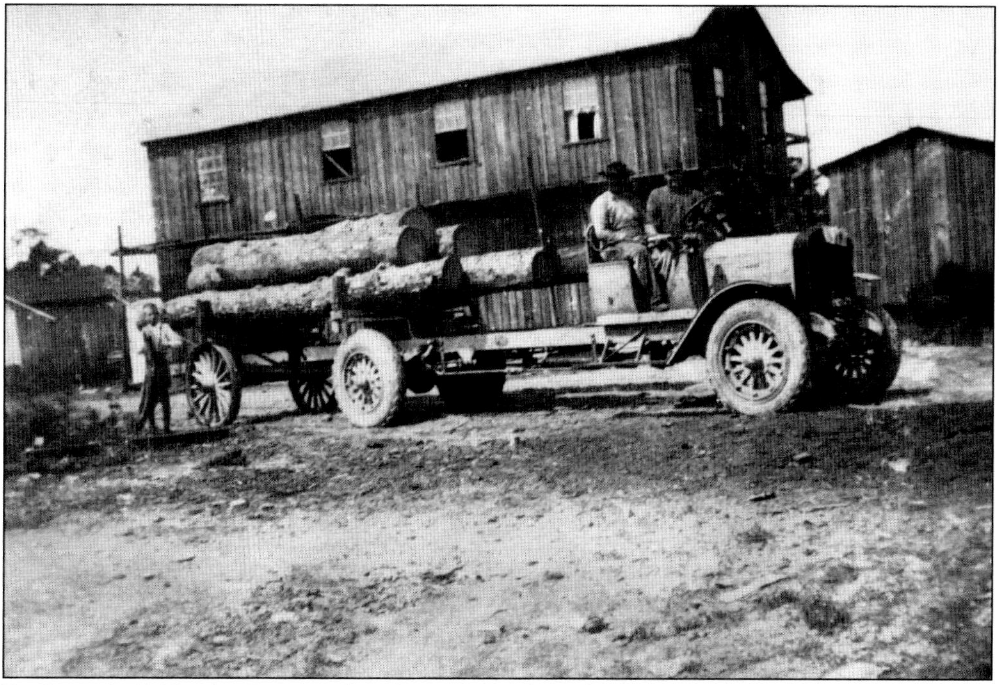

By the early 1900s, the Owen and Little Company leased 1,000 acres to the west and established a turpentine camp and lumber mill. Logs were pulled by mule and were loaded onto log cars. Loggers were often prisoners or escaped convicts, and they camped out in the woods to cut down the trees. In a 1911 postcard simply signed "Roy," he writes, "The three standing next to me in the picture are murderers, and the other is charged with stealing a cow." (Courtesy of Lennon Guy Jordan Jr.)

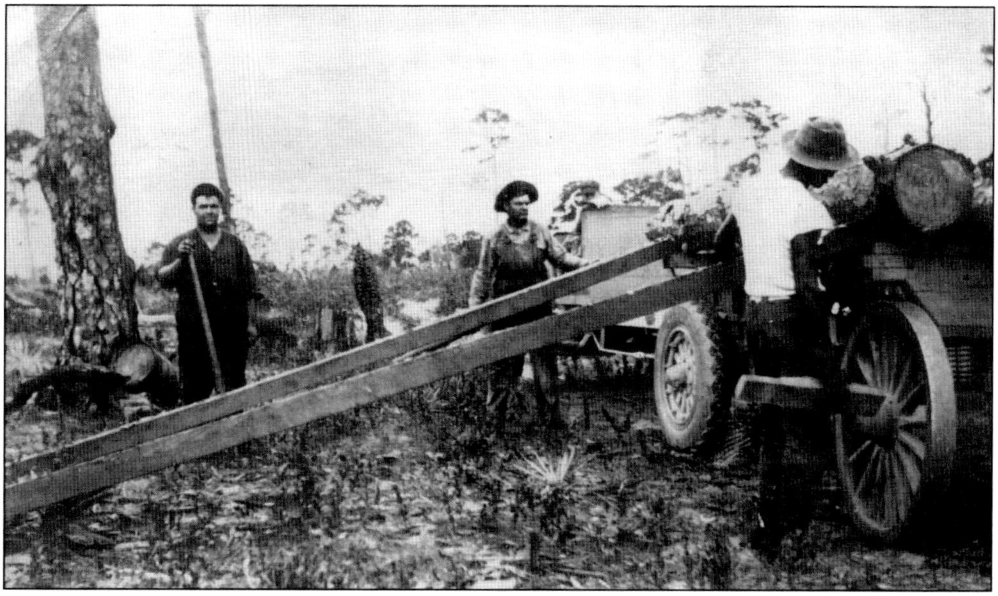

Eddie Jordan and his wife, Amanda, also owned a sawmill. Once loaded, the logs were hauled to a nearby lumberyard, where the process of cutting them into lumber continued. (Courtesy of Lennon Guy Jordan Jr.)

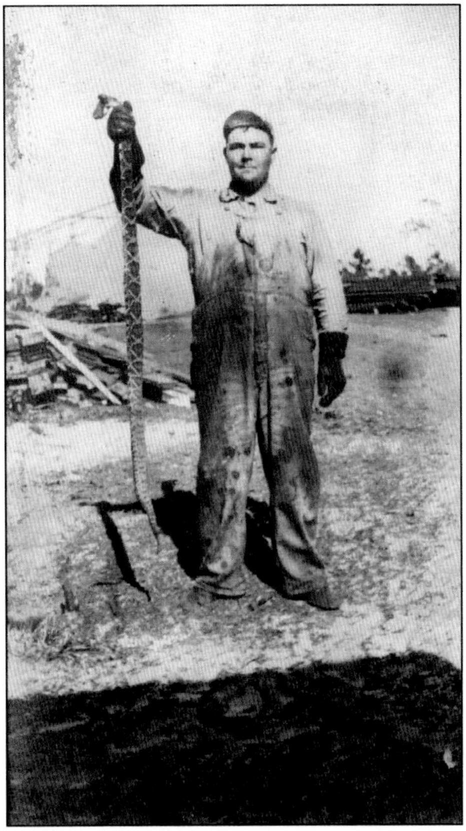

The intense heat from the Florida sun and pesky mosquitoes were not the only difficulties the laborers encountered. This unidentified worker won the battle with a diamondback rattlesnake. (Courtesy of Lennon Guy Jordan Jr.)

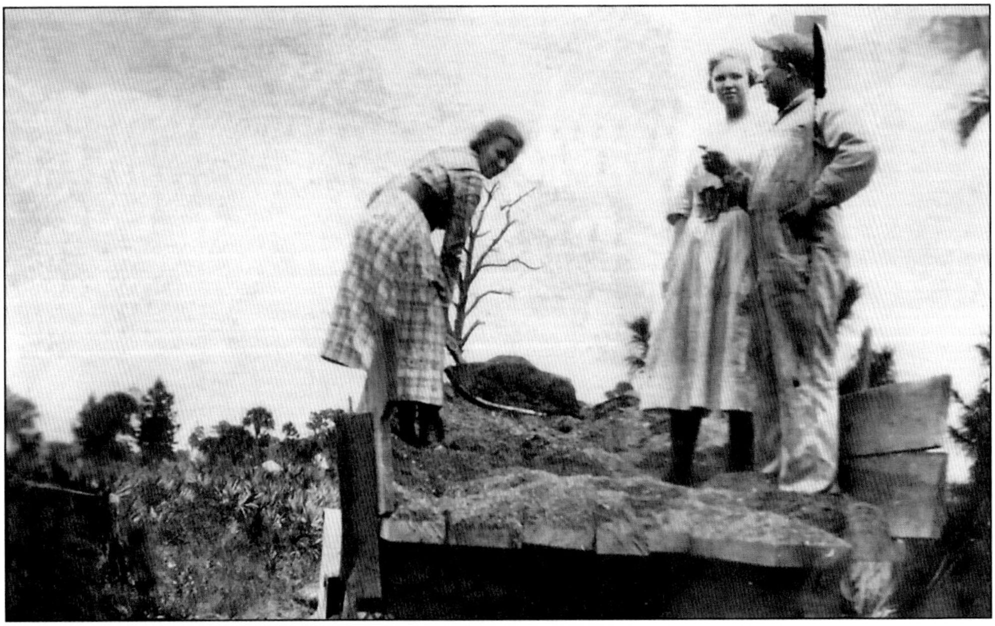

Even the ladies participated in unloading the sawdust, a by-product of the lumbering operation. The kilns were fired by sawdust to provide power for the frame shanties built for the workers. (Courtesy of Lennon Guy Jordan Jr.)

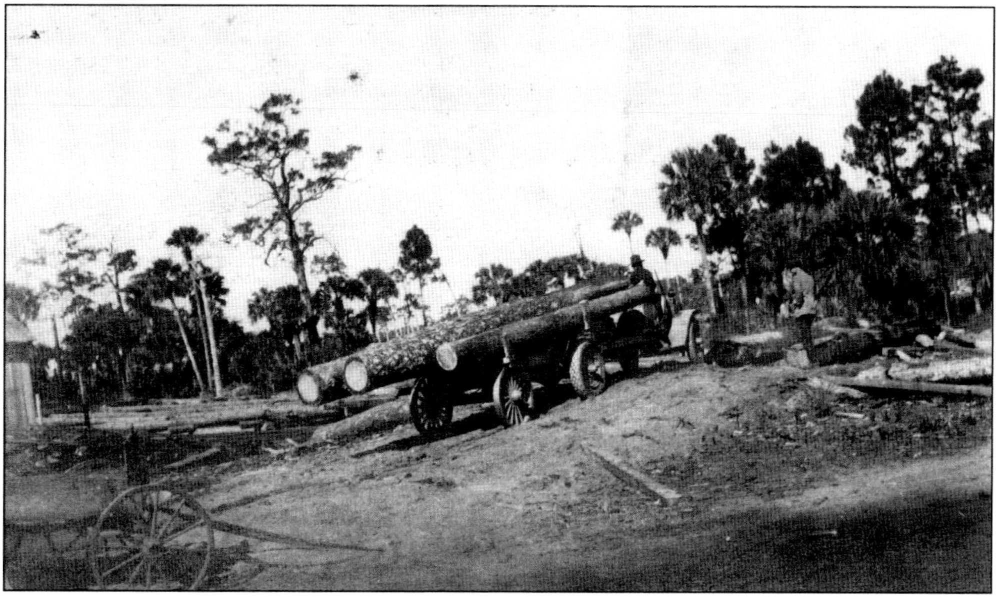

Laborers were paid daily with company coins in the hope that they would spend their earnings at the company store, known as the commissary. The wage at the time was $1 for an 11-hour day. (Courtesy of Lennon Guy Jordan Jr.)

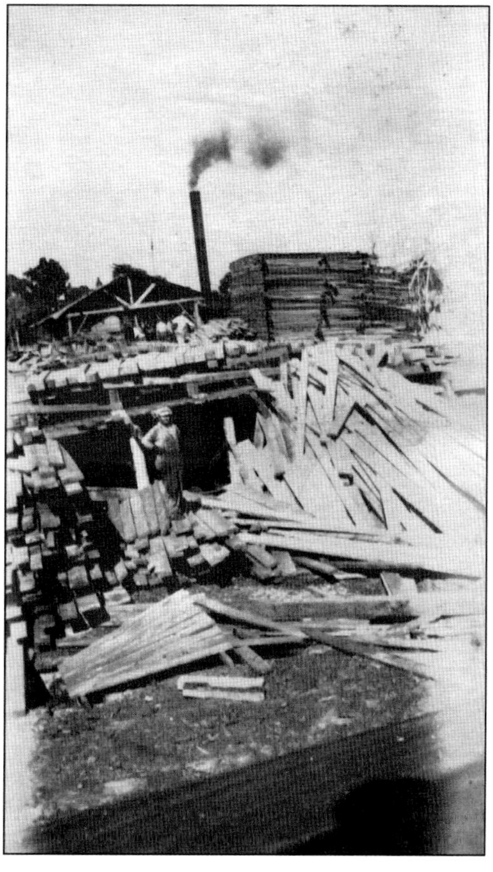

The smoke in the background indicates that the mill was in full operation because the boilers were producing the power for the saws to cut the timber, which was then loaded onto railroad cars and shipped out. (Courtesy of Lennon Guy Jordan Jr.)

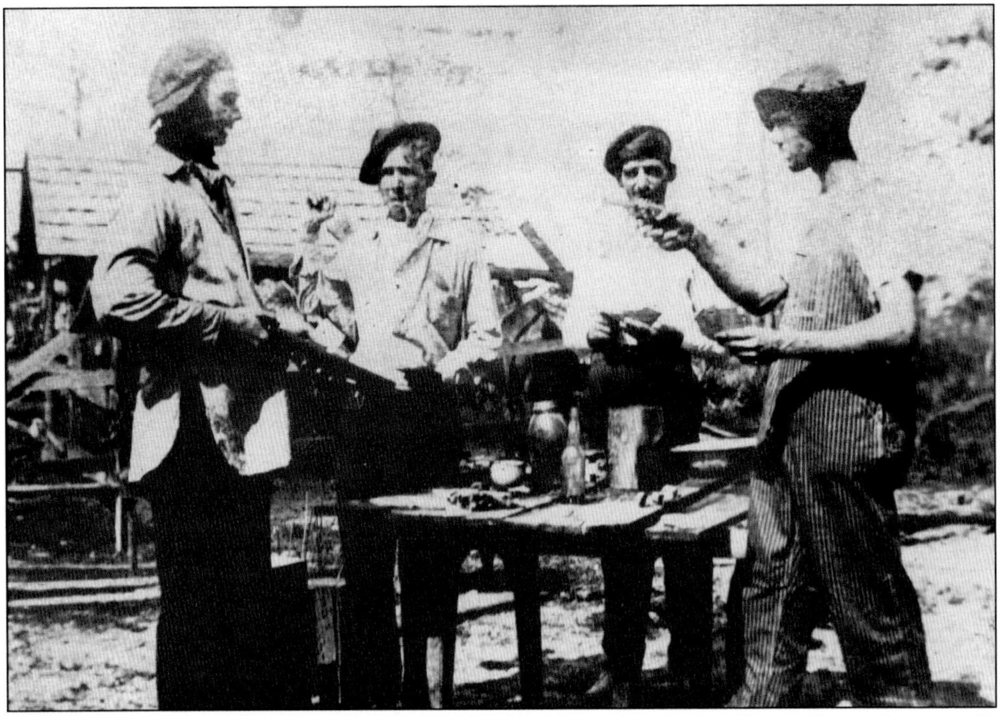

Unidentified laborers offer a glimpse of what their break time might have been like at the sawmill. (Courtesy of Lennon Guy Jordan Jr.)

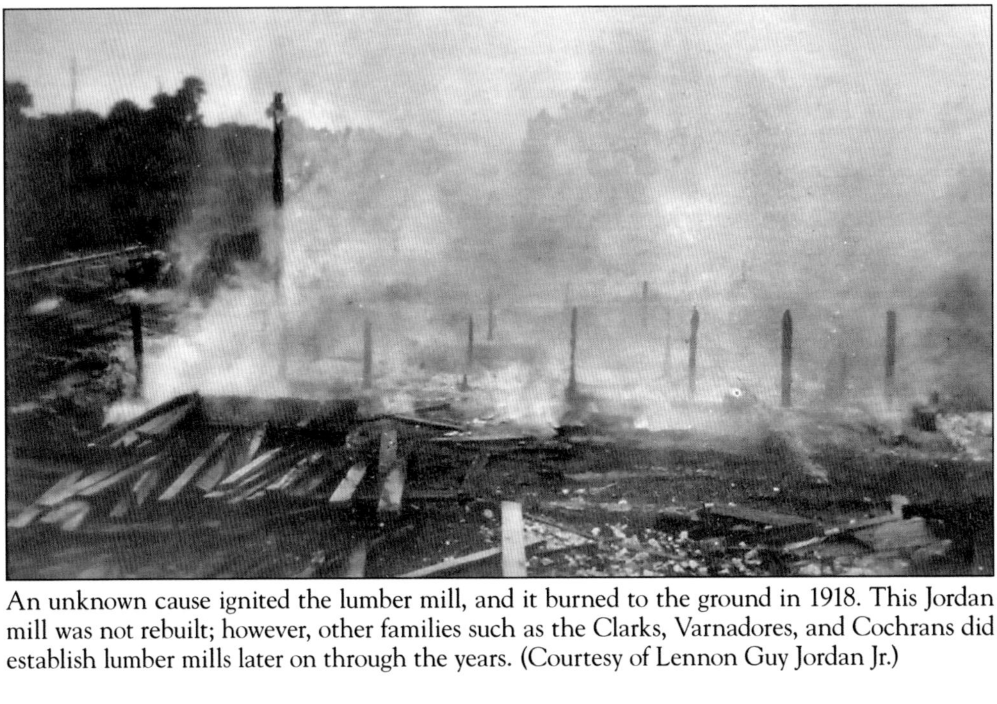

An unknown cause ignited the lumber mill, and it burned to the ground in 1918. This Jordan mill was not rebuilt; however, other families such as the Clarks, Varnadores, and Cochrans did establish lumber mills later on through the years. (Courtesy of Lennon Guy Jordan Jr.)

Born on September 11, 1832, John Darling Vann was a private in the Florida Infantry, Company E, 2nd Battalion, Confederate States of America. While working on a sailing ship after the Civil War, John met Hannah, an immigrant from Denmark, who was traveling on his ship. They married and moved to an island in Mosquito Lagoon, still known today as Vann's Island. Once they built a house and settled on the island, Hannah never left. They had three children: John (born 1889), Mabel, and Leon. The family grew vegetables and sold them to people going up and down the river. (Courtesy of Dot Burch.)

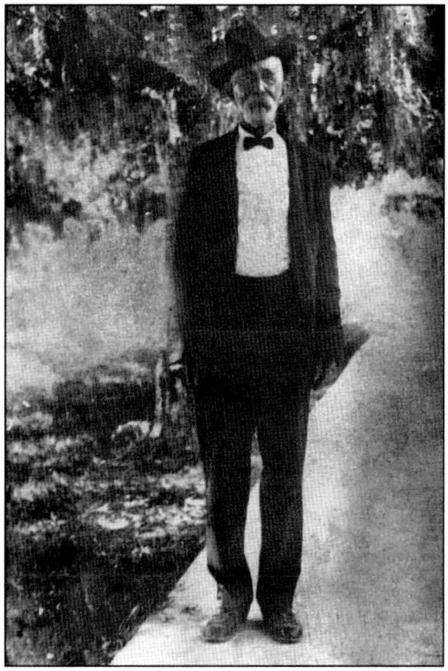

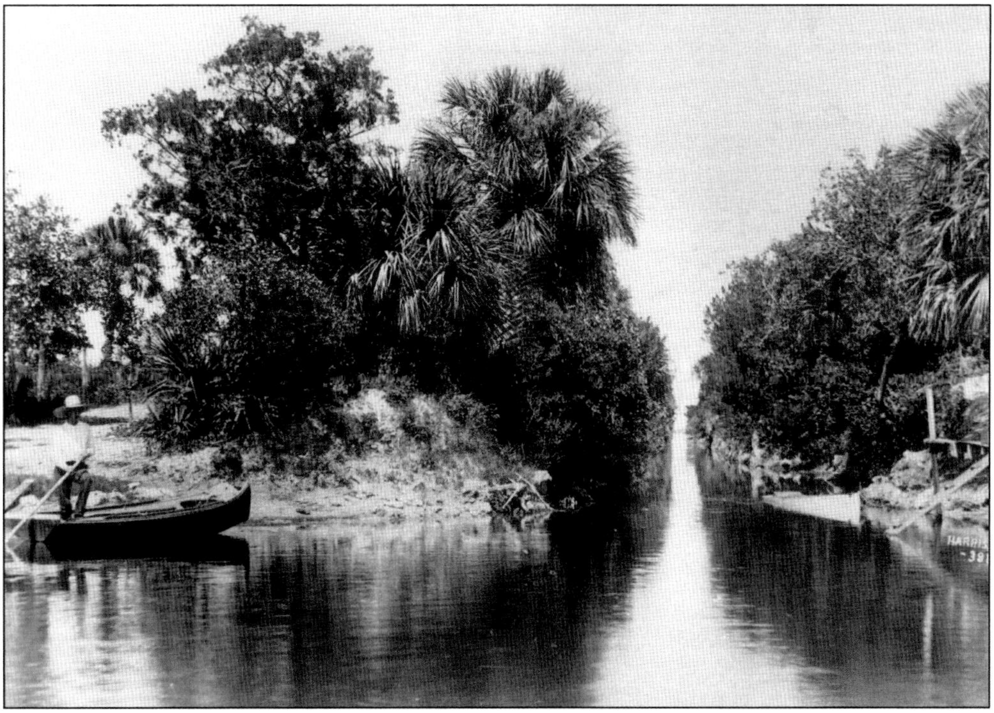

John Vann worked as one of the first haulers at Haulover Canal, where boats were hauled over the mainland from Mosquito Lagoon to the Indian River. There was a system of rollers and skids implemented to drag schooners from the lagoon to the river across half a mile of sand and scrub. As early as 1824, James Gadsden, aide to Gen. Andrew Jackson, advised the building of a canal at this location. Again in 1840, Gen. Zachary Taylor advised the need for a canal, but it took 10 more years before a small 8-foot-wide, 2-foot-deep, 725-yard-long canal was dug with shovels.

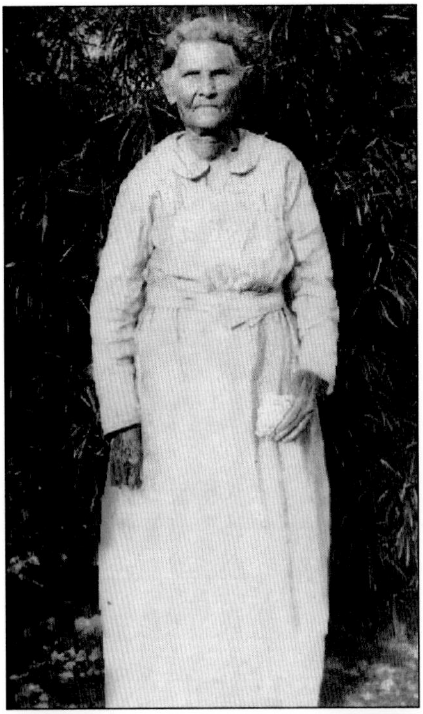

Julia Ann Osteen Hagin lived on Orange Island, just north of Vann's Island. She was married to Edward Hagin and had a daughter named Lena. Since it is believed these were the only two families that claimed residence on the Lagoon Islands, it seems only natural that Johnny Vann and Lena Hagin were destined to fall in love. (Courtesy of Jimmie Vann.)

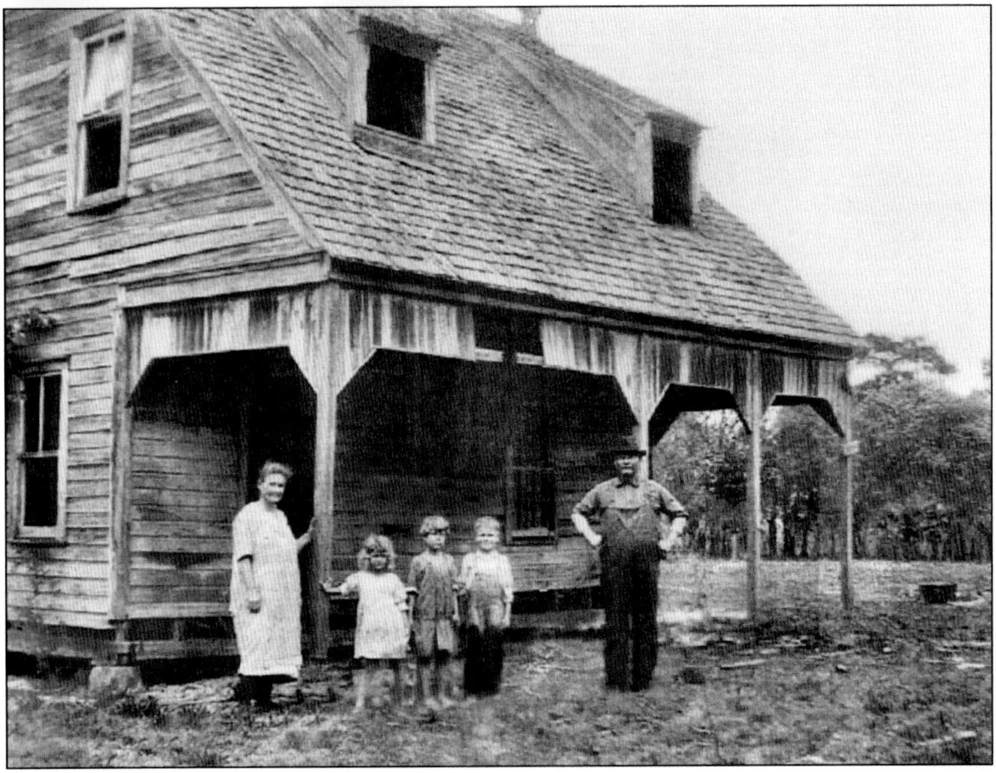

The Hagin House on Orange Island was always a busy place. Standing between their parents are (from left to right) Lena, Mable, and Wyatt. (Courtesy of Jimmie Vann.)

Young Johnny Vann moved to the mainland when he was 14 years old to attend school. He became a commercial fisherman and later owned a fish house. However, most locals remember stories of his "rum-runnin'" days, with more than 30 moonshine stills on the Lagoon Islands he knew so well. He also ran a boat to the Bahamas to sell his moonshine and pick up bonded whiskey. He was paid $300 a boatload until Al Capone's men offered him $600 to work for them exclusively. (Courtesy of Dot Burch.)

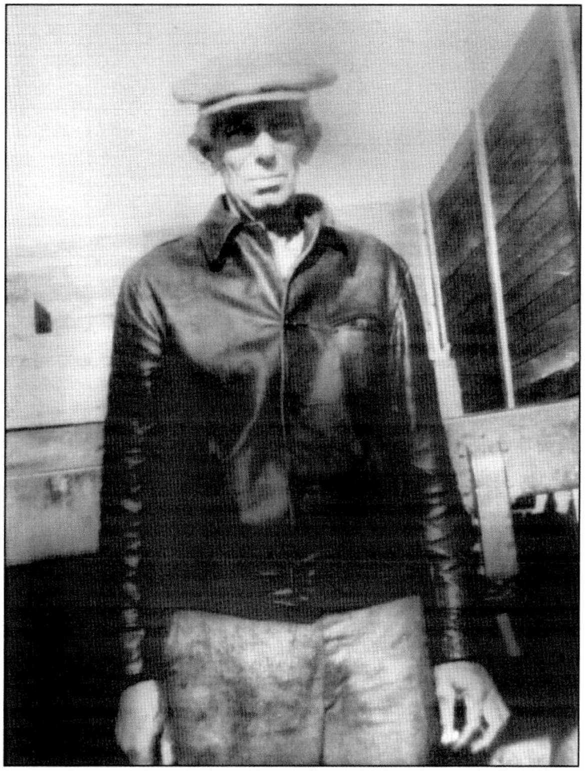

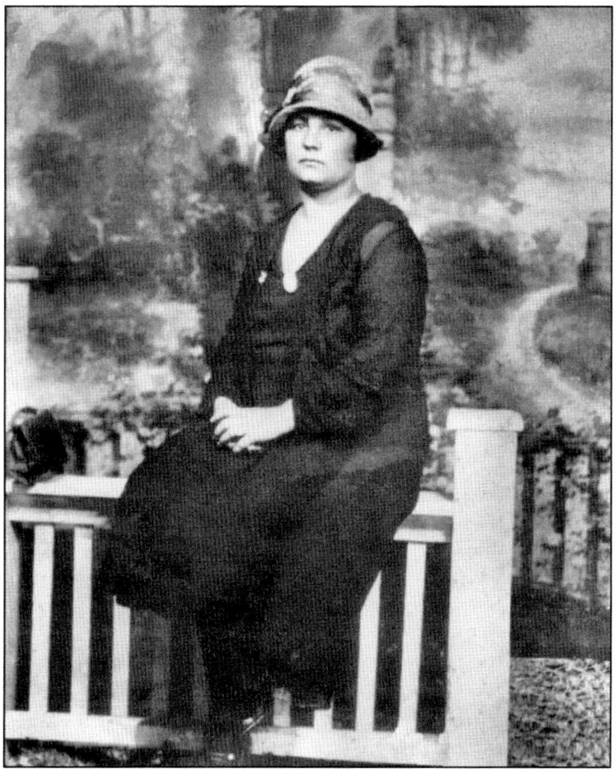

Lena Hagin Vann of Orange Island married Johnny Vann of Vann's Island in 1911, and they had 11 children: Gertrude (1915), Lenora (1917), Lucille (1919), Viola (1920), John D. Jr. (1922), Leona (1924), Edward (1925), Curtis (1927), Merle (1930), Arnold (1932), and James (1934). (Courtesy of Jimmie Vann.)

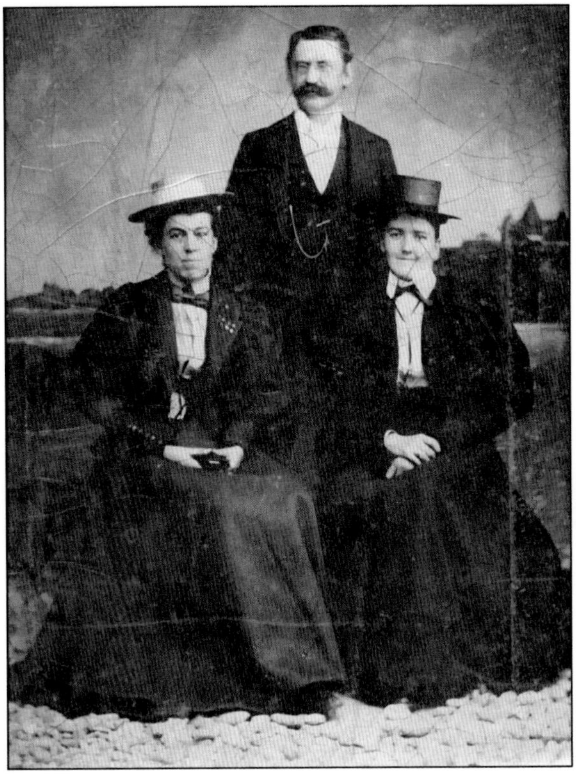

In 1863, Jonathan Washington Fountain and his wife, Sarah Ferdict Fountain, came to Oak Hill from Thomasville, Georgia, and settled on the riverfront. There were only three white families and one black family living in Oak Hill at this time. William Williams, a black ex-slave, arrived about six months later with his family and settled near the Fountains. This area is still known today as "Bill's Hill." The Fountains had three boys—James Walter, Rudulpho, Alanzo Thomas—and two girls—Ella and Elizabeth (who lived only nine days). Jonathan Fountain rode to "high ground" to bury his child. This was the first grave in the Oak Hill cemetery. In 1884, Jonathan died and was buried beside his infant child, Elizabeth. Prior to his death, Fountain homesteaded 80 acres west of U.S. 1 and planted orange groves. Jonathan, Sarah (left), and their daughter, Ella, are pictured at left. (Courtesy of Ida Haverly.)

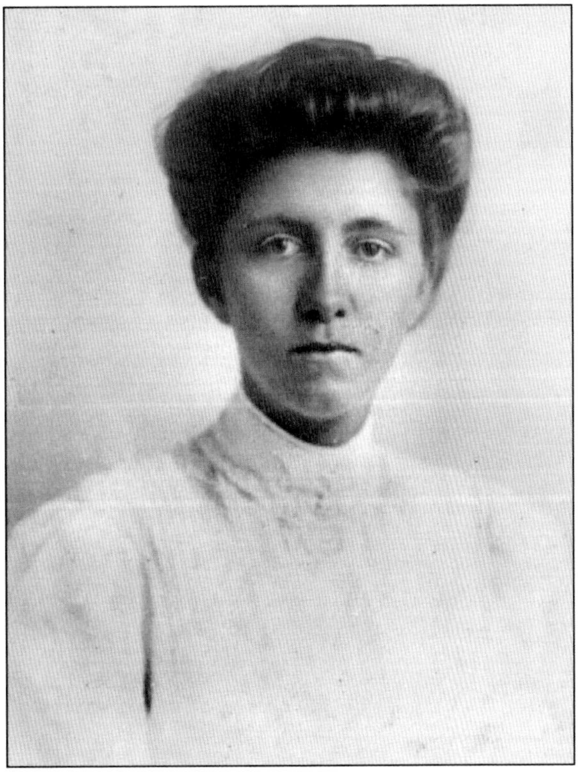

The widow Sarah Fountain married Lawrence John Johnson in 1888 in Oak Hill, and they moved to the resting place of her loved ones. Lawrence was born in Sweden and "worked in the swamps riving out shingles from cypress." In 1889, the Johnsons gave up 10 acres of their land to the Florida East Coast Railroad, realizing the impact it would have on the community. Their first daughter, Mary, was born that year and grew up watching the men lay the railroad tracks through Oak Hill and listening for that train whistle every day for the next 95 years. Mary Johnson Anderson is pictured at right. (Courtesy of Ida Haverly.)

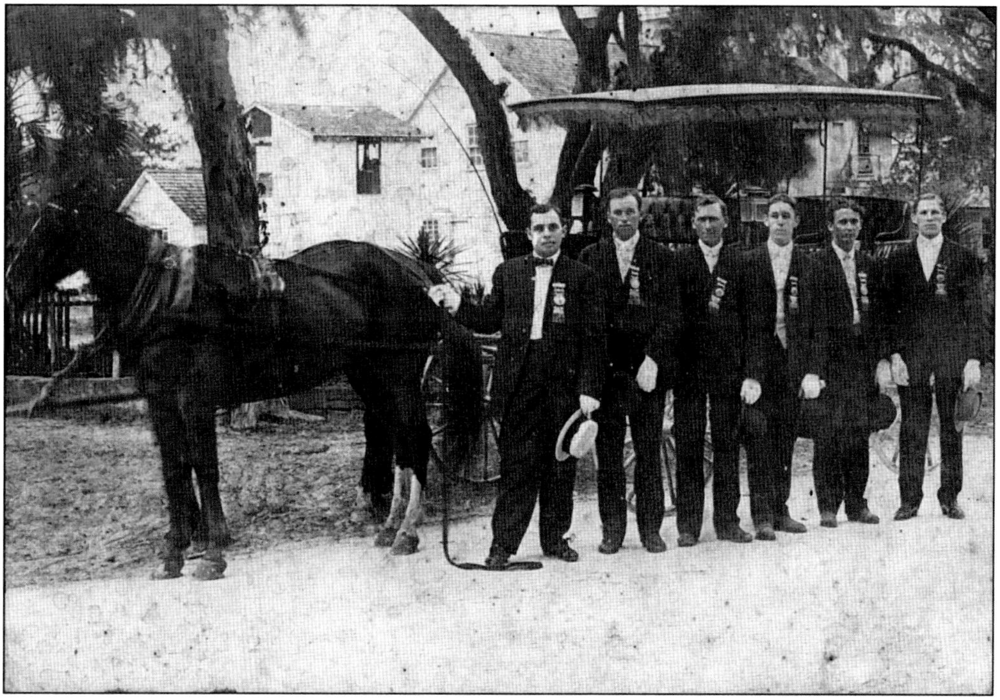

Joseph Harold Anderson is pictured third from the left around 1900. He was a Swedish fisherman who moved to Oak Hill in 1919. Although Mary had vowed never to marry, she fell in love with Joe when she was 30. She was determined not to be like her sister, Clara, who married Anchor Damgaard and had a child every year until the count totaled 10. However, Mary did marry Joe, and they had one son, Lloyd Harold Anderson. (Courtesy of Ida Haverly.)

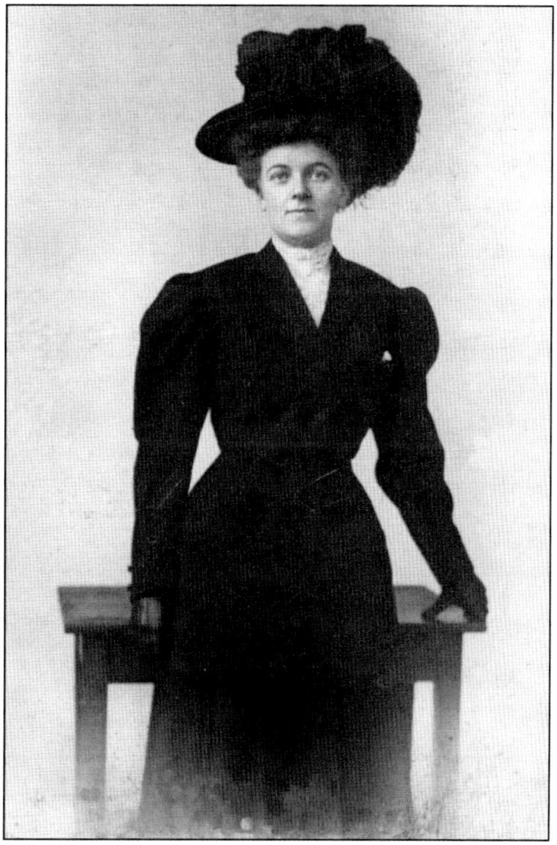

Joe Anderson's sister, Maria Josephina Anderson, arrived in Oak Hill from her home in Sweden to see her brother and visit her new relatives.

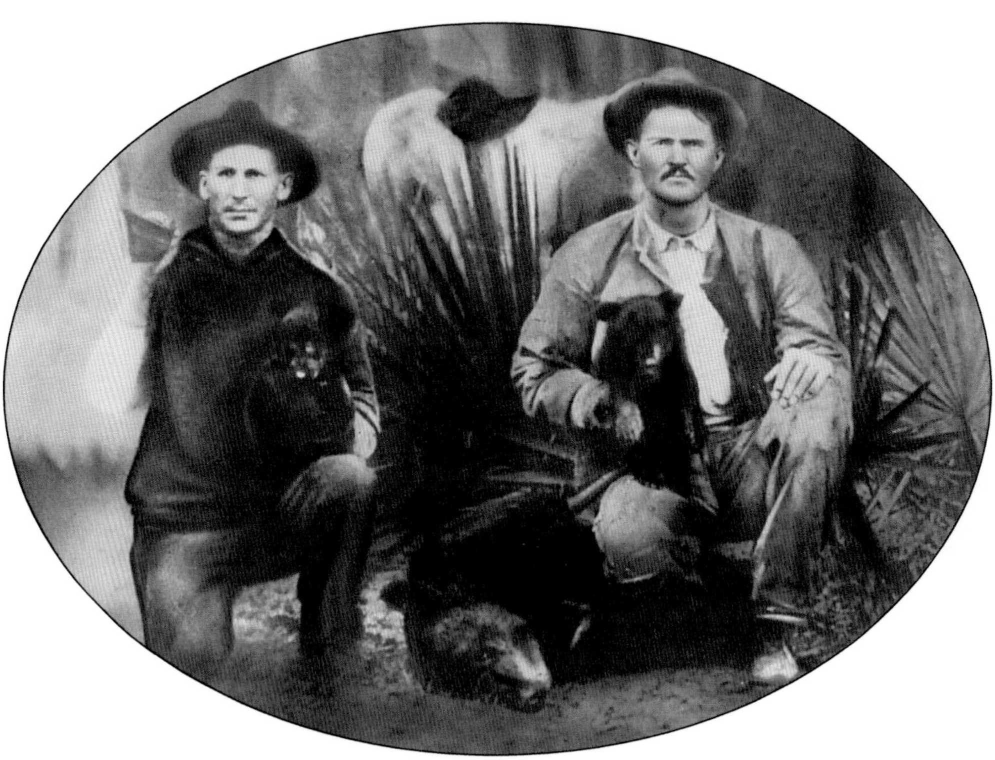

At the start of the 20th century, the Simmons brothers, Charles (left) and Perry (right), finally put a stop to the thief stealing the honey from their apiary business. Much to their surprise, two baby bear cubs came out looking for their mother, so the boys agreed to take over the care of the two cubs until they could be released into another area of the woods. (Courtesy of Bill McGee.)

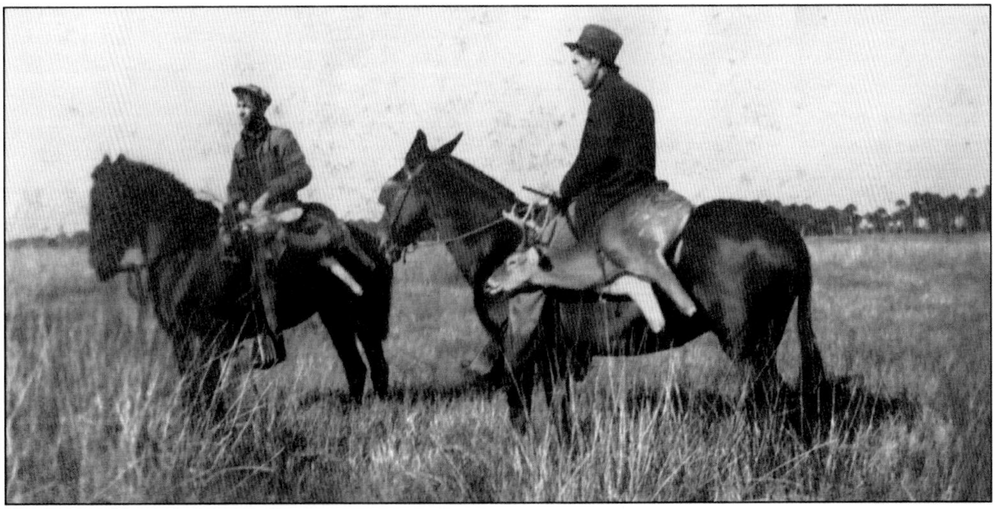

Two unidentified hunters represent the many nameless Northerners who came to Oak Hill to stay at the Atlantic Hotel, a hunting and fishing lodge. Tom McMurray and Henry J. Faulkner of New York built this lodge in 1882. They hired Frank Sams to manage the lodge, located on the lagoon just north of the Seminole Rest Indian Mounds. The Atlantic Hotel, which burned in 1893, provided lodging, food, horses, and guns for guests for the fee of $4 a day. (Courtesy of Ida Goodrich.)

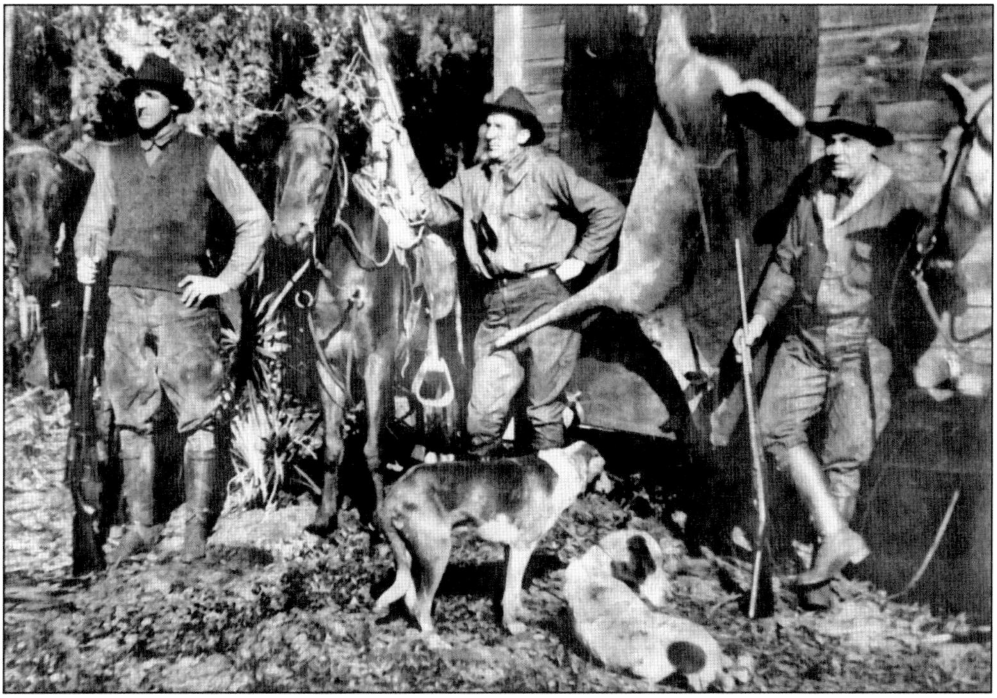

Visiting hunters had great stories to tell about deer hunting in Oak Hill when they returned to their Northern homes. (Courtesy of Harlen Hutchins.)

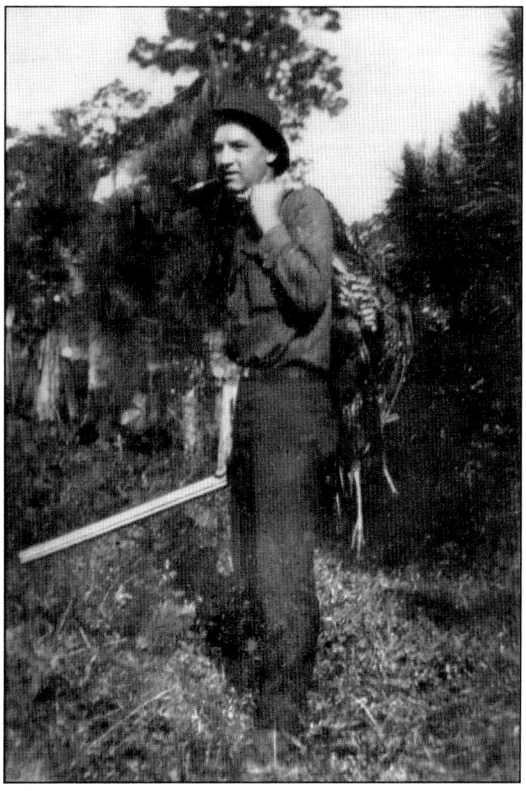

Bill Wright, a family member of the early Wright settlers, is shown here with his turkey after a morning hunt. (Courtesy of Harlen Hutchins.)

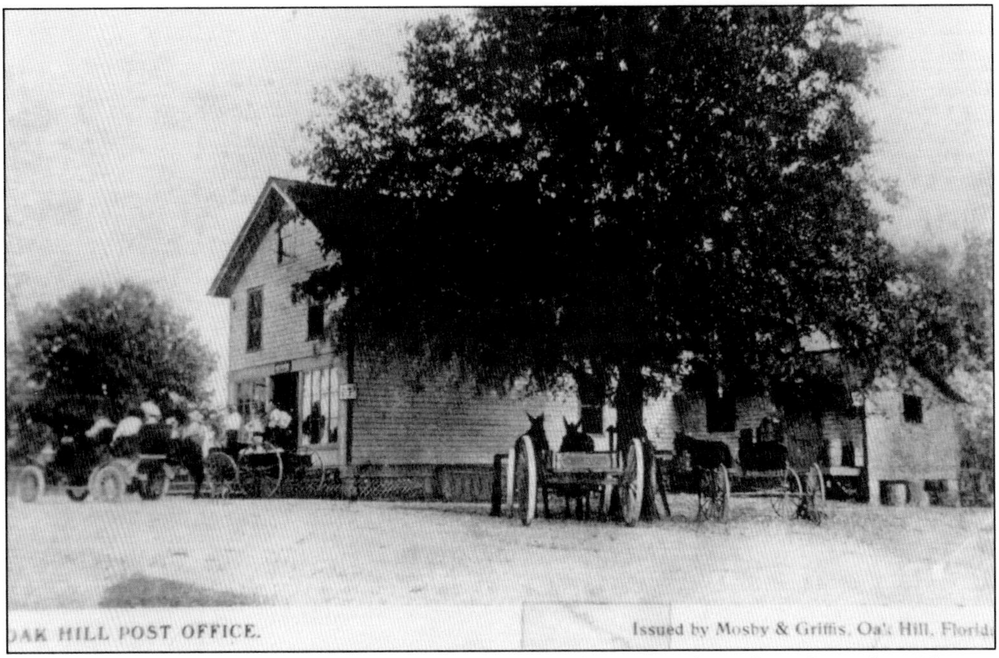

Local businesses no longer had to rely on the river to bring supplies when the railroad began operation through Oak Hill. W. C. Howes moved his store and post office from the river to be closer to the railroad. He built this building at the top of the hill, which soon became the center of town.

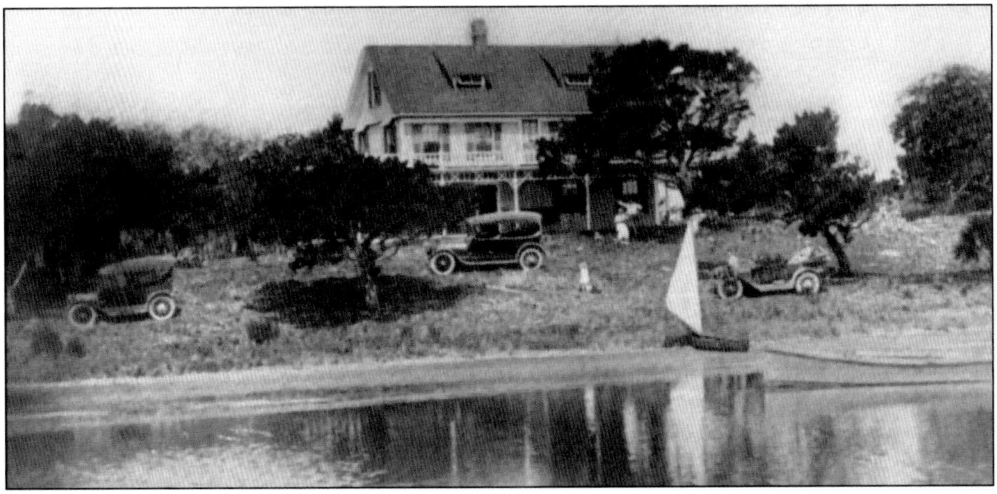

By the 1890s, Lady and Lord Hatton Turnor from England built two houses on the Native American mounds, later to be known as Seminole Rest. Turnor was a minister, and his neighbor to the north was W. C. Howes, a store owner and postmaster. The mail and supplies for Howes's general store came by sailboat up the river from Titusville between 1894 and 1908. At this time, Oak Hill was referred to as a "flourishing post-office settlement." In 1911, the Turnors sold their houses and property for $2,000 and returned to England. (Courtesy of Harlen Hutchins.)

In 1872, Axson Quarterman Goodrich came by wagon from Bradford County at the age of 15 with his father, Charles, and three brothers, Mitchell, Charles, and Gus. The family claimed 168 acres and started raising cattle on the open range, planted citrus trees, and always had a family garden. Axson said, "You gotta have something growing while you are sleeping." In 1884, W. C. Howes officiated at the wedding of Axson to Annie Cleopatra Wilson, who had come with her family down the river on a boat from Fernandina. They had six children: Lula May (1885), Sam (1887), Clarence (1892), Jeff (1894), Annie (1897), and Elmer (1900). (Courtesy of Dot Burch.)

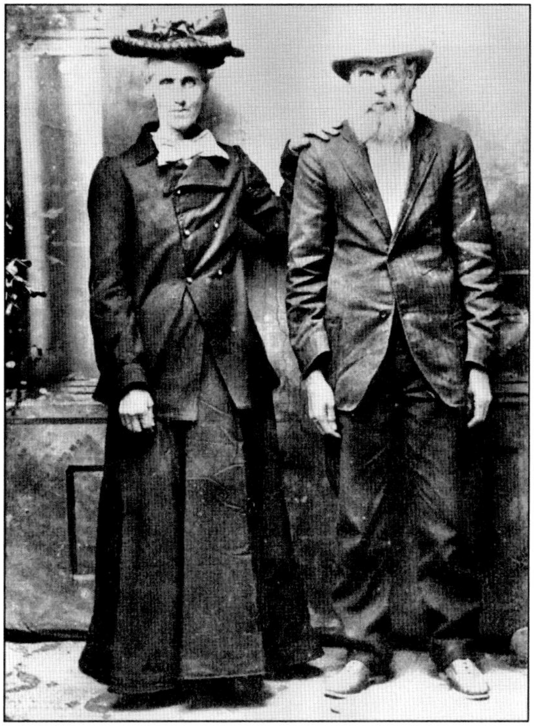

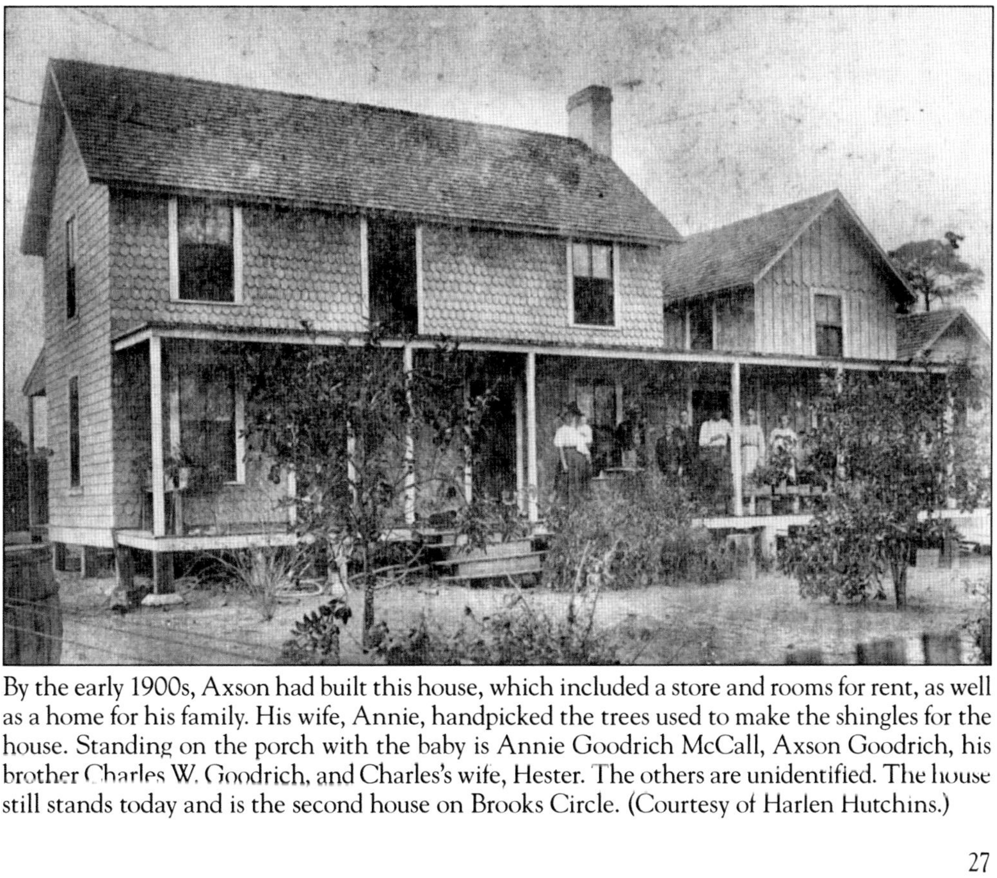

By the early 1900s, Axson had built this house, which included a store and rooms for rent, as well as a home for his family. His wife, Annie, handpicked the trees used to make the shingles for the house. Standing on the porch with the baby is Annie Goodrich McCall, Axson Goodrich, his brother Charles W. Goodrich, and Charles's wife, Hester. The others are unidentified. The house still stands today and is the second house on Brooks Circle. (Courtesy of Harlen Hutchins.)

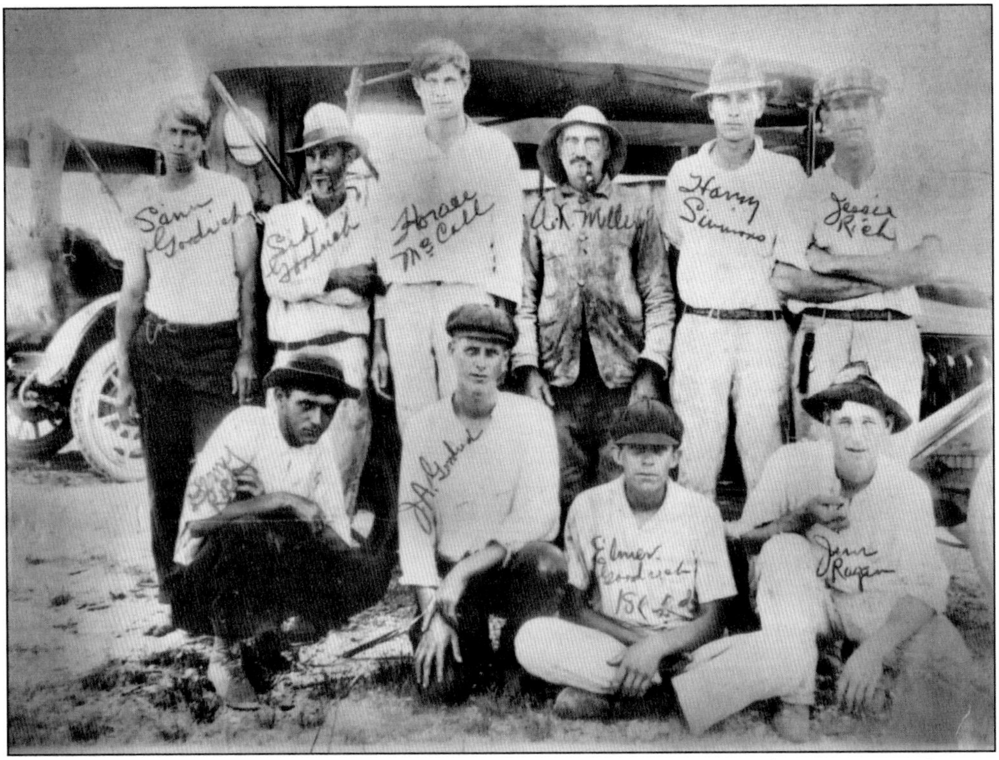

By 1908, commercial fishing was beginning to take on more importance because, according to Axson's son Clarence, "orange groves only paid off for you once a year, but fishing put money in your pockets twelve months a year." Clarence started fishing at age 17, soon to be followed by his brother Jeff. The locals who knew these waters best included, from left to right, (first row) Benny Rich, Jeff Goodrich, Elmer Goodrich, and Jim Ragan; (back) Sam Goodrich, Sid Goodrich, Horace McCall, A. X. Miller, Harry Simmons, and Jessie Rich. (Courtesy of Vernon Goodrich.)

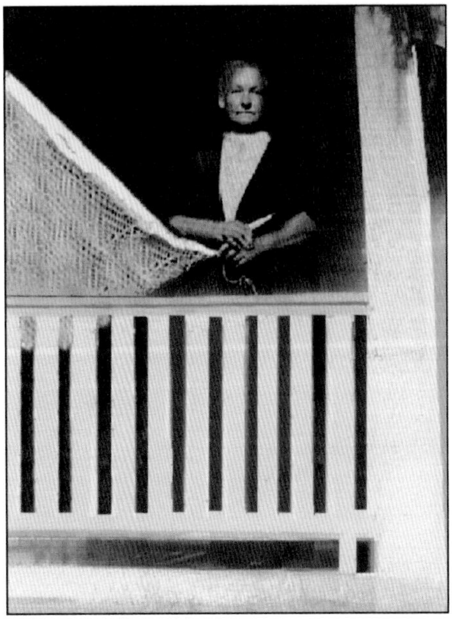

Grandma Julia Hagin represents many women who made the nets for the commercial fishermen. Most of the fish caught in the early days were mullet, which sold for 3¢ a pound. According to many locals, the river seemed to be the only industry that had any future in it. The severe winters destroyed many orange trees, and the new "dipping law" required cattle to be immersed in a solution to kill fever-causing ticks. This put many out of the cattle business when the cows escaped this process. (Courtesy of Jimmie Vann.)

Howard G. Putnam's family suffered under the hand of Gen. William T. Sherman, who burned their gristmill on his march through Georgia. His father, John, and mother, Mary Gresham Putnam, left the devastation behind in 1886 and came south, settling in Oak Hill with their children. In 1888, their father died of tuberculosis, and by 1892, Mary has also died, leaving the responsibility for seven younger siblings to Howard, now age 19. He started early in the citrus industry and became a leader, owning 150 acres of orange groves. (Courtesy of Bill Dyall.)

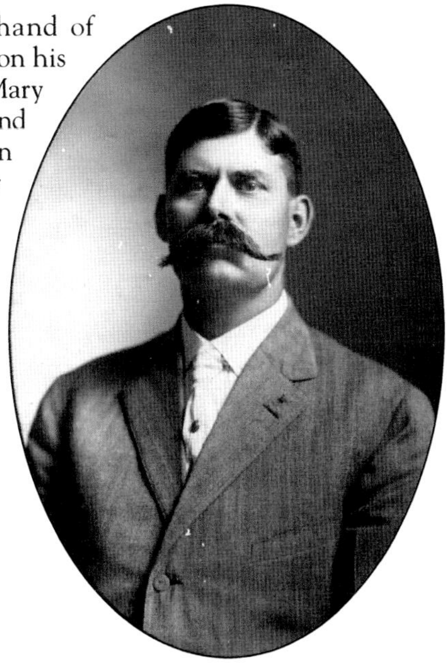

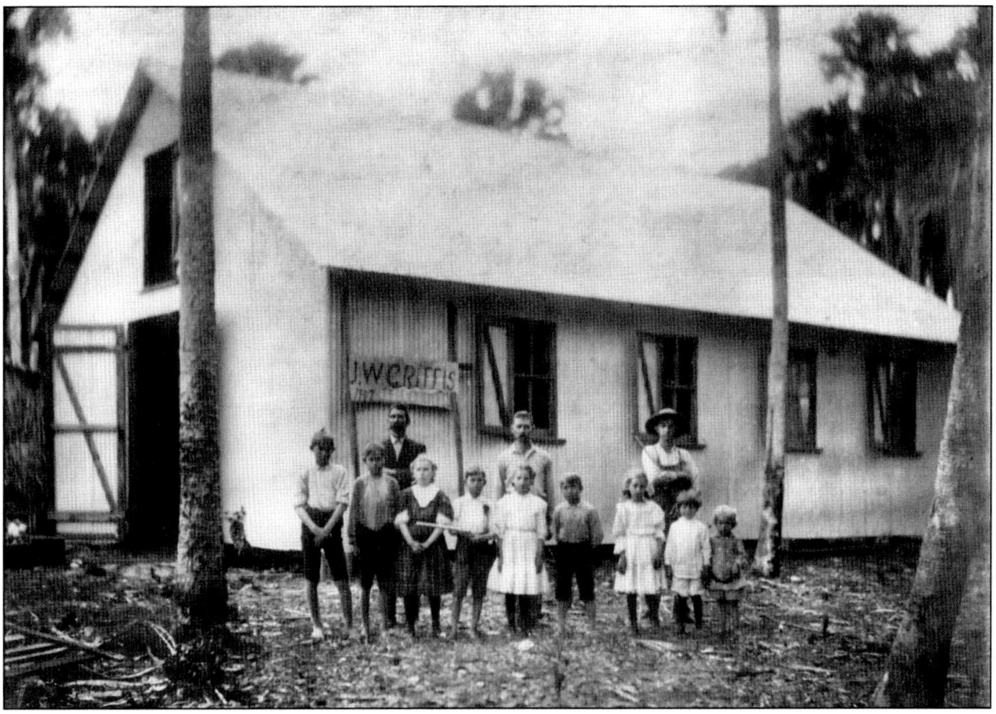

In 1870, S. D. Mitchell's son, Jacob Davy Mitchell from Massachusetts, built a house on family land near the river and planted the state's second citrus grove. The Dummett Grove, just north, was recorded as the first grove. J. W. Griffis established this citrus packinghouse in the early 1900s, and it was reported that there were more than 130 acres of producing groves in the Oak Hill area. Pictured in front of the packinghouse are, from left to right, (first row) Roy Harmond, Willy Griffis, Cora Bennett, Aaron Taylor, Mary Mosby, Travis Harmond, Olivia Taylor, Dan Taylor, and Truman Taylor; (second row) DeWitt Taylor, J. W. Griffis, and David Taylor.

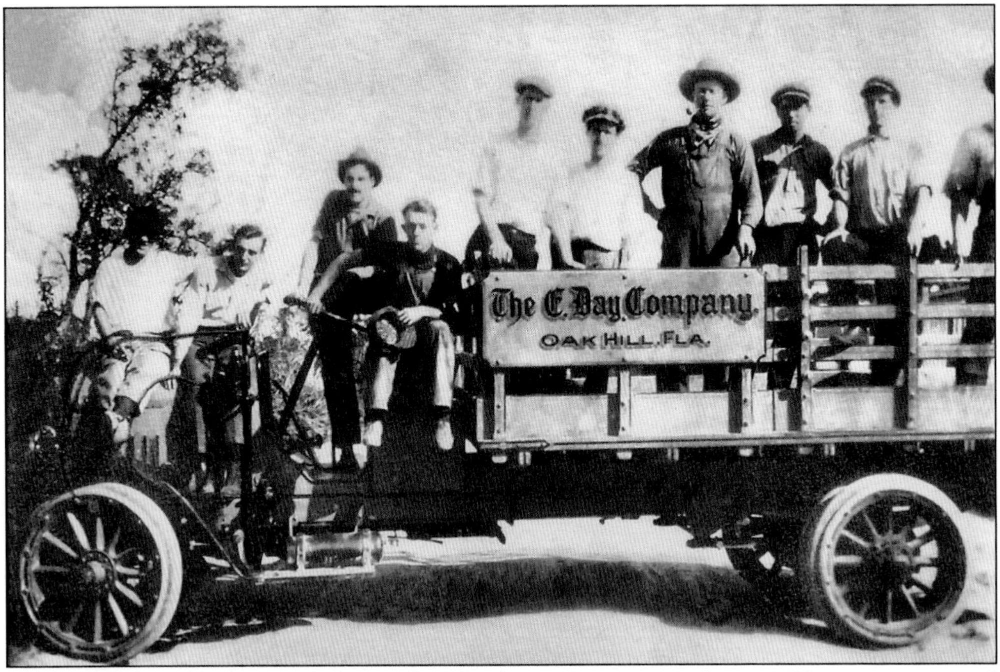

The E. Day Company provided fruit pickers for the many groves in the area. The mosquitoes and sun made this a difficult job. These unidentified workers are being transported to their workplace. As more settlers came to plant groves, families like the Putnams and Fred Hatch, Henry Barker, A. J. Wilson, Phillip Wright, Zack Williams, Axson Goodrich, George Magruder, A. A. Montgomery, John McCarthy, and John Johnson expanded the industry. (Courtesy of Bill Dyall.)

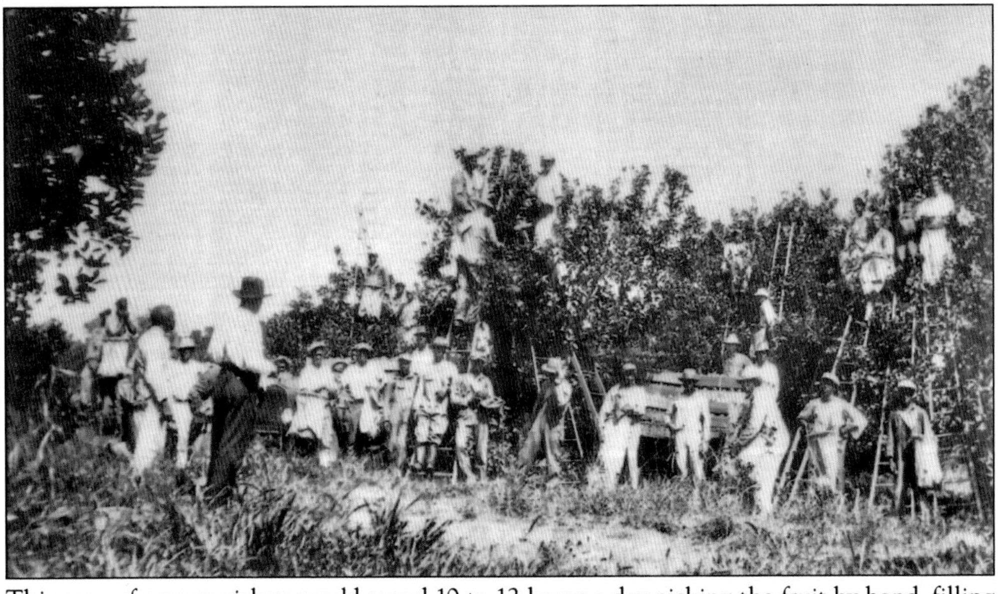

This crew of orange pickers would spend 10 to 12 hours a day picking the fruit by hand, filling picking sacks that were emptied into fruit boxes and taken to the packinghouses. The freezes of 1894 and 1895 killed many fruit trees in some colder outlying areas, but some farmers replanted and started over. Others turned to fishing or sought a new livelihood with the railroad. (Courtesy of Betty Bellamy.)

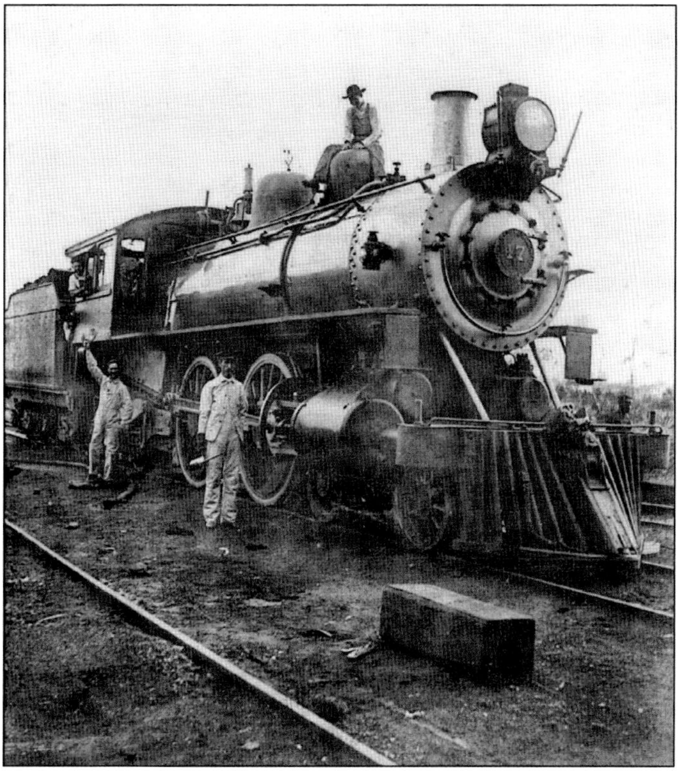

John Putnam (pictured below) was the younger brother of Howard Putnam. He was fascinated by the trains and went to work on them as soon as he was old enough. He is shown standing next to a train (at right) with his arm raised. The railroad lines were extended south through Oak Hill by 1892. (Courtesy of Bill Dyall.)

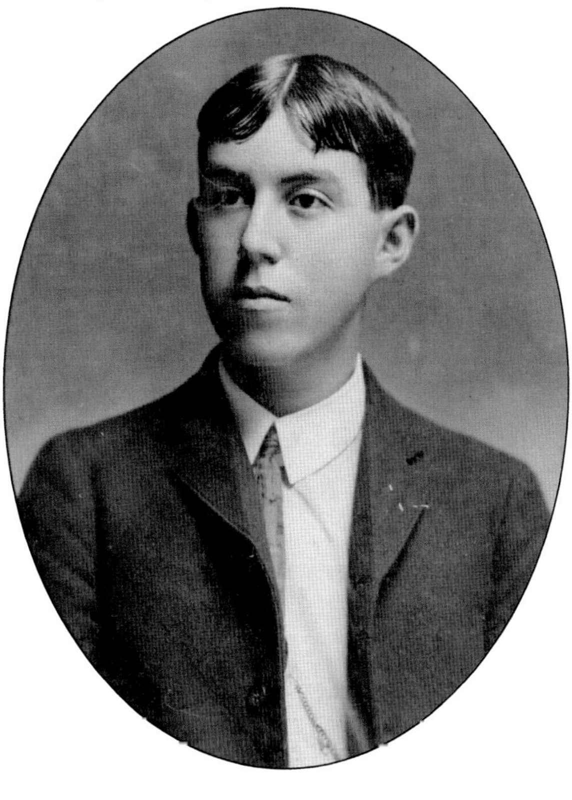

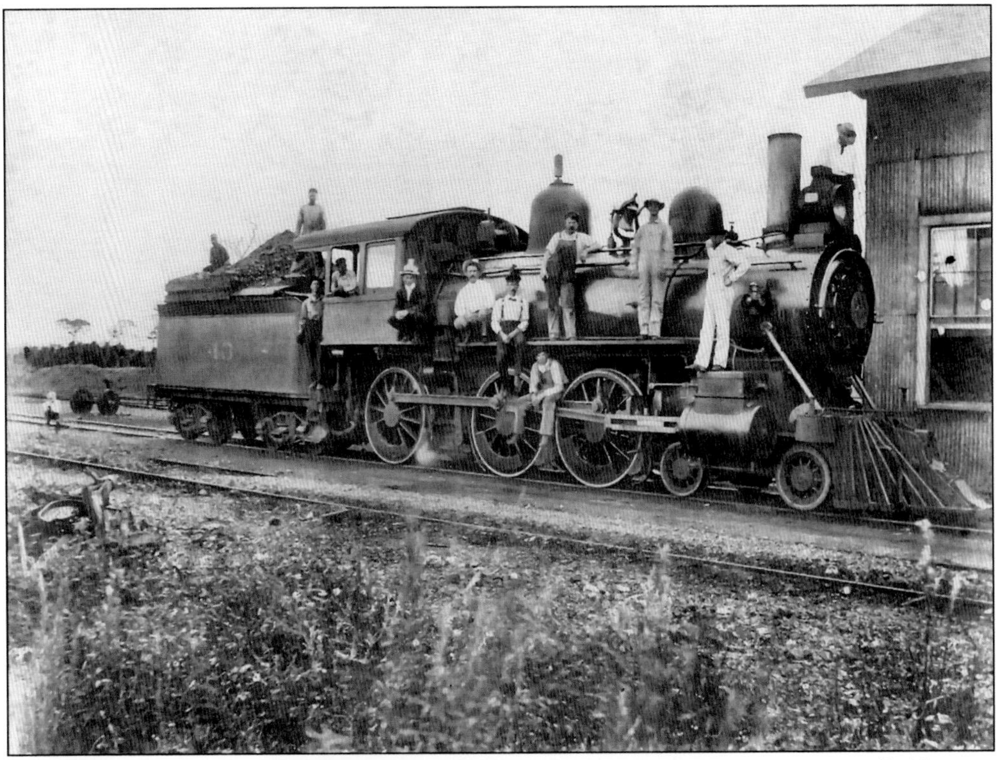

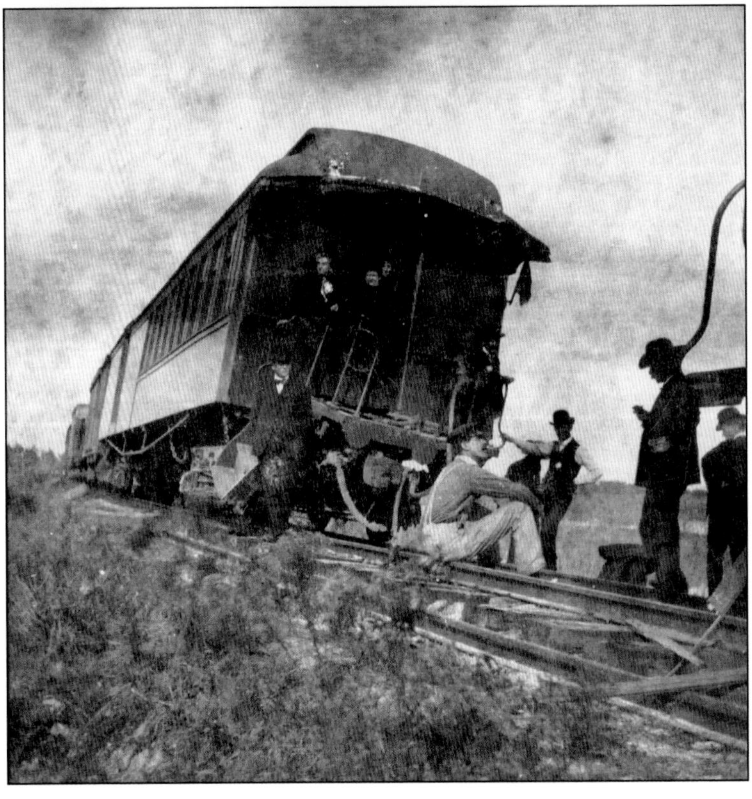

Trains pulled by steam engines, powered by wood or coal, were vital to the town's commerce, bringing in needed supplies and carrying out carloads of sweet Indian River fruit from Oak Hill to Northern markets.

Train wrecks, such as this one in Oak Hill in the 1920s, occurred occasionally when the train derailed or "jumped the track" because of an open switch or objects in its path.

Three

CHANGING TIMES

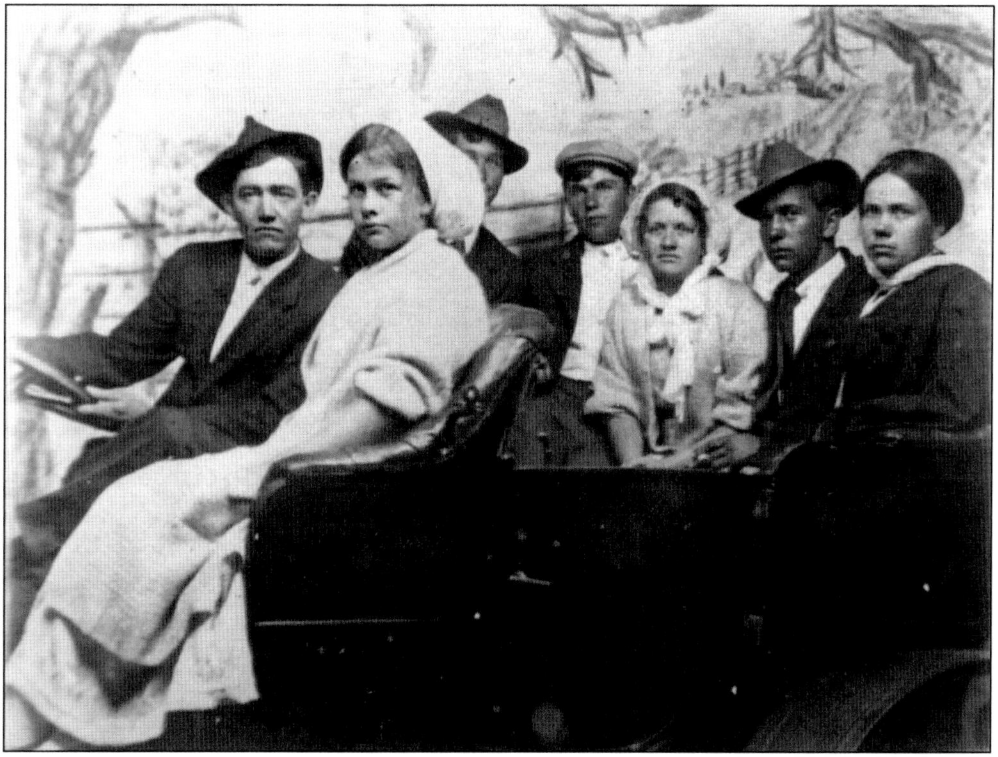

The automobile brought many changes to the area. Photographers used this popular background for memorable photographs taken of families and friends. Pictured from left to right are Craig and Annie Goodson, Sid Goodrich, Horace Bennett, Ida and Harry Simmons, and Katie Goodrich. (Courtesy of Ida Goodrich.)

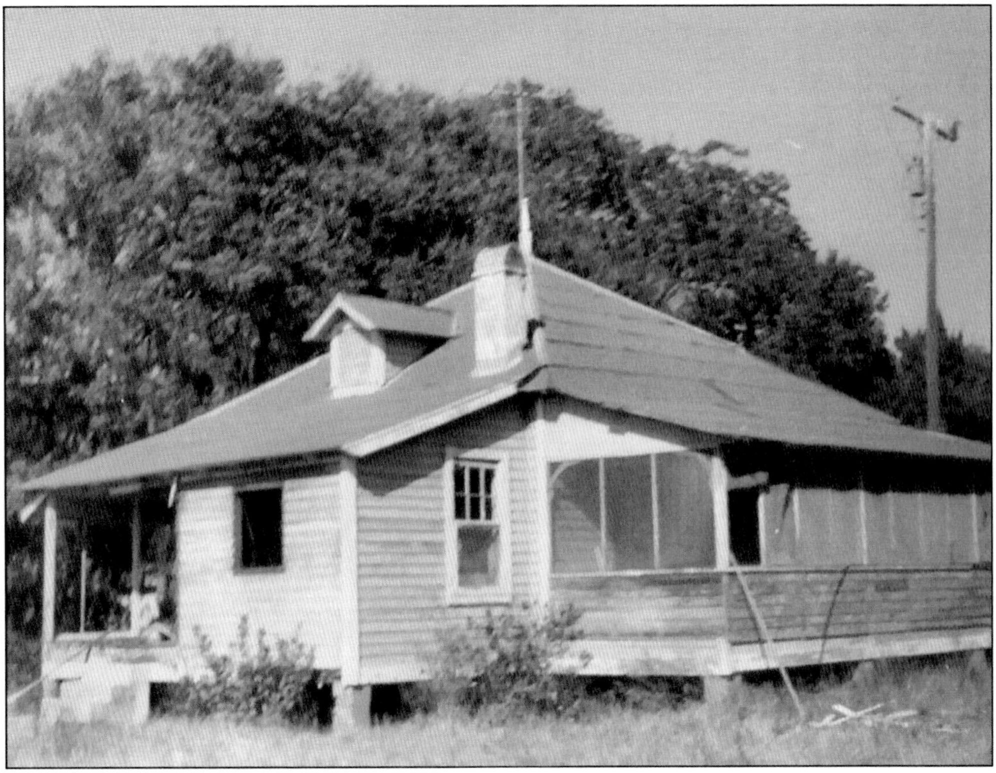

Depot agent Alfred G. Basch lived in this house across the tracks from the depot. Besides managing the railway station, Basch also operated the telegraph system, decoding dots and dashes when telegrams came for local residents. (Courtesy of Ida Goodrich.)

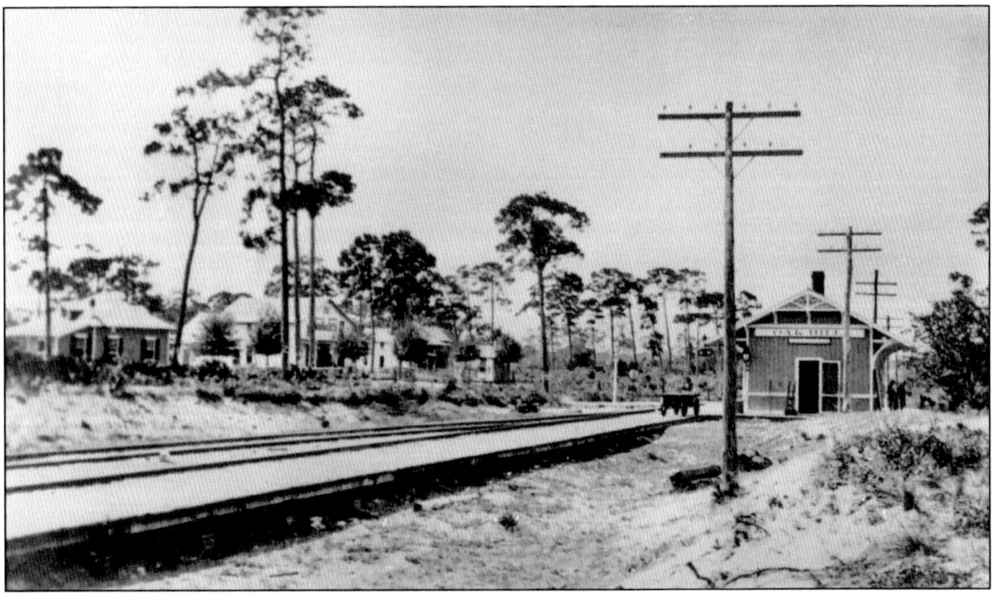

A handcart is ready to pick up mail when the train arrived at the Oak Hill depot. Across the tracks can be seen the station house and the Goodrich Store, which had rental apartments in the second story. (Courtesy of Ida Goodrich.)

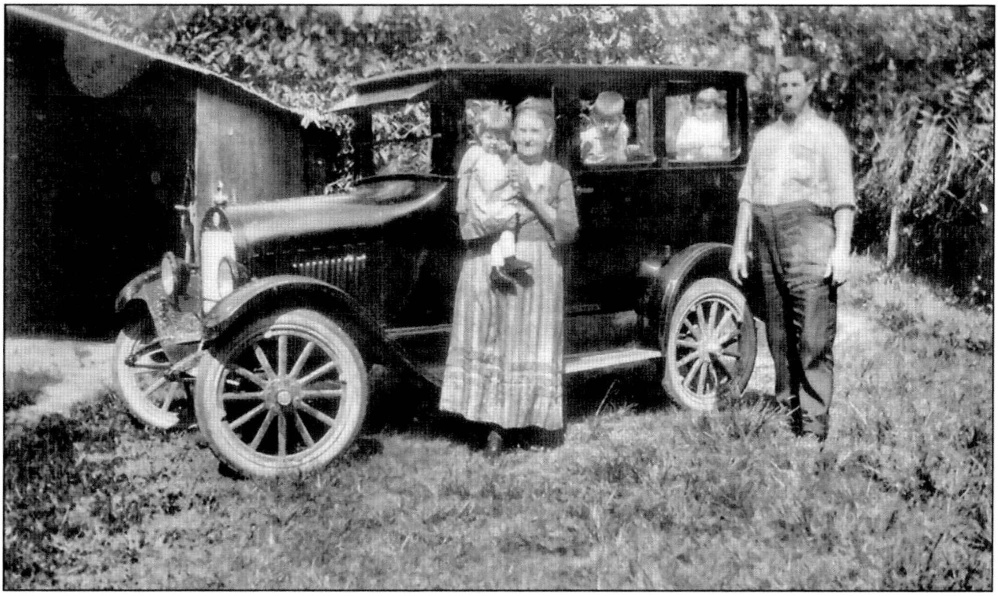

Jesse and Amanda Mosby take their three grandchildren for a ride in their new car. The small child being held is Frances Baldwin (Johnson), and the other grandchildren in the car are Van Buren Baldwin Jr. and his sister, Jeanne Baldwin (Wheeler).

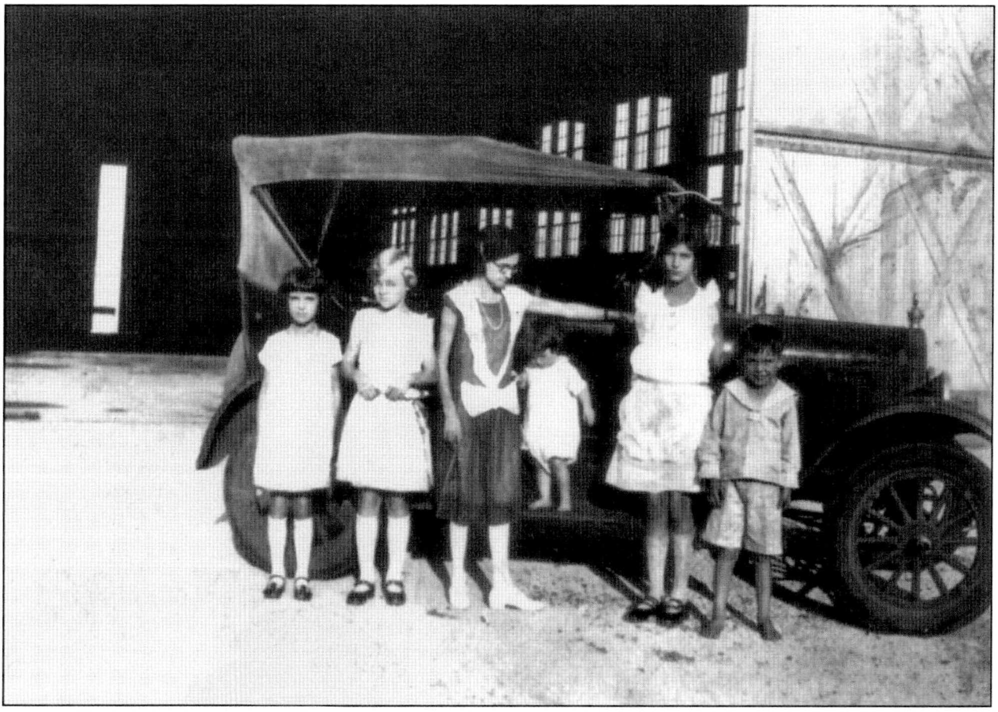

The Floyd Jones family goes for an afternoon ride with friends. They are, from left to right, two unidentified friends, Ethel Bessinger Jones, and her children, Beatrice, Martha Sue, and Pharold. (Courtesy of Jean Vann.)

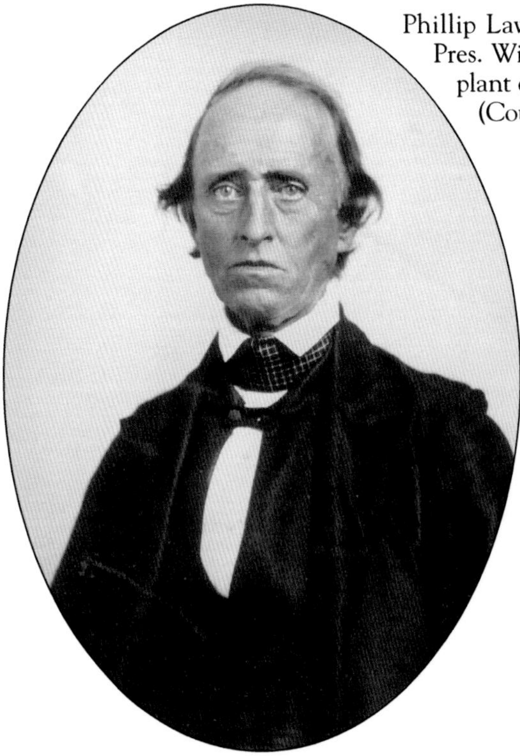

Phillip Lawrence Wright received a land grant from Pres. William Henry Harrison in 1884 and began to plant citrus groves on hammock land west of town. (Courtesy of Sally Bayles.)

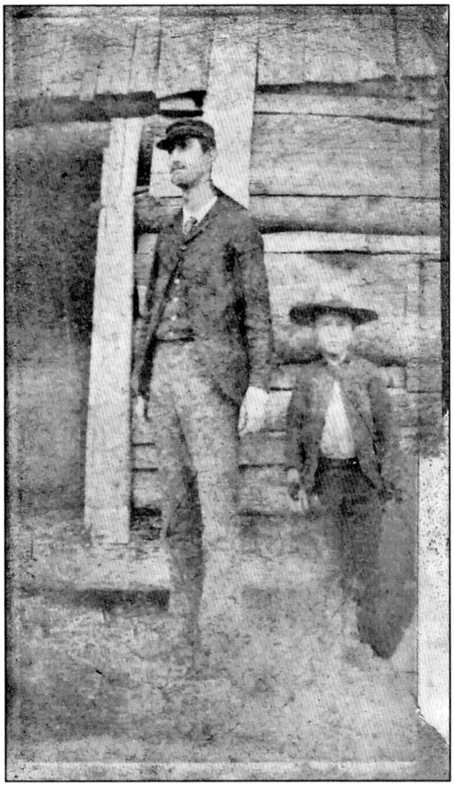

During the early days, Phillip Wright spent time with his younger brother, Willie, because he had the responsibility of teaching Willie many skills to provide for himself as he grew older. (Courtesy of Sally Bayles.)

Phillip Lawrence Wright married Ruth McPherson in 1896. They are pictured with their older daughter, Cora Belle, who later married John Deal. (Courtesy of Sally Bayles.)

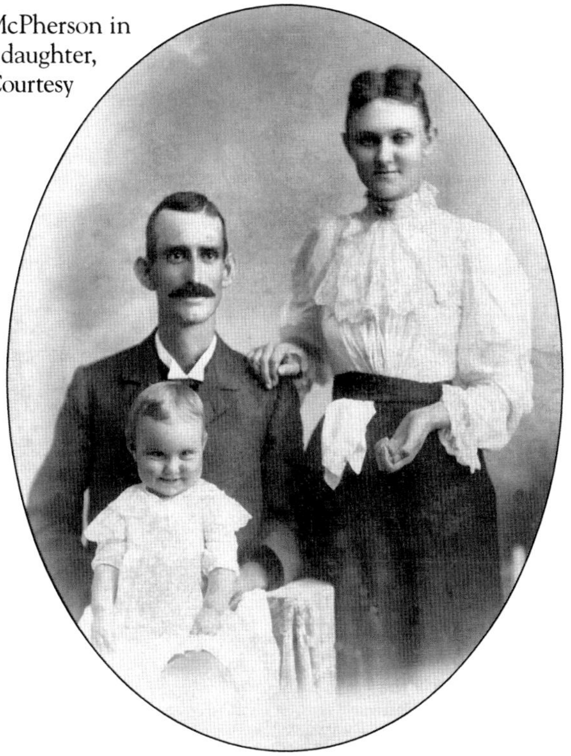

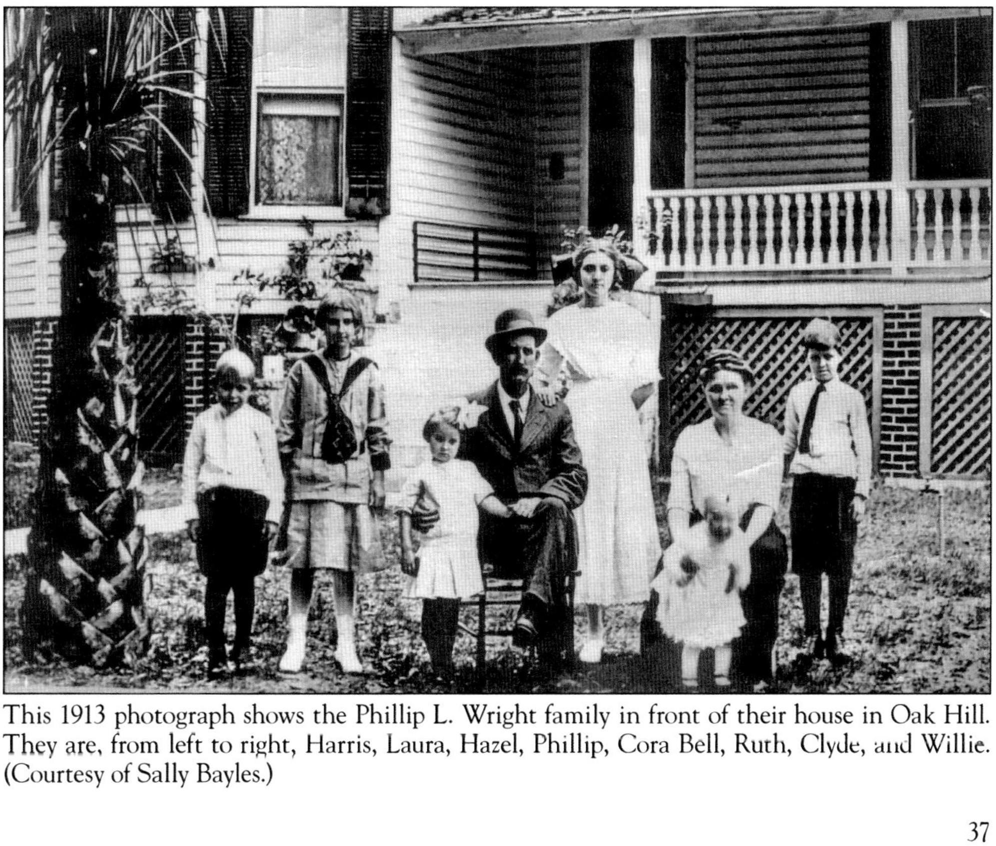

This 1913 photograph shows the Phillip L. Wright family in front of their house in Oak Hill. They are, from left to right, Harris, Laura, Hazel, Phillip, Cora Bell, Ruth, Clyde, and Willie. (Courtesy of Sally Bayles.)

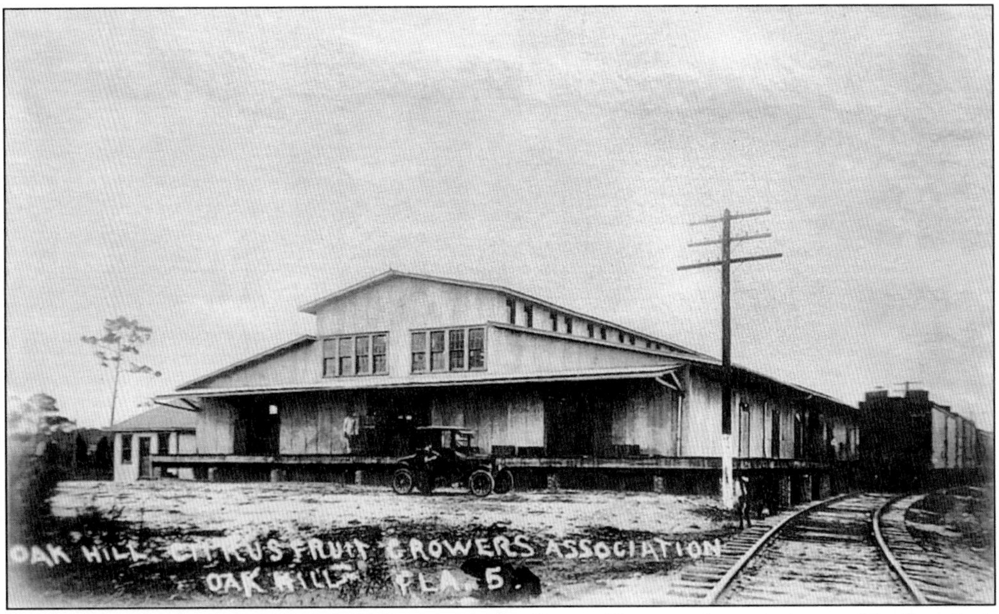

As the citrus industry grew, Oak Hill organized a Citrus Growers Association and built a fruit packinghouse close to the railroad. Locally grown citrus could now be shipped to many Northern markets. (Courtesy of Betty Bellamy.)

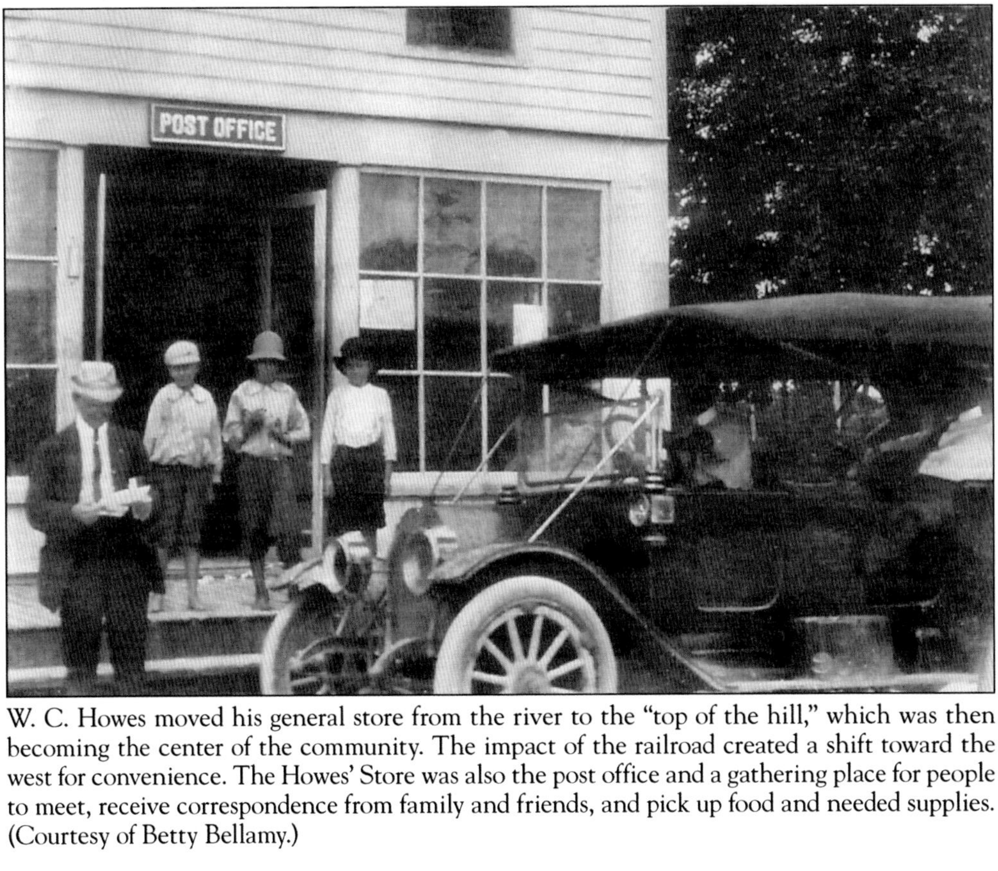

W. C. Howes moved his general store from the river to the "top of the hill," which was then becoming the center of the community. The impact of the railroad created a shift toward the west for convenience. The Howes' Store was also the post office and a gathering place for people to meet, receive correspondence from family and friends, and pick up food and needed supplies. (Courtesy of Betty Bellamy.)

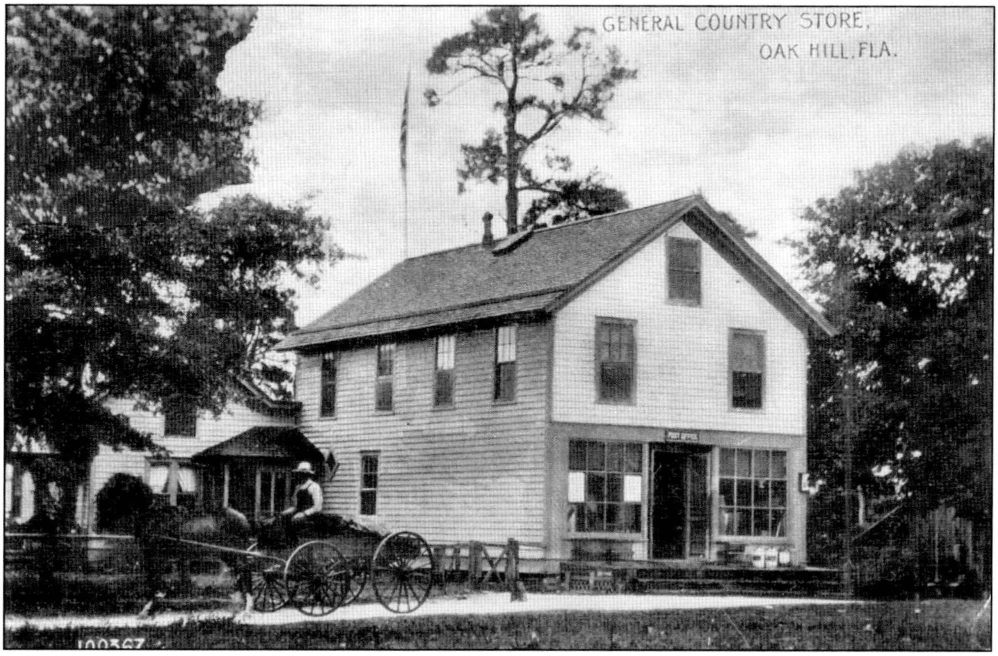

Leonard Mosby bought the Howes' Store in 1912. He and his wife, Muriel, built a house close by where they raised five children: Leonard Jr., Evelyn Marie, Mary Freida, Patty, and Donald.

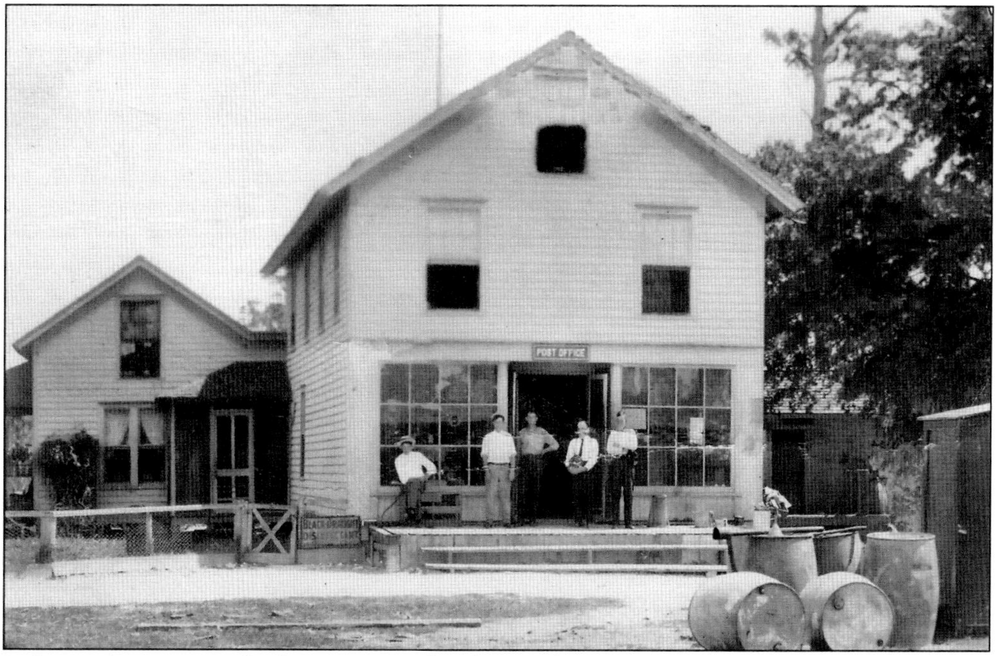

Influential community leaders seem to solve the problems of the day while standing on the store porch. Pictured on the right is Charles Ebenbeck, justice of the peace. Ebenbeck and his family are pictured on the cover.

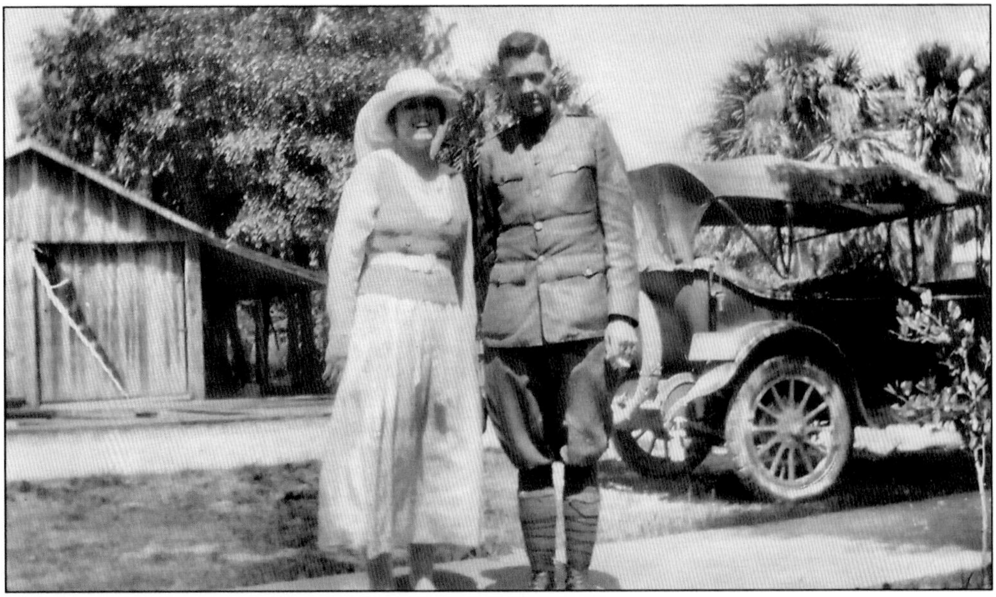

Leonard Mosby must say good-bye to his wife, Muriel Keebler Mosby. He was the first man to be drafted from Volusia County to fight in World War I. (Courtesy of Patty Nelson.)

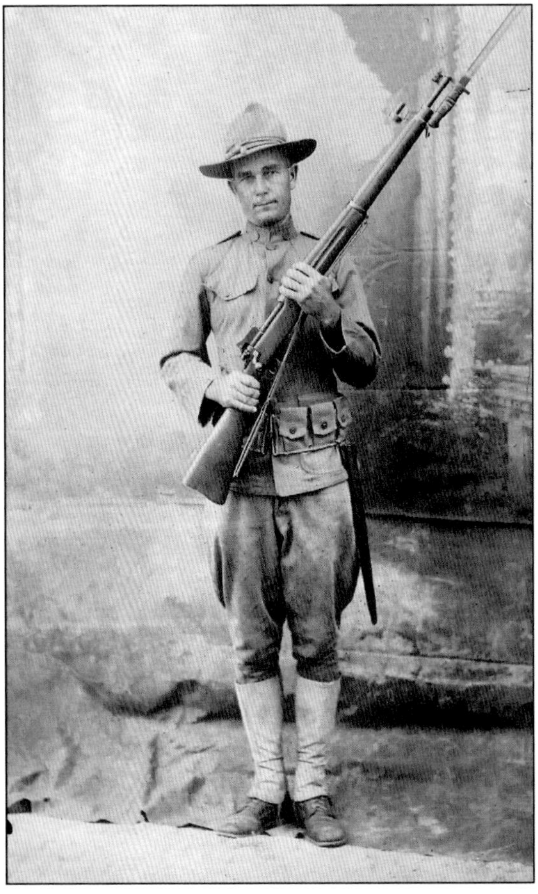

Archie Smith, pictured here, left Oak Hill to serve in World War I. Not long after, Clarence Goodrich Sr. also left to serve in the army. (Courtesy of Eddie Smith.)

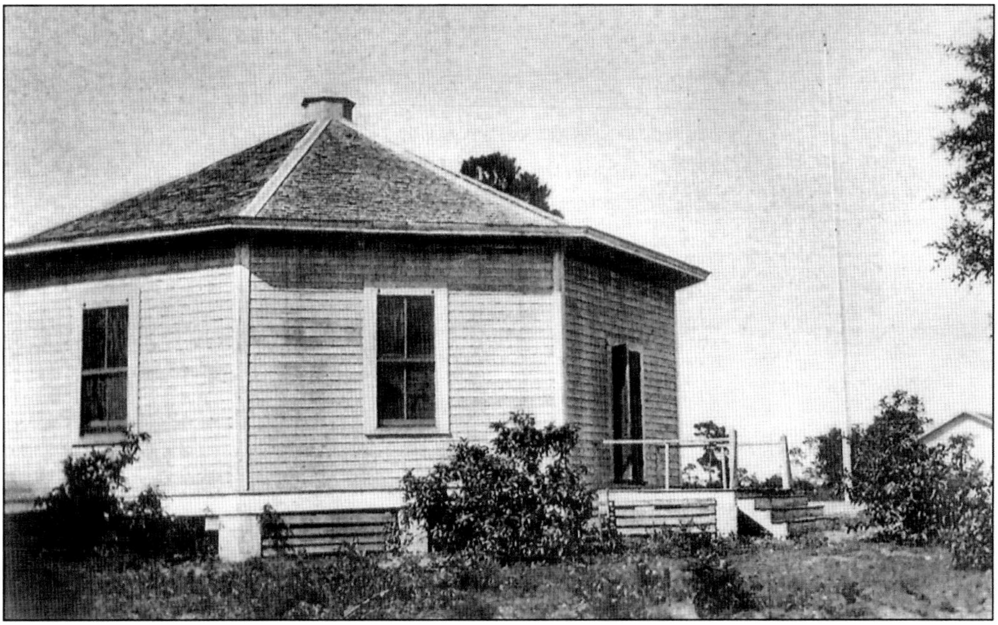

By the dawn of the 20th century, F. W. Hatch, H. J. Magruder, and L. L. Mosby formed the Village Improvement Association and served as the first trustees. This organization was a forerunner to city government, and members met regularly to plan community events and solve problems. Originally, their meeting place was an octagonal structure built at 146 U.S. Highway 1 on land donated by F. W. Hatch in 1906. (Courtesy of Betty Bellamy.)

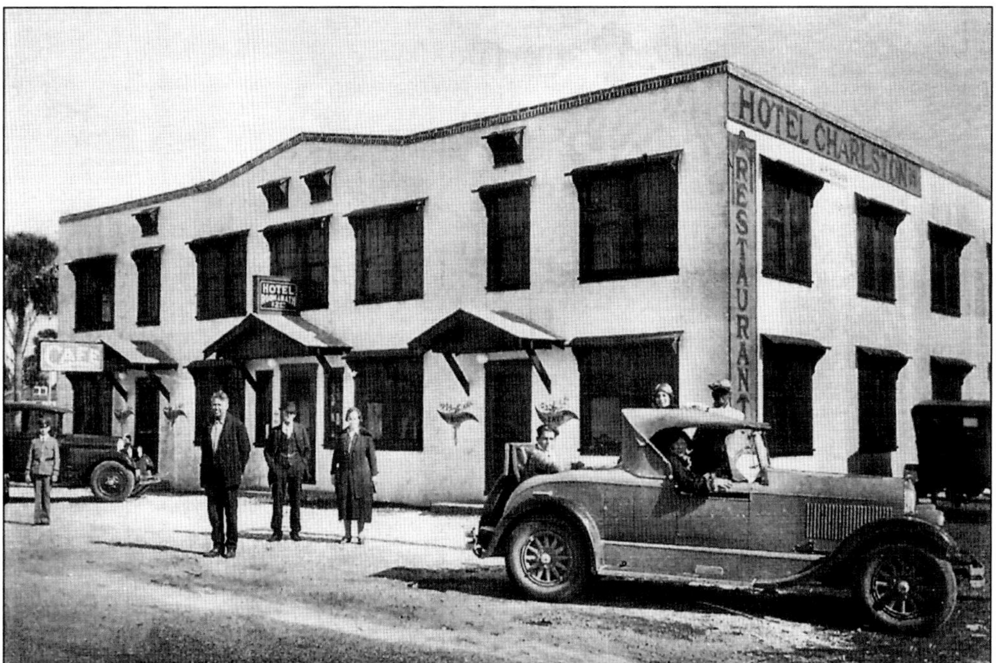

John Somerset built Hotel Charlstown in the early 1900s. As the citrus industry expanded, workers came from the Carolinas to find seasonal work in the groves picking fruit. He decided it would be a good investment to provide a place for them to stay. (Courtesy of Bill Dyall.)

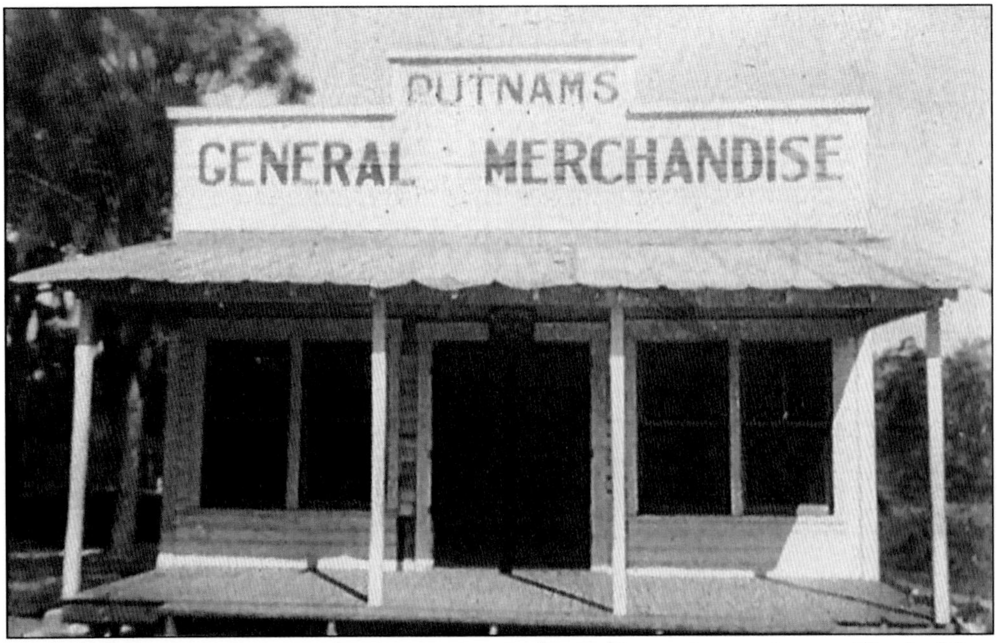

With the growth of the town, Jim Putnam opened an additional general store. The building was originally a commissary for the turpentine company that operated just west of town in the Maytown area. (Courtesy of Ida Goodrich.)

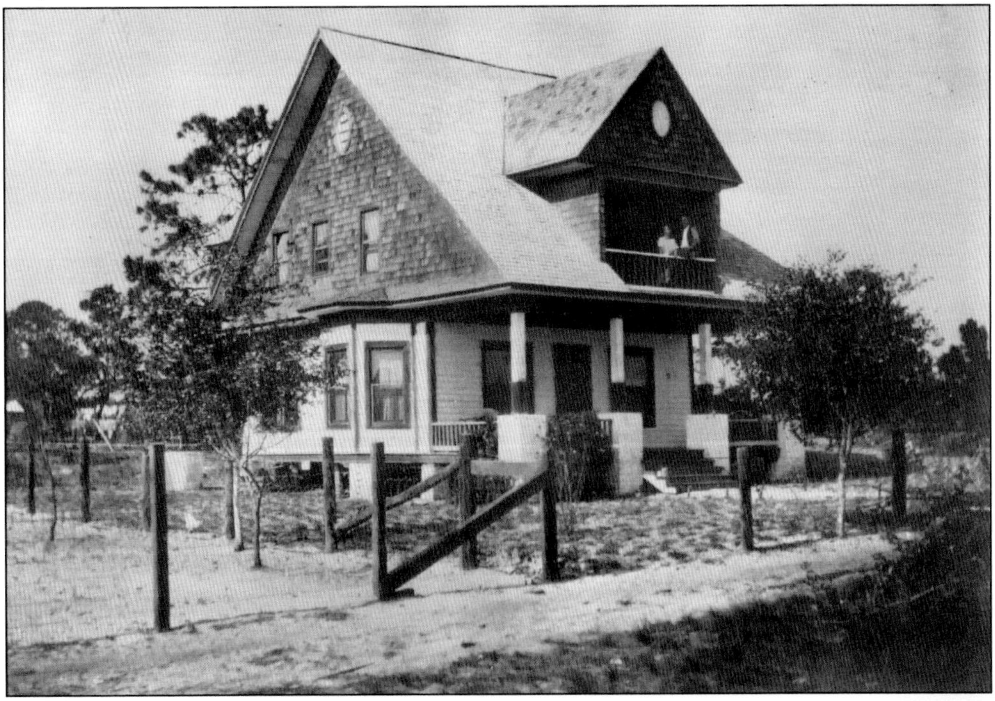

Archie Smith built this house in 1912 for $500 on land identified today as Campton Street. It was a Sears and Roebuck Catalog house, actually constructed by Walter Null and Mac Clinton. Sears shipped the kit by railroad, which included the precut lumber and plans. Eventually, Sears offered 70 different kits from which to choose. (Courtesy of Eddie Smith.)

William Abraham Simmons came from South Carolina in the early 1860s, riding on a raft down the St. Johns River from Jacksonville. (Courtesy of Marie Goodrich.)

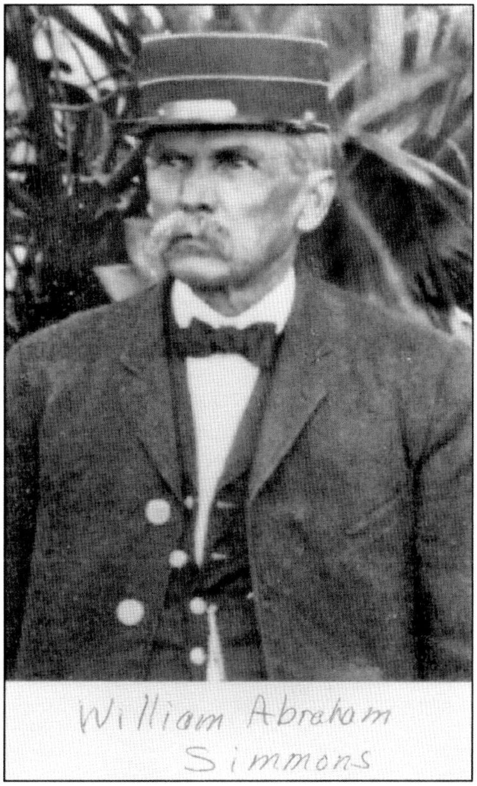

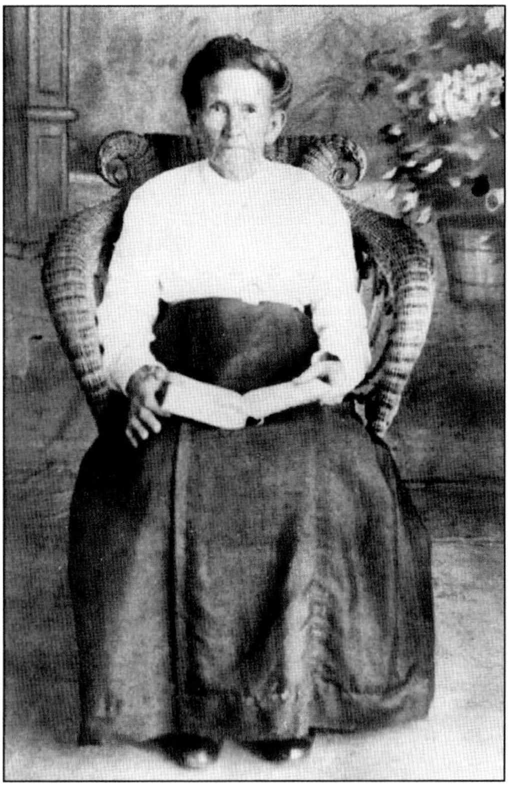

In 1865, Mary Ann Curry Underhill married William Abraham Simmons. Earlier, when her family was living near Lake Harney, Union soldiers confiscated the family's livestock. (Courtesy of Marie Goodrich.)

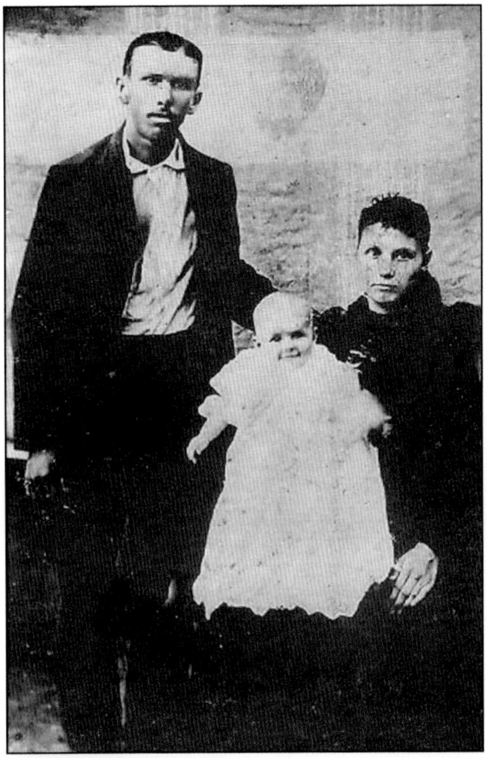

William and Mary Ann Simmons are pictured here with son Perry, their first of nine children. Mary was born in Kissimmee, and it was said "she could shoot a gun like a man, and was able to hit a Bruton snuff can at 100 yards." Their older children included Charles, Cleve, and Thurlow, all of whom raised their families in Oak Hill. (Courtesy of Marie Goodrich.)

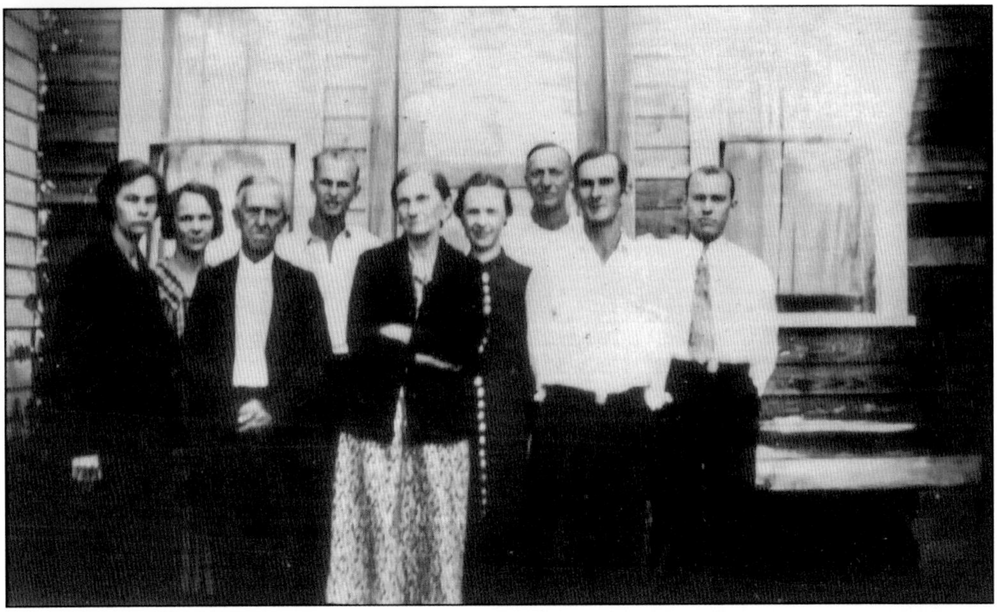

Pictured above is the Perry Simmons family. From left to right are (first row) Perry and Melinda; (second row) Annie, Pearl, Howard, Margaret, Harry, Bill, and Buddy. When oldest son Harry was out hunting, a rattlesnake bit him. To save his own life, he had to tie a rope around his leg, cut an X over the bite, and watch the poisonous black blood run out. Mounting his horse, Harry headed for his home at Blue Ridge, changed his shirt, and was taken to the Hawks Park Hospital by a friend. He was treated and survived the bite. (Courtesy of Marie Goodrich.)

Thurlow Simmons married Mary Smith. They were the parents of Alvin, who married Doris Treadwell, and Alice, who married Bennett Lopez. (Courtesy of Eddie Smith.)

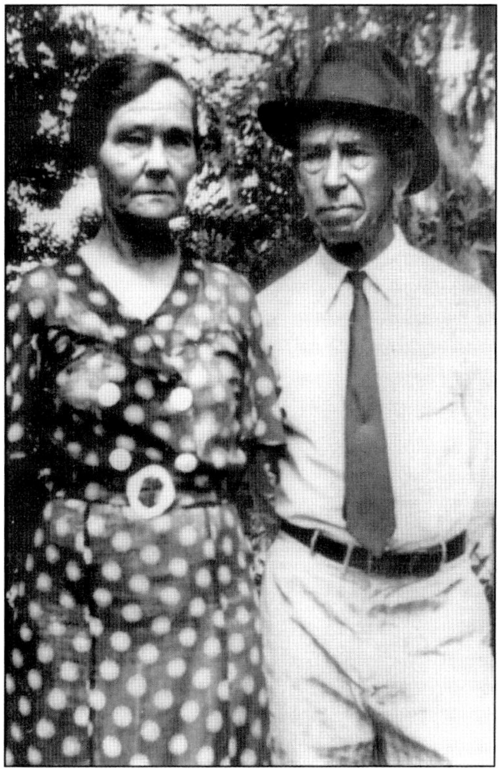

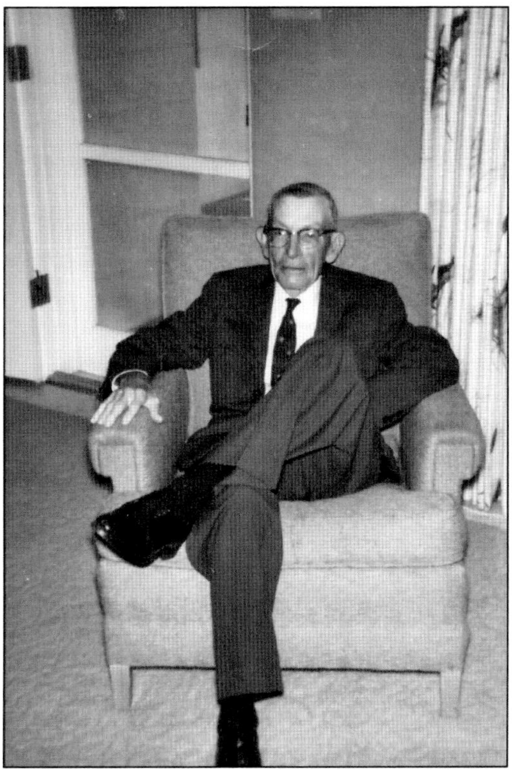

Cleve Simmons married Jeanetta Moore, whose family had come from England. He was custodian for the Oak Hill School for many years. He arrived early in the morning to light the furnace so children would have warm classrooms in the winter. (Courtesy of Ann Simmons.)

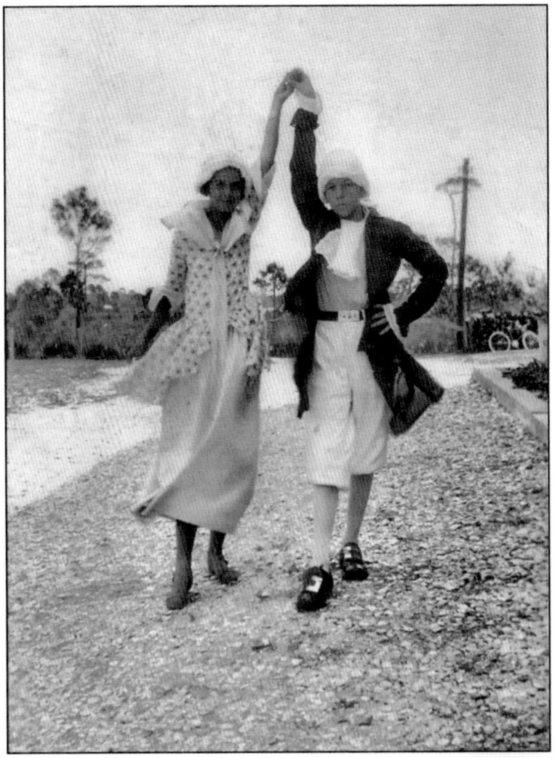

Sarah Slaughter (left) and Arthur Simmons (right) are dressed for the school play, which was always a highlight for the children who were participating and for their parents, who enjoyed the show.

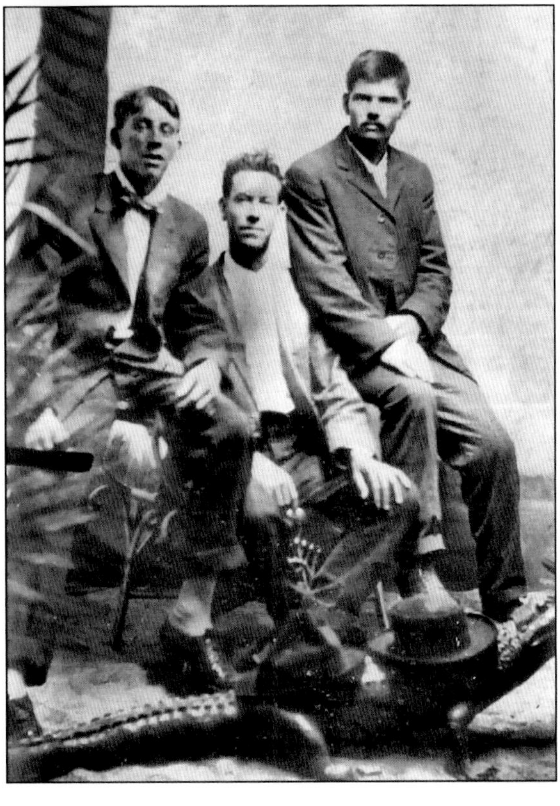

From left to right, Clarence Goodrich, Glen Montgomery, and Ankor Damgaard were community leaders from the start of the 20th century whose families are still in Oak Hill today. (Courtesy of Ida Goodrich.)

Lenora Coward was born in North Carolina and married Charles Simmons. Lenora is remembered as "a Godly woman" who taught Sunday school and was active in the First Baptist Church. They had six children: Clyde, Evelyn, Guy, Edna, John Henry, and Nina. (Courtesy of Bill McGee.)

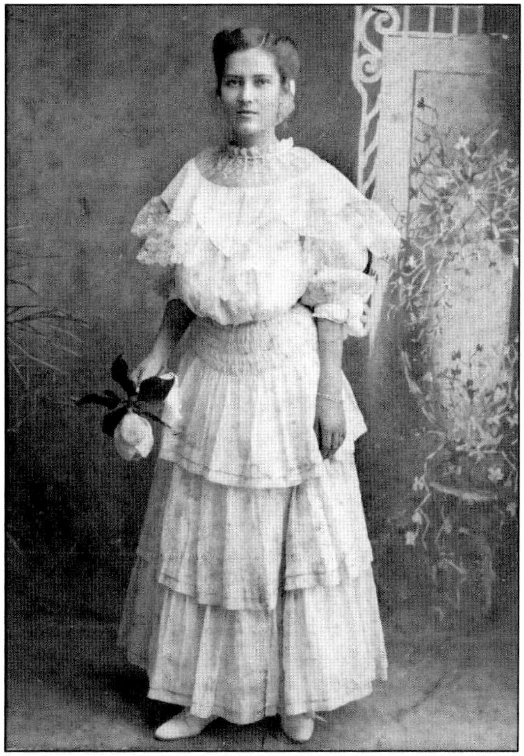

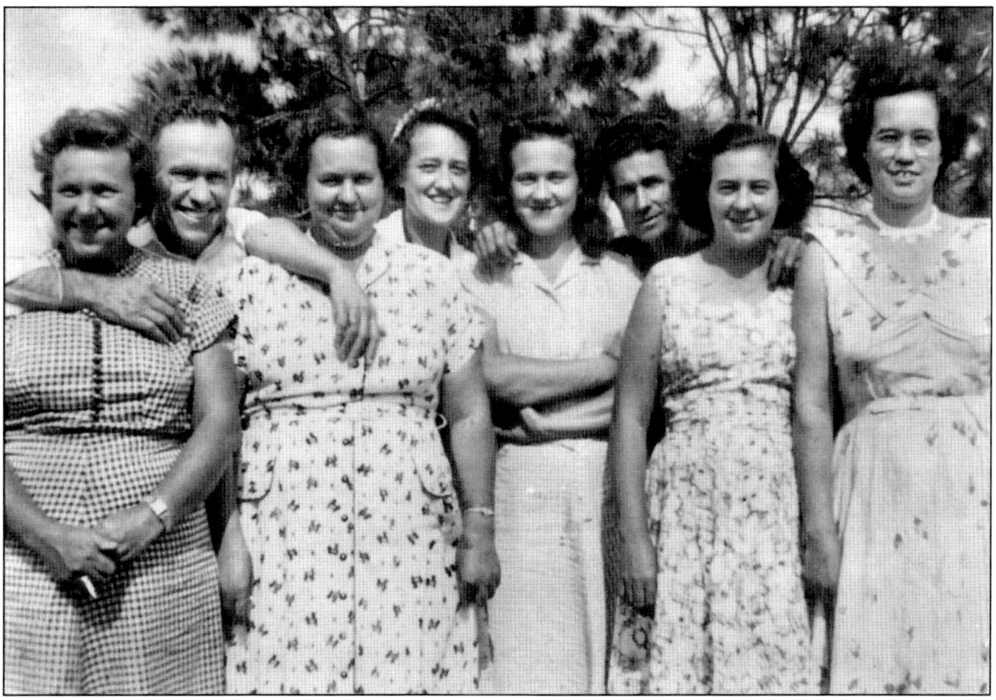

Charlie and Ola Harris were early settlers in Oak Hill. Their children are, from left to right, Annabelle, Woodrow, Maybell, Myrtle Lee, Marie, Oliver, Evelyn, and Iona. (Courtesy of Margie Shine.)

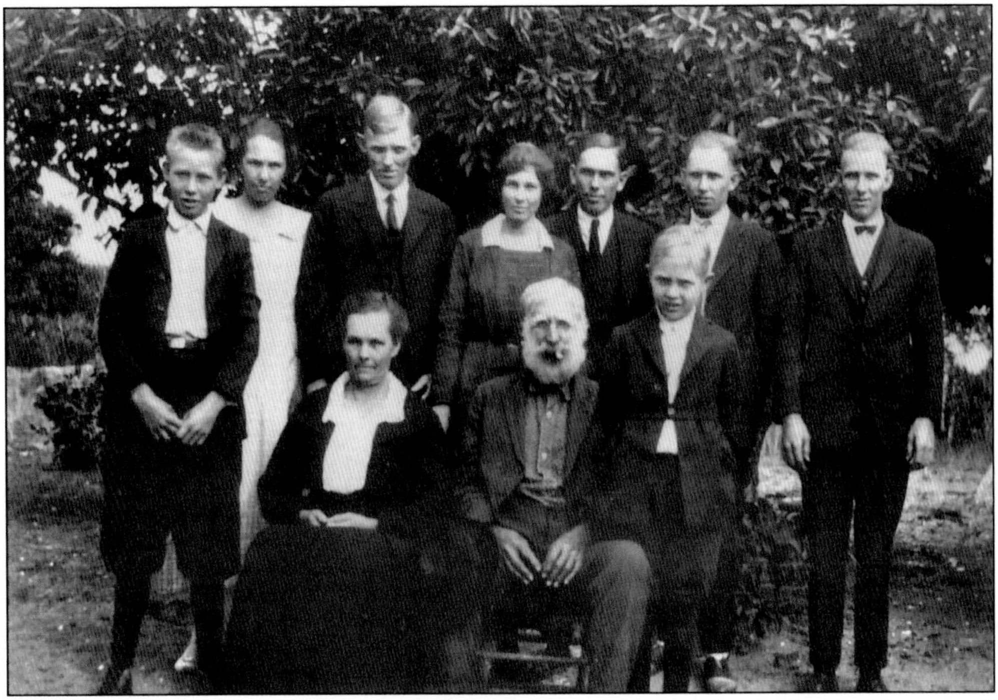

Another early family that settled in Oak Hill was that of John and Annie Osteen. They put all of their belongings on a small raft in 1905, and John and his sons poled up the river from Fort Lauderdale to Oak Hill. Annie and her daughter, Nancy, came by train. The cost of two tickets was $5. John Osteen provided for his family by working in the cattle and orange industries, and he carried the mail to nearby settlements. (Courtesy of Bill Dyall.)

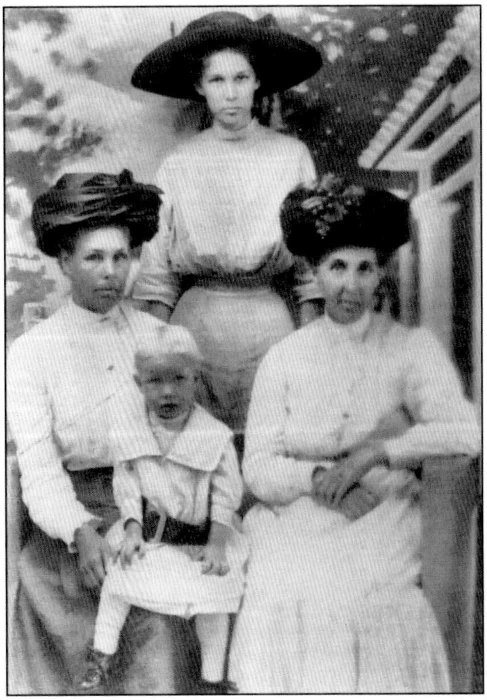

These Osteen ladies were Nancy Osteen Dyall (standing), Annie Brooke Osteen (left), and her mother, Nancy Prevatt Brooke, along with Kenneth Osteen. (Courtesy of Bill Dyall.)

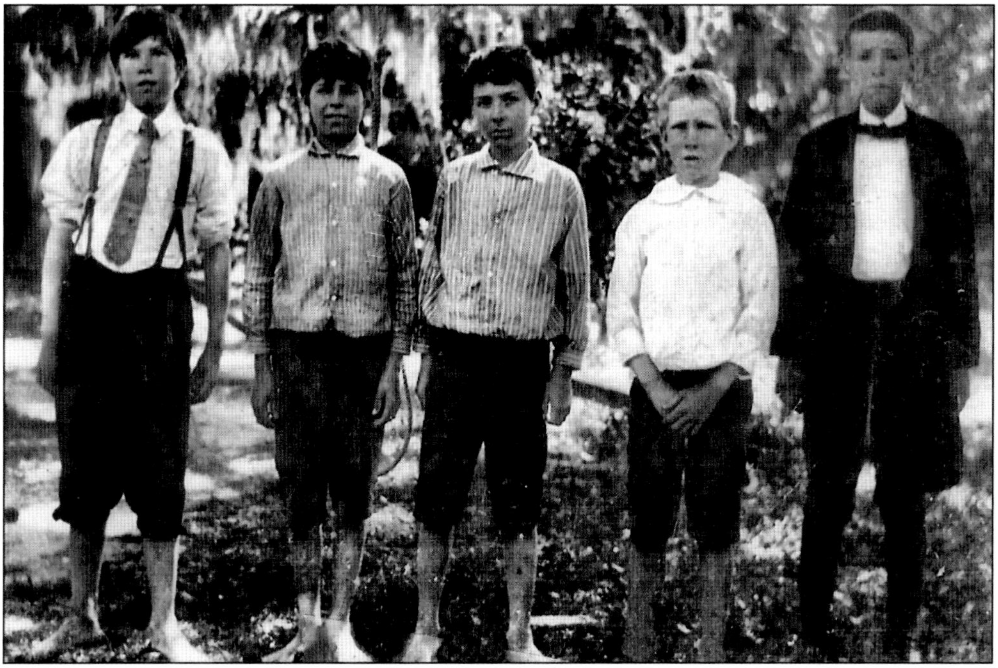

Annie Osteen's nephews, pictured here, only wore shoes when made to do so by their parents. From left to right are Edward Burch, Cortez and Dewey Brooke, Edgar Osteen, and Gilbert Brooke. (Courtesy of Bill Dyall.)

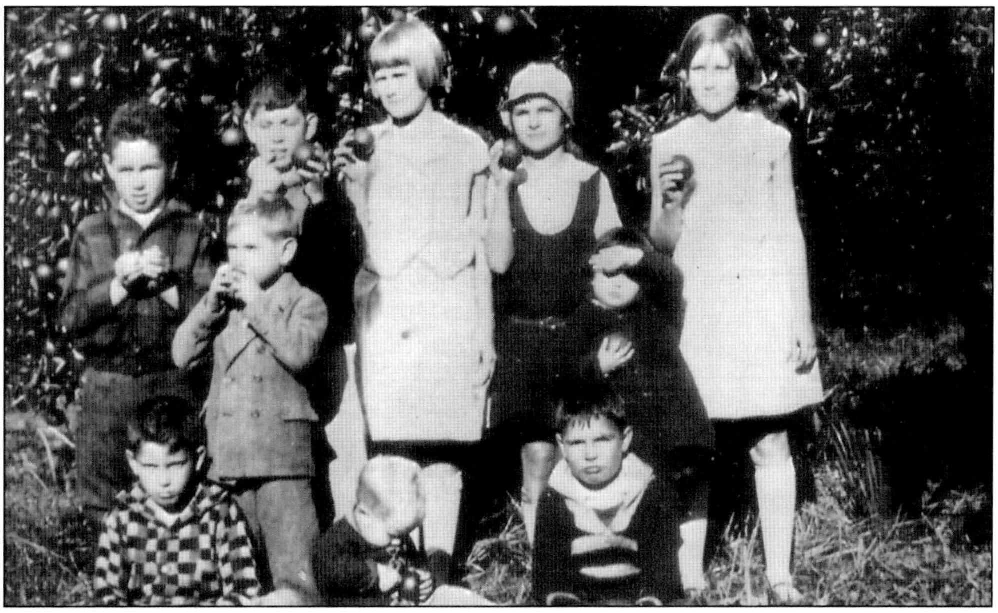

Forte Jones married Eva Bass in 1915, and his brother, Floyd, and Ethel Bessinger were also married the same year. They came to Oak Hill from Georgia to work for the E. Day Grove Company. The Jones children are pictured in the groves with friends. From left to right are (first row) Everett Jones, Madlow, and Pharold; (second row) Roy and Martha Sue (Bufford); (third row) Marion Jones, Harold Jones, Eunice Dyall (Solana), Beatrice Jones (Stewart), and Bobbie Dyall Somerset. (Courtesy of Jean Vann.)

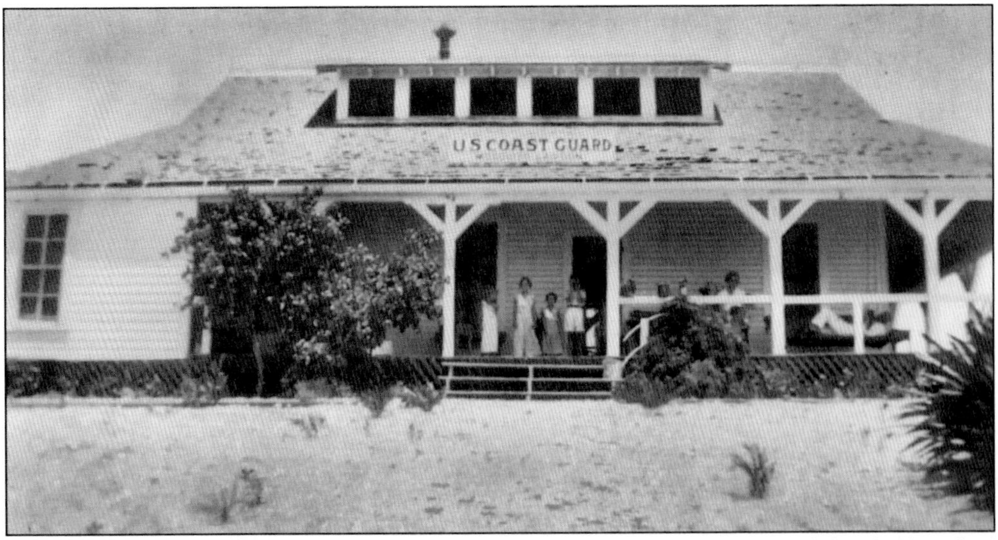

Capt. Jarvis Midgett and his family lived at the U.S. Coast Guard Station, and the children had to take a boat across the river to attend school. The station remained active until 1935, when the services moved to Ponce Inlet between New Smyrna and Daytona Beaches. (Courtesy of Bill Dyall.)

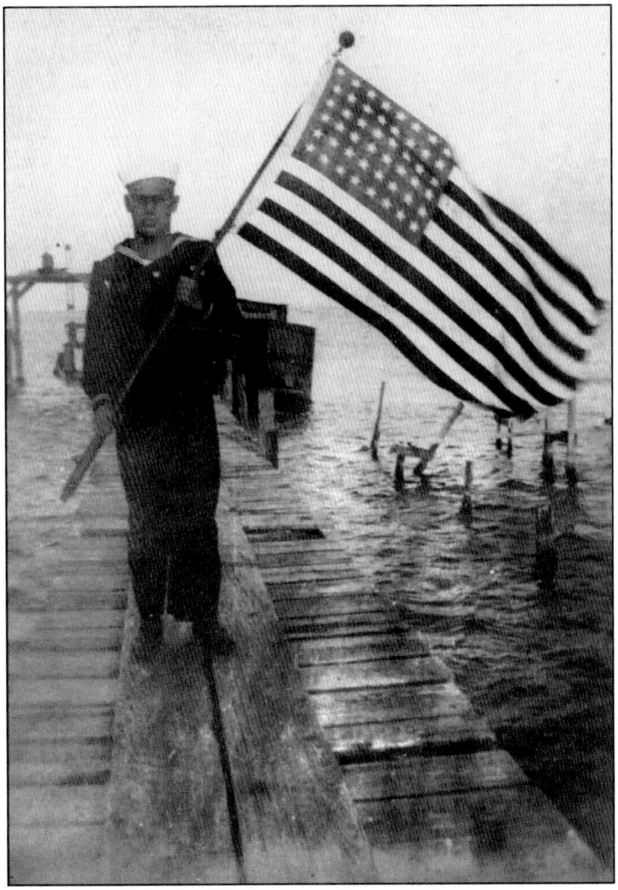

Pictured is an unidentified U.S. Coast Guard serviceman carrying a 48-star flag on the dock of the Oak Hill Station. (Courtesy of Bill Dyall.)

Pictured right are unidentified members of the U.S. Coast Guard during the early 1920s. (Courtesy of Bill Dyall.)

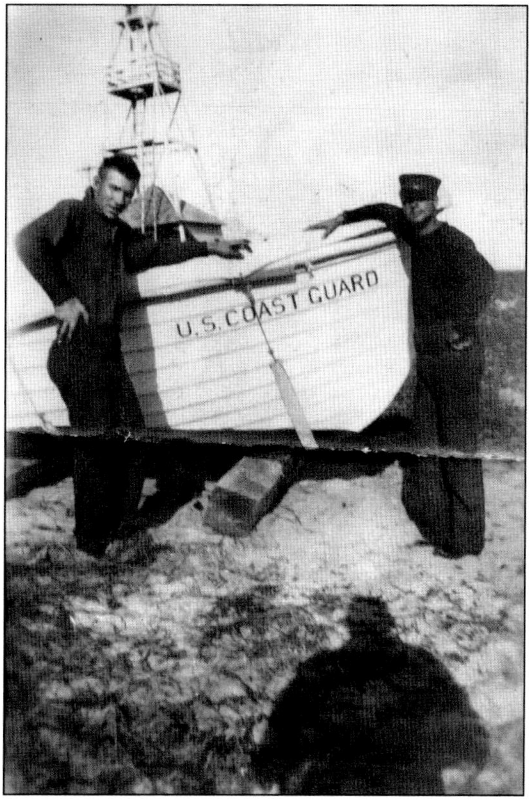

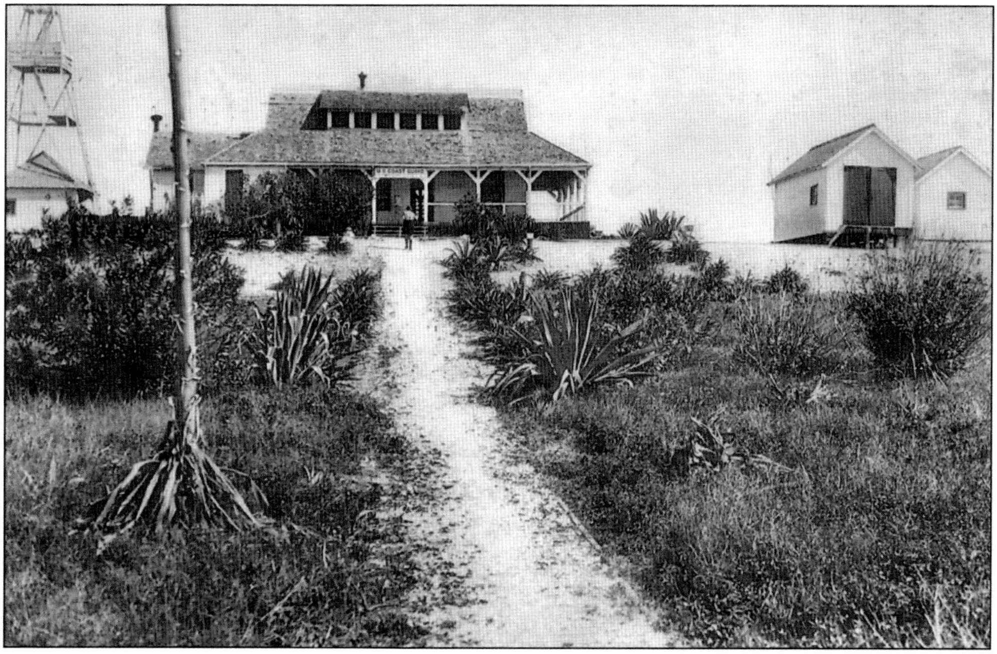

A lifesaving station was built on the ocean in the late 1860s. It was first established as a "House of Refuge" before officially becoming a U.S. Coast Guard Station. John D. Vann was a beach watcher at the House of Refuge. (Courtesy of Ida Goodrich.)

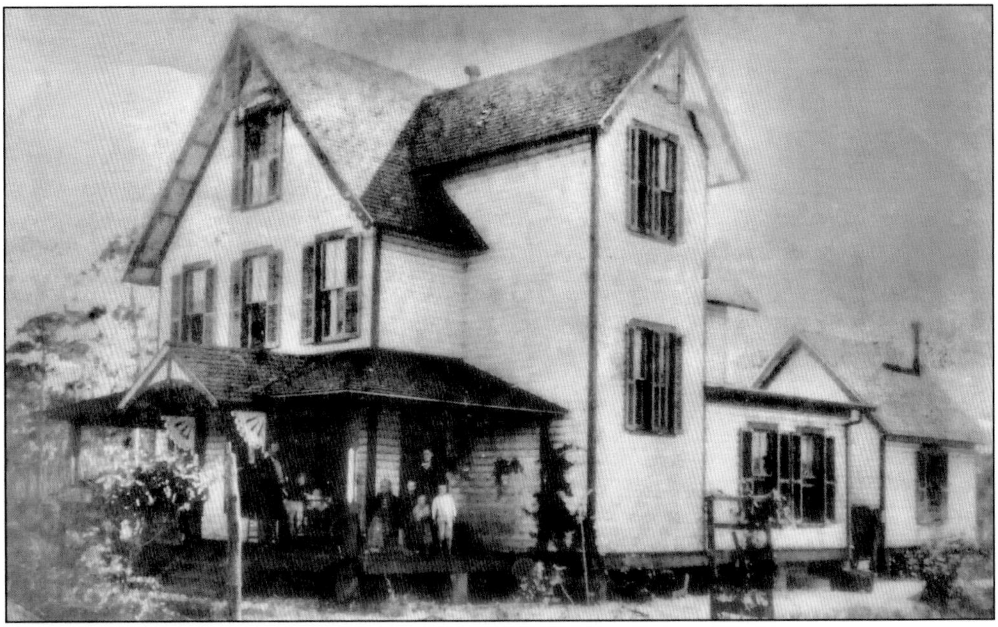

Capt. John Coleman came to Oak Hill from Texas in the 1800s. Traveling with him was his sister, Fannie who was carrying $30,000 in her bustle to invest in Florida citrus groves. Captain Coleman's daughter, Sidney, met and married Zack Williams. The Williams family continued in the citrus industry until the great freeze of 1896, which destroyed most of the groves in the area. Axson Goodrich's groves were not destroyed by the freeze, so he furnished trees to others to replant their groves. The picture above is the home of Zack and Sidney Williams, where they raised their children: Zack Taylor Jr., Warren, Lee, Effie, Coleman, Sidney, Preston, and Annie Belle. It remains a residence today. (Courtesy of Dorothy Lee Hutchinson.)

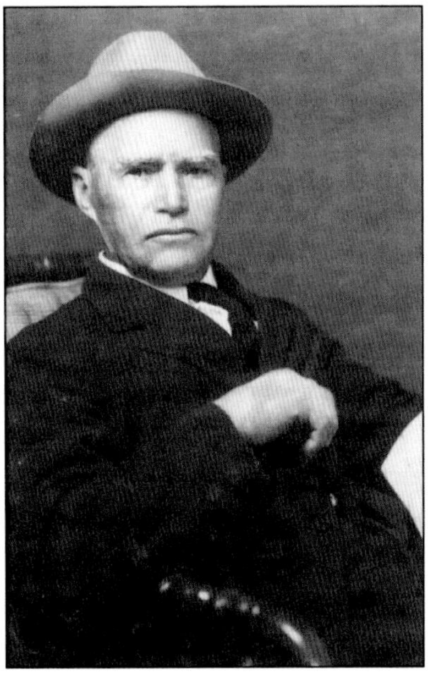

John C. "Papay" McCullough left South Carolina in 1900 with his two sons. They rode bicycles to Florida, where they settled in Oak Hill. He was a builder and is remembered for the construction of the McCullough House on East Halifax Avenue, the Somerset Hotel, and several stores. His two daughters were Eva McCullough (Brooke) and Jessie McCullough (Fogle). (Courtesy of Betty Bellamy.)

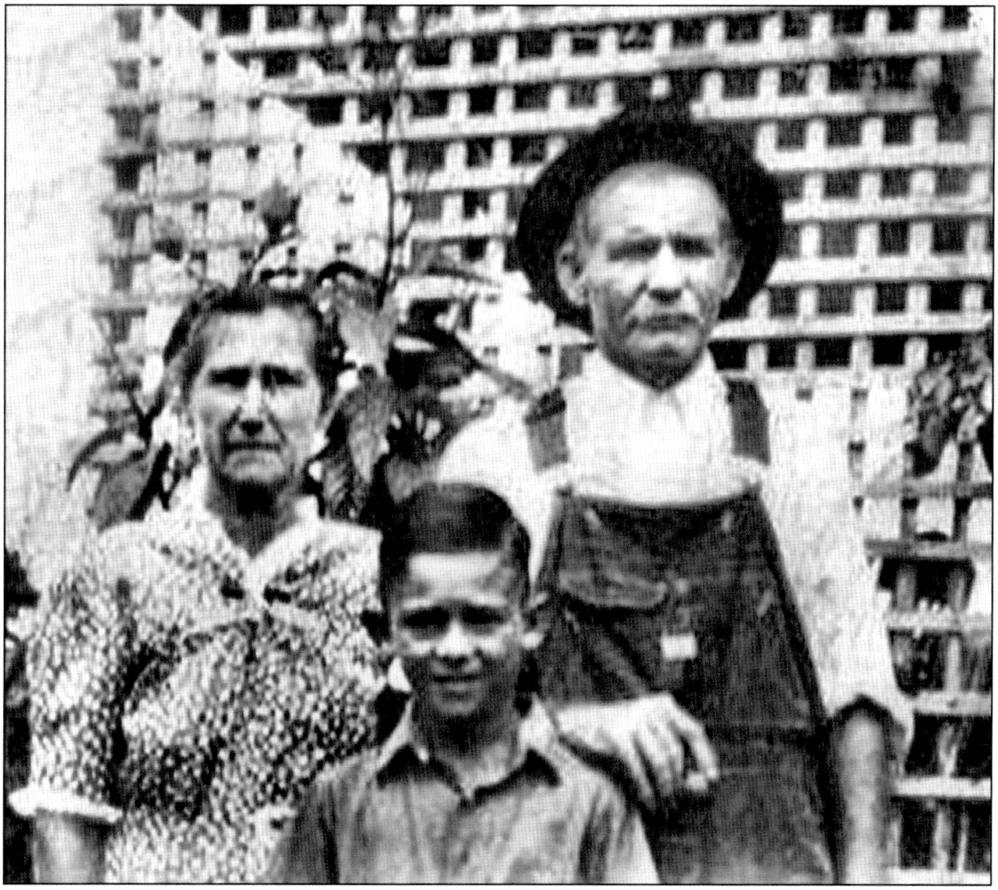

Will and Emma Bellamy and their son Jack are pictured above. Will Bellamy tended citrus groves. Other Bellamy children were Lonnie, Ethel, and Esther. (Courtesy of Betty Bellamy.)

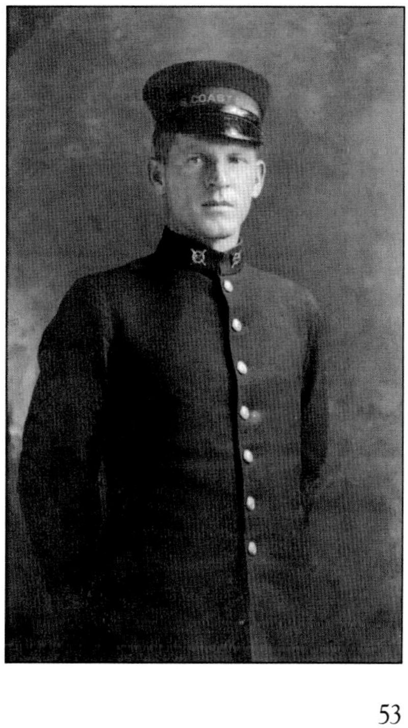

Doc Robinson served in the U.S. Coast Guard during World War I. He moved from Sanford, joining his brother, William Allen Robinson, to settle in Oak Hill. He never married. (Courtesy of Juanita Robinson.)

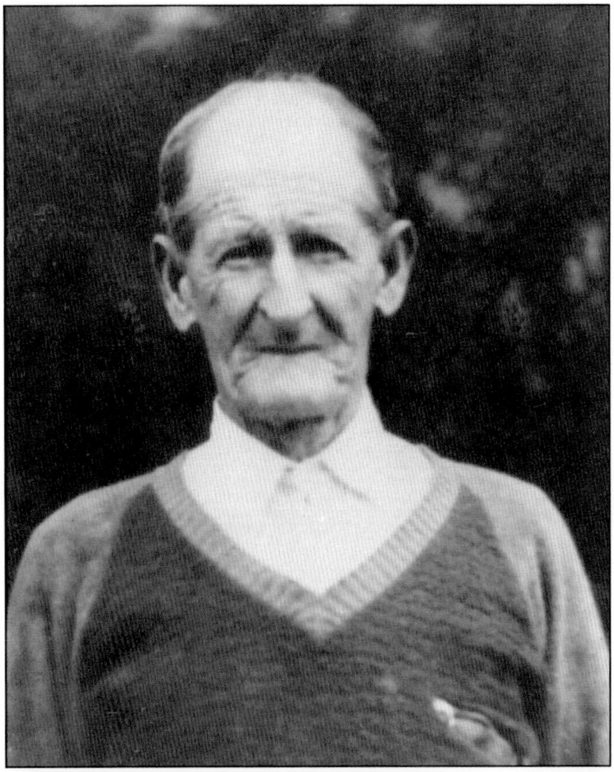

William Allen Robinson was born in Orlando, Florida, in 1880. He moved to Oak Hill in 1916 and became a commercial fisherman. He met Lillie Park, and they were married on November 10, 1917. They raised eight children: William, Lamar, Earl, James, Rosie, Dick, Annie, and Everall. His brothers were Jessie James, Christopher Columbus, Eugene, and Doc. (Courtesy of Juanita Robinson.)

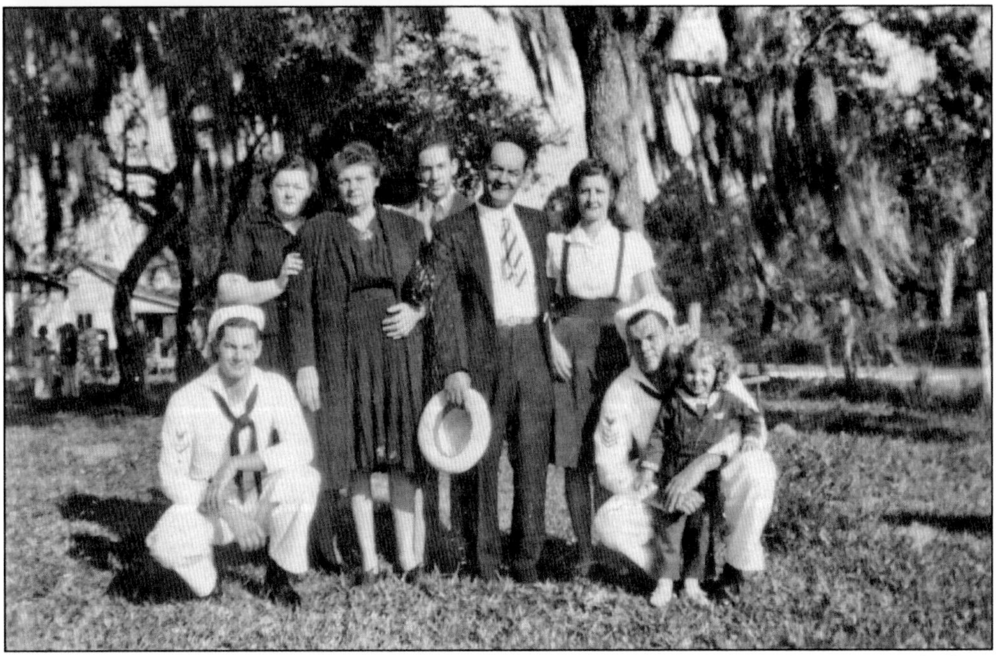

Sailors Russell Robinson (far left) and his brother Carl Robinson (far right) pose with their family before leaving for military service during World War II. Others pictured are (from left to right) Eleanor Robinson, Rose Robinson, Davis "Chippy" Robinson, Eugene Robinson, Glennis Robinson, and "Baby Glennis" in the arms of her father, Carl.

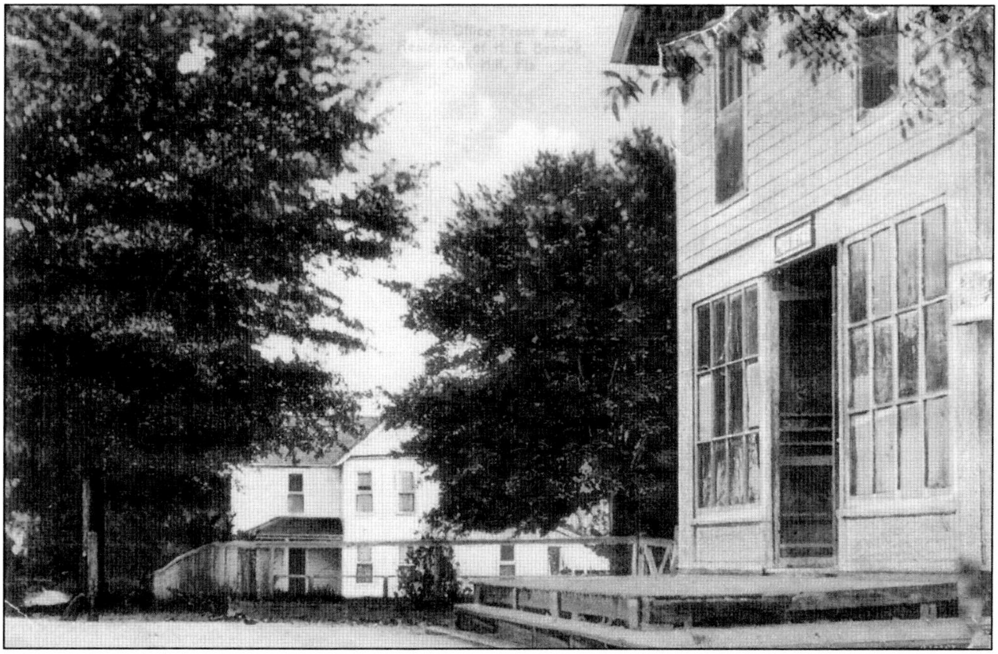

This postcard displays the original Howes' Store and post office, which was bought by Leonard Mosby. When he was drafted into the military, he sold his business to his brother-in-law, Van Buren Baldwin Sr. Baldwin and his wife, Mary, lived above the store and raised six children here. The house seen in the background belonged to Mary's sister, Gertrude, and her husband, Horace Bennett. The Bennetts were owners of several large citrus groves.

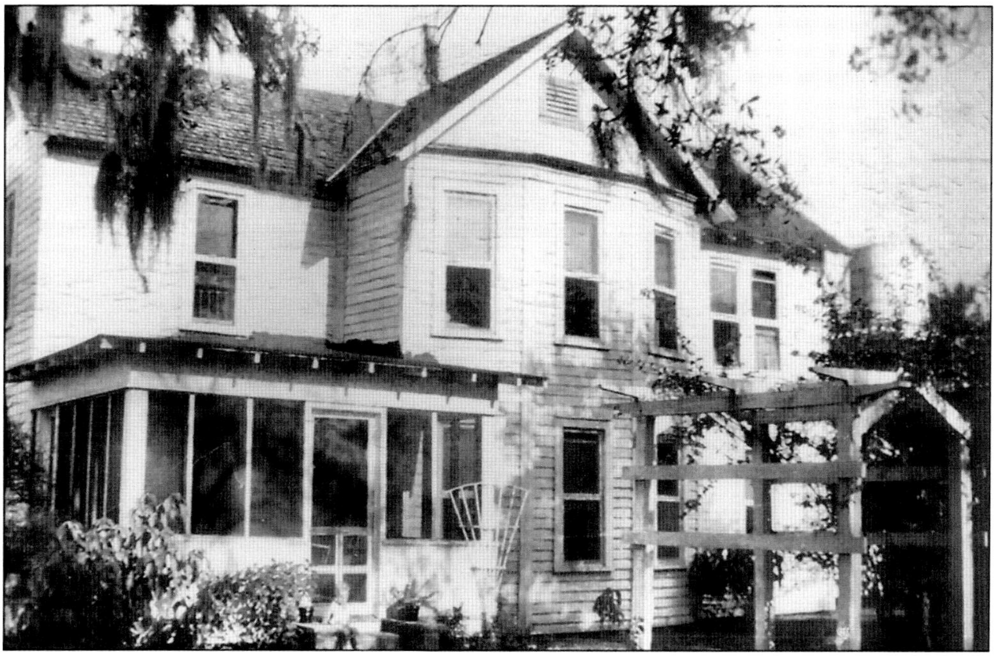

This is the same house in the 1930s, with an addition. Horace Bennett had a large generator and supplied electricity for several neighboring houses. Florida Power and Light did not provide power for businesses until 1931.

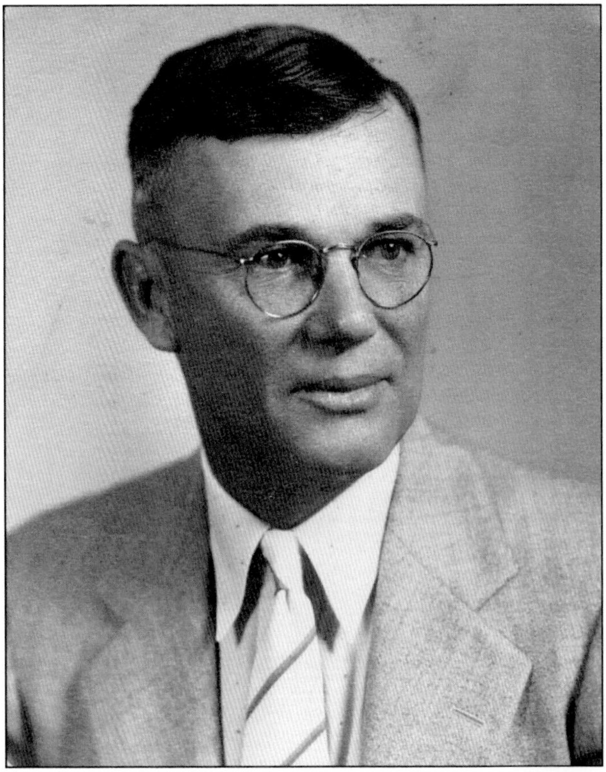

Horace Bennett and his wife, Gertrude, had three children: Breece, Marion Louise (always called "Sis"), and Horace Jr., who attended Julliard and became a professional musician. Horace Sr. died of a heart attack at a young age, leaving his widow in charge of the large grove business. (Courtesy of Martha Ann Parks.)

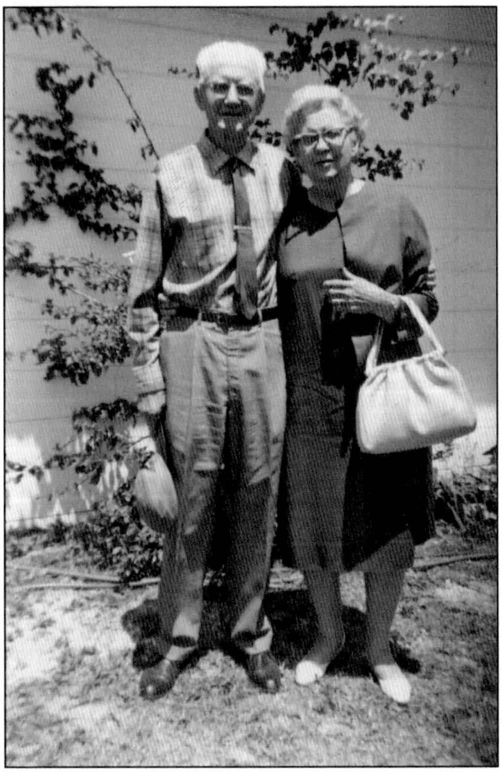

Gertrude later married Percy Threlkeld, and they lived in this house until their deaths. They were active in the First Baptist Church, where she placed an arrangement of fresh flowers on the altar every Sunday for more than 30 years. (Courtesy of Martha Ann Parks.)

Breece Bennett, son of Horace and Gertrude, married Pauline Simmons, and they had three children: Sue, Barbara, and Breece Jr. Like his father, Breece went into the citrus business, managing the Blue Goose Packing House. Tragedy struck this prominent family when Breece Jr. was in the woods hunting with his father and was bitten by a rattlesnake. Knowing what to do, Breece saved his son's life, but the leg had to be amputated. Not long after that, Breece Sr. was thrown from a horse and killed. (Courtesy of Martha Ann Parks.)

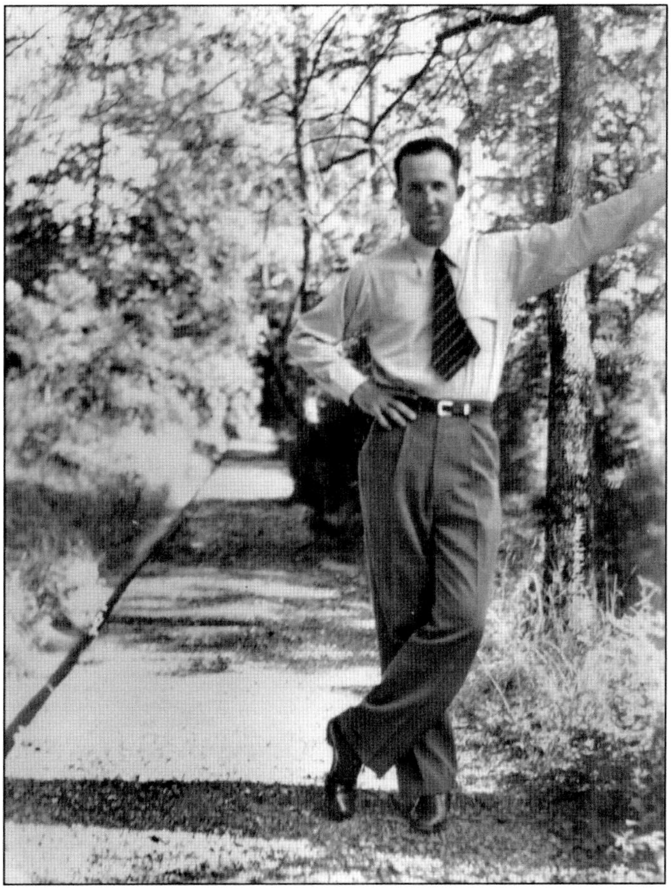

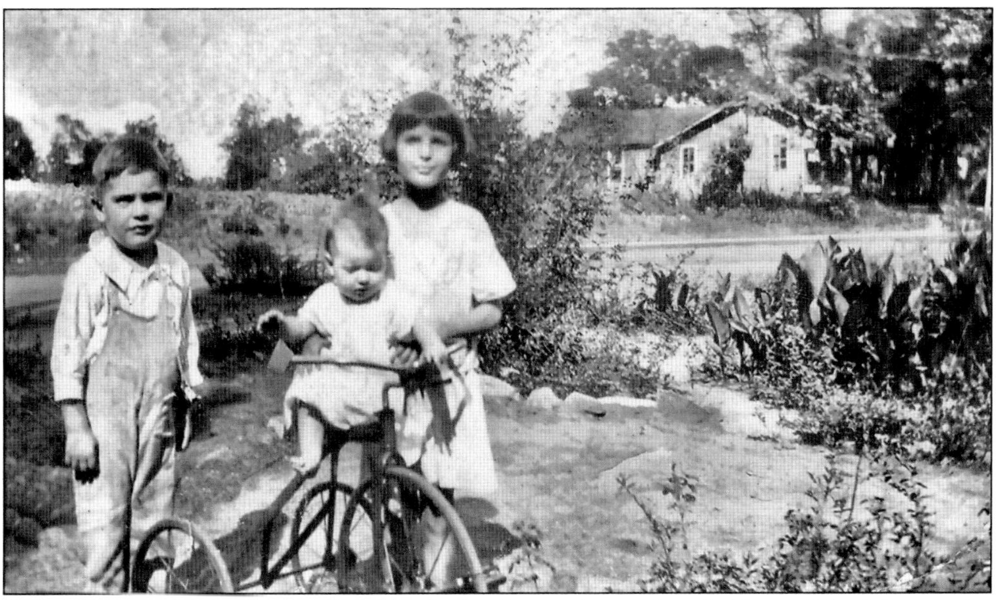

Pictured from left to right are Pharold, Martha Sue, and Beatrice, children of Floyd Jones, who was also involved in the citrus industry. (Courtesy of Jean Vann.)

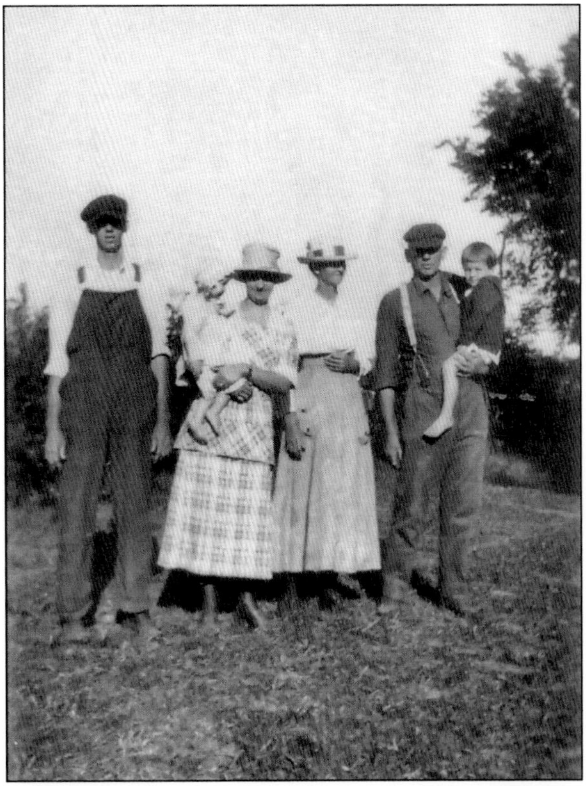

Van Buren and Mary Baldwin moved to Oak Hill from Titusville in 1917 to take over the Mosby grocery store at the top of the hill when her brother, Leonard, left for war. From left to right are Van Buren and Mary Baldwin, holding Jeanne; and Florence and Robert Baldwin, parents of Van Buren, holding Van Buren Jr.

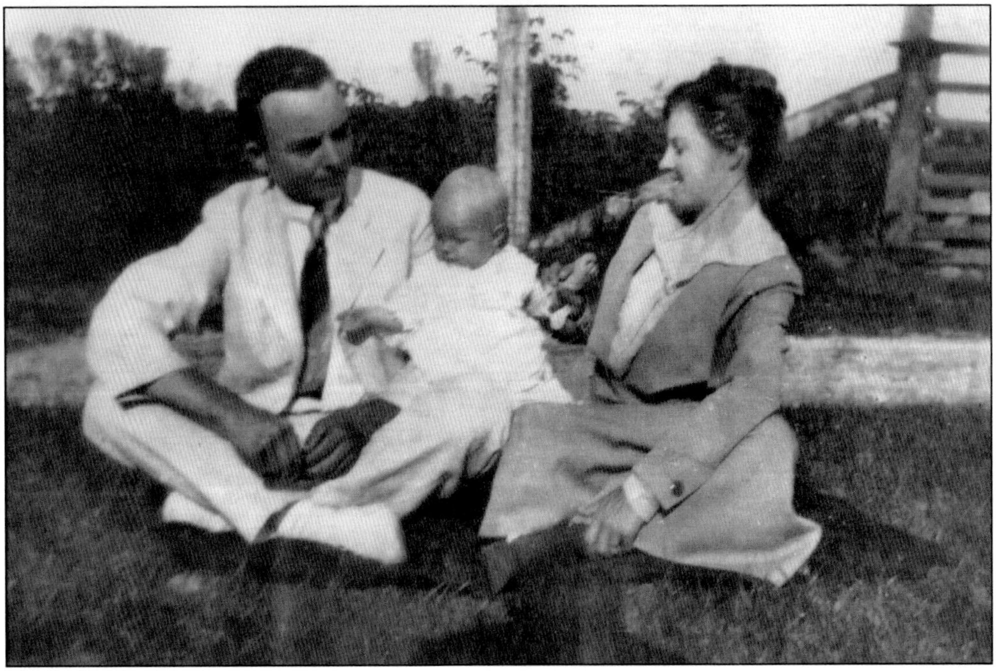

Oscar and Mamie Alderman are pictured with their first child, Inez, in 1918. Oscar was the meat cutter at the Baldwin Store, and the two families were close friends. (Courtesy of Euda Mary Alderman.)

Four

"The Good Ole Days"

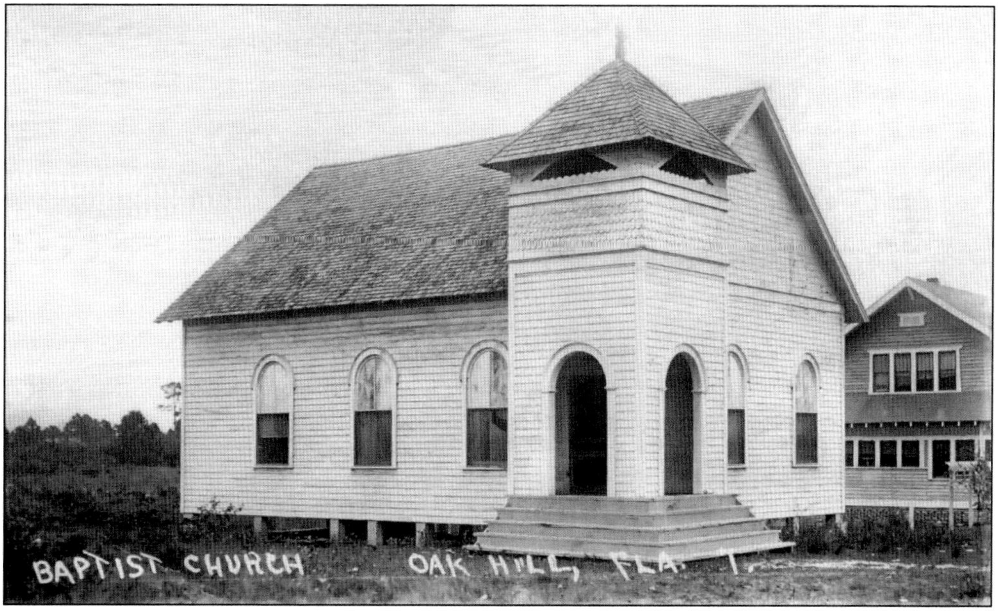

On May 18, 1889, Mary Putman, Jennie Putman, Mary Gaines, A. B. Curfry, Lee Ann Curry, J. A. Wright, H. C. Wright, Phillip Wright, and Sydney and Zack Williams met with Rev. S. T. Gove to establish the Oak Hill First Baptist Church. W. C. Howes donated the land to construct a church building. John and Annie Osteen were among those who helped organize cake and ice cream socials to raise money for the building. (Courtesy of Ida Goodrich.)

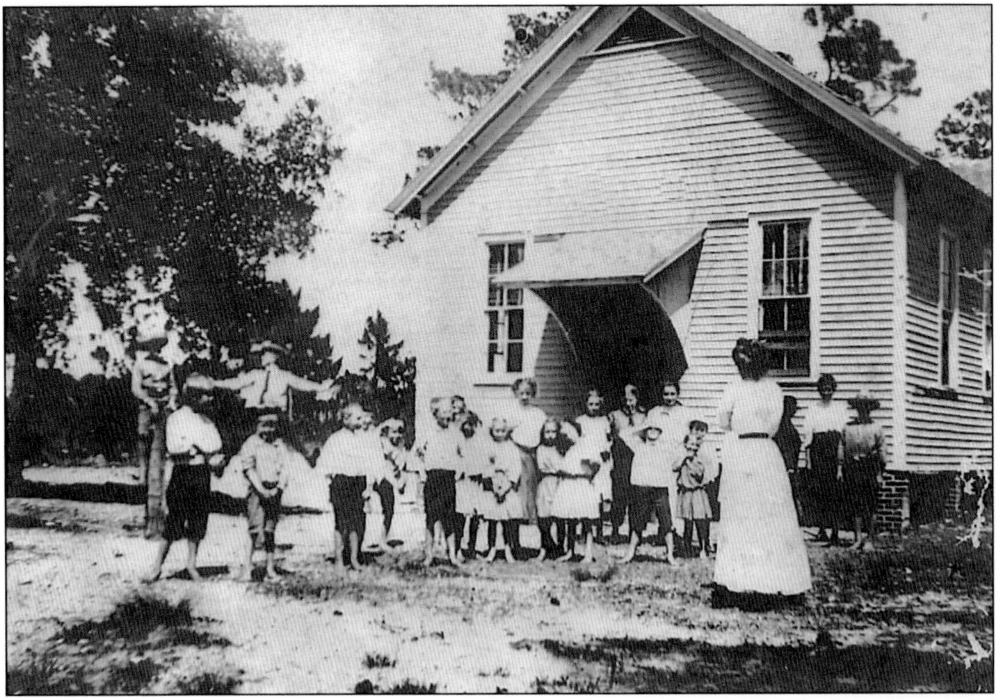

The local citizens also established a volunteer school board that would provide educational opportunities for local children. Volunteers built this early school. (Courtesy of Betty Bellamy.)

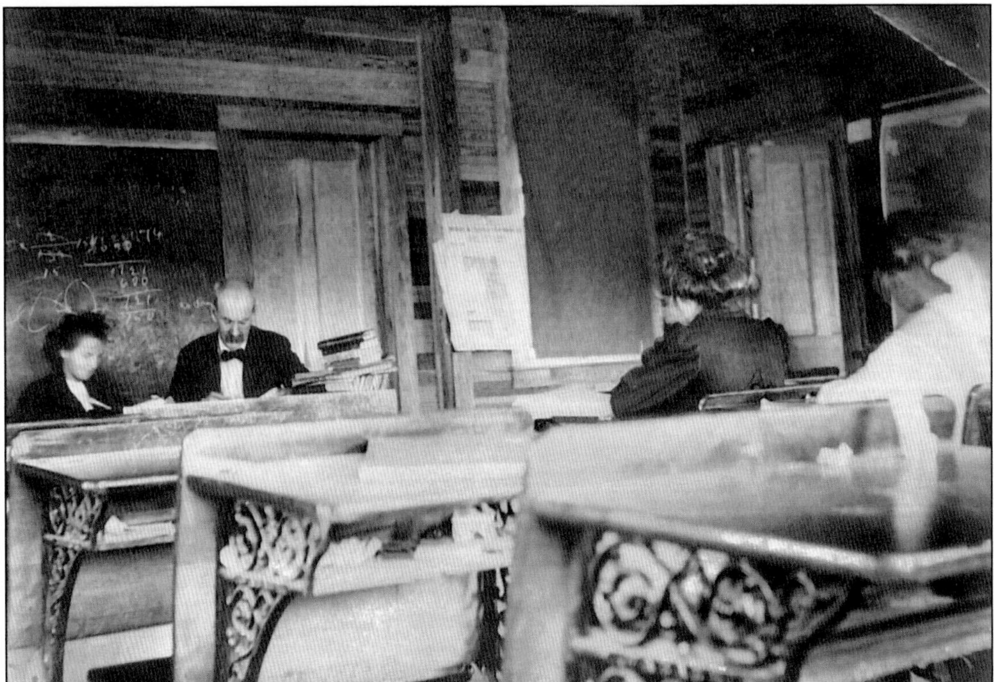

Take a look inside the first schoolhouse in Oak Hill. Ada Stanley was a teacher, as were Patty Howes and Ethel Williams, who taught two generations of Oak Hill children. Principal John Story is pictured above helping a student. (Courtesy of Betty Bellamy.)

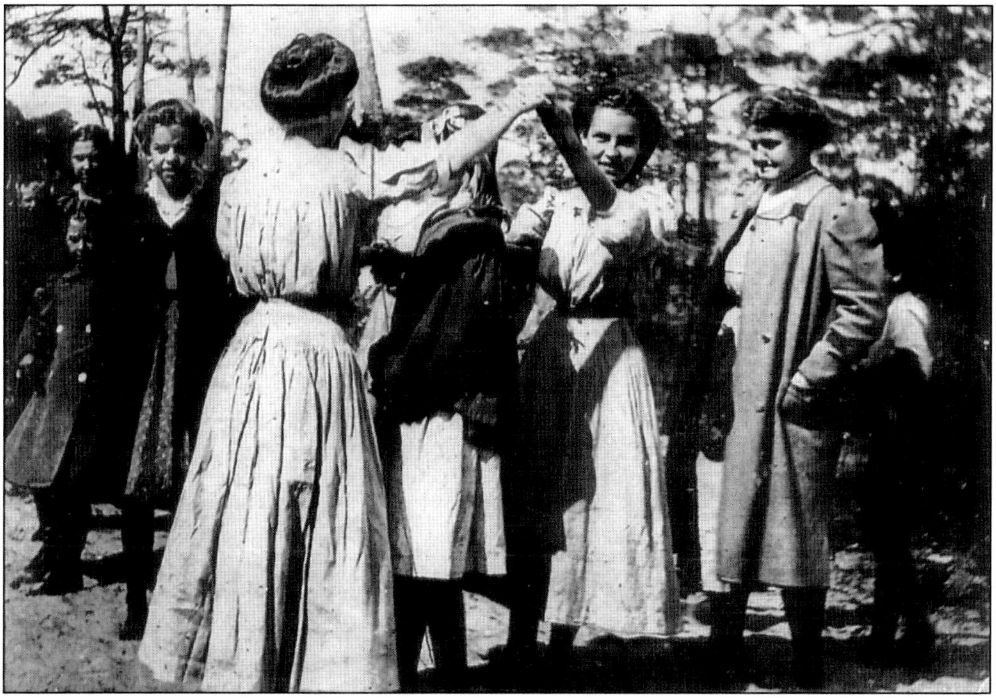

Students enjoyed simple outside games during recess. (Courtesy of Betty Bellamy.)

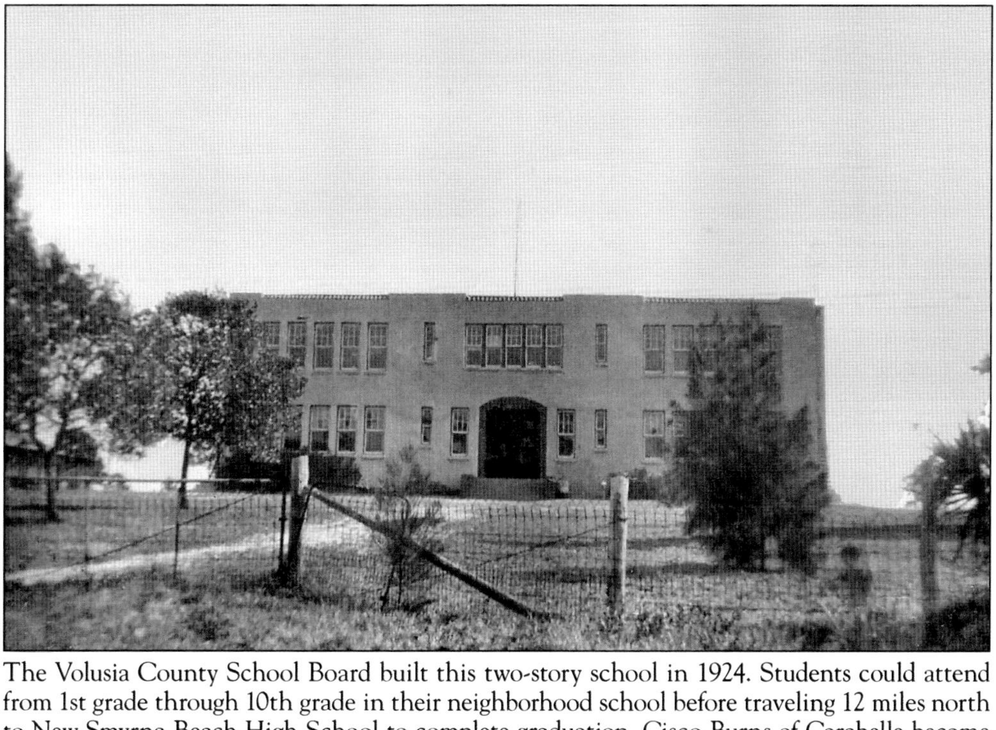

The Volusia County School Board built this two-story school in 1924. Students could attend from 1st grade through 10th grade in their neighborhood school before traveling 12 miles north to New Smyrna Beach High School to complete graduation. Cisco Burns of Carabelle became this school's first principal. T. DeWitt Taylor followed him as principal in 1927. William F. Burns began a long career as principal in 1938. (Courtesy of Marie Goodrich.)

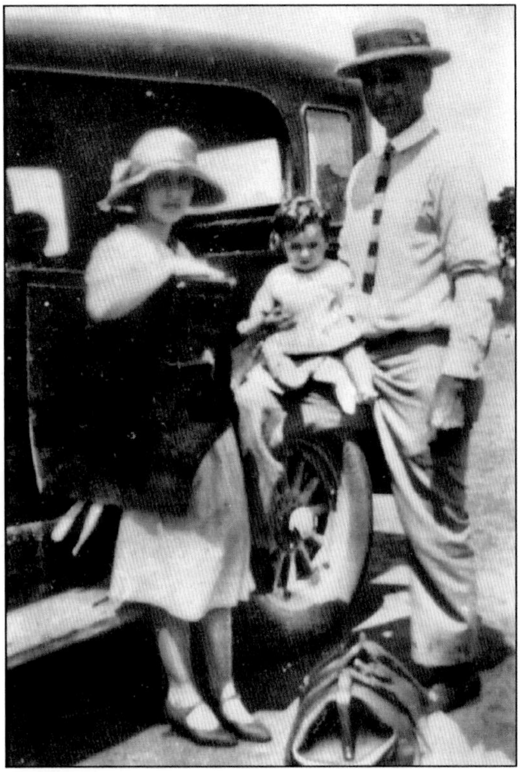

Archie Smith and his wife, Ruby Gordon Smith, take daughter Betty Lou for a ride in their new car. Archie met Ruby at her father's restaurant in Orlando when he was delivering whiskey during Prohibition. The 18th Amendment, ratified in 1919, introduced the era of Prohibition by outlawing the manufacture, sale, or transportation of alcohol. This new law created a profitable occupation for Archie Smith and many other locals. They called it the "whiskey business." (Courtesy of Eddie Smith.)

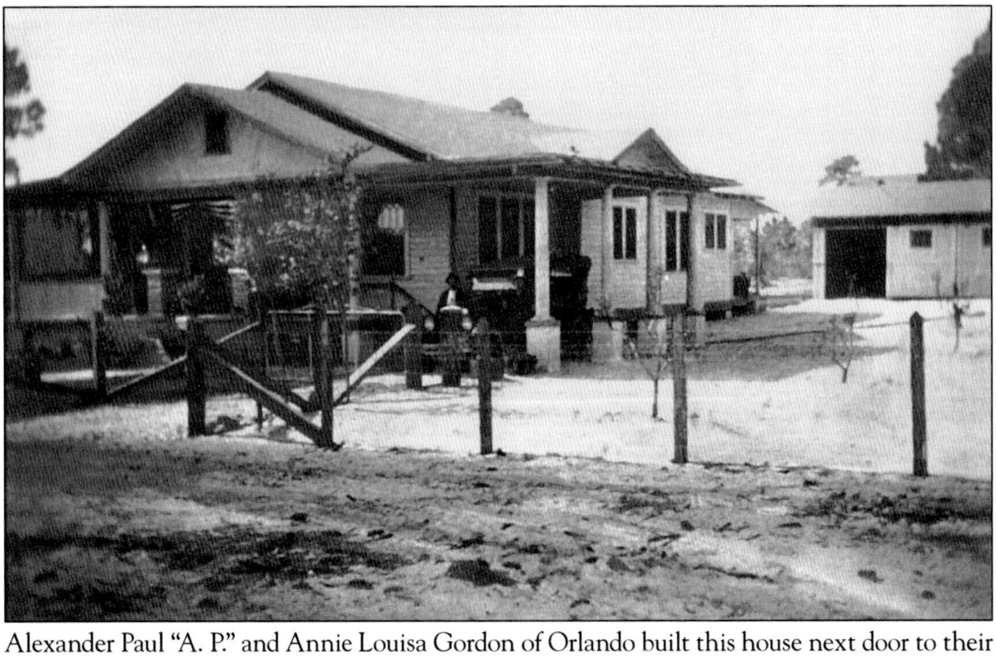

Alexander Paul "A. P." and Annie Louisa Gordon of Orlando built this house next door to their daughter, Ruby. It became the unofficial headquarters for an illegal whiskey operation during Prohibition days. The taste for alcohol spread, and the lure of the forbidden seemed to draw in more of the youth. Many churchgoers felt that fewer would drink were it not illegal. Whiskey was hidden in the attic and garage floor of this house. (Courtesy of Eddie Smith.)

A. P. Gordon (back) is pictured with his sons, Alexander J. Gordon, Edward Gordon, and Tommy Gordon, and step-grandson, Eddie Smith, in the front. (Courtesy of Eddie Smith.)

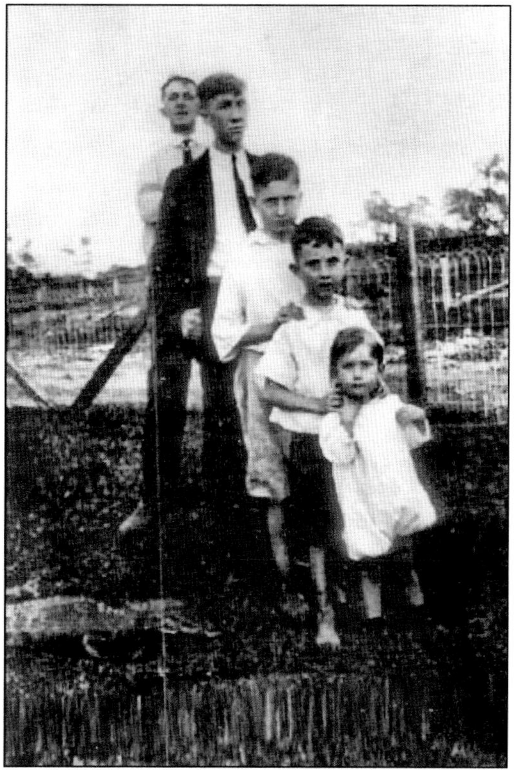

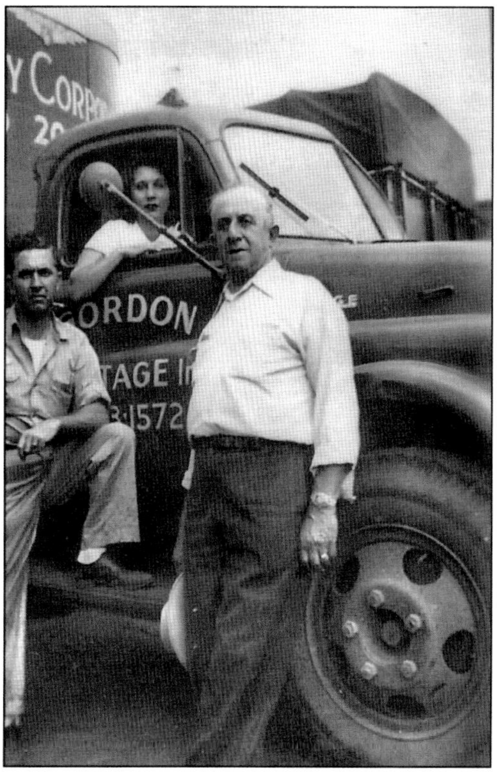

A. P. Gordon owned a trucking company, and he is remembered for building an ice plant and bringing electricity to the community. The Gordon family moved back to their home in Detroit in the 1930s, and Van Buren Baldwin bought their house in 1935. (Courtesy of Eddie Smith.)

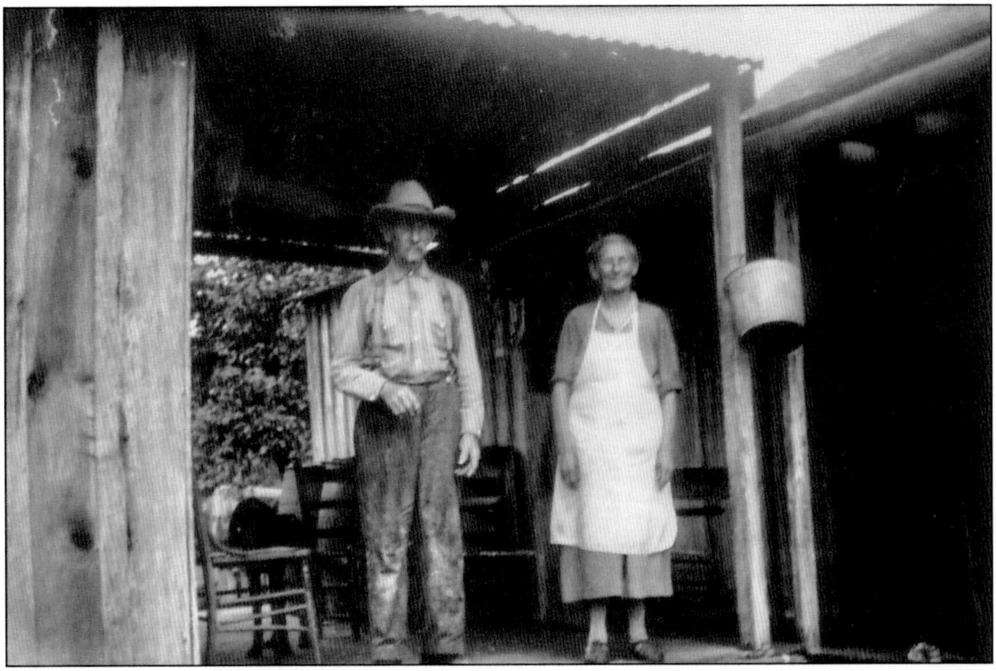

Henry and Annie Clark settled in the area just west of Oak Hill, known as Maytown, in 1900, where he raised stock and farmed. Annie Clark ran the first post office in Maytown in 1905. (Courtesy of Edward Clark.)

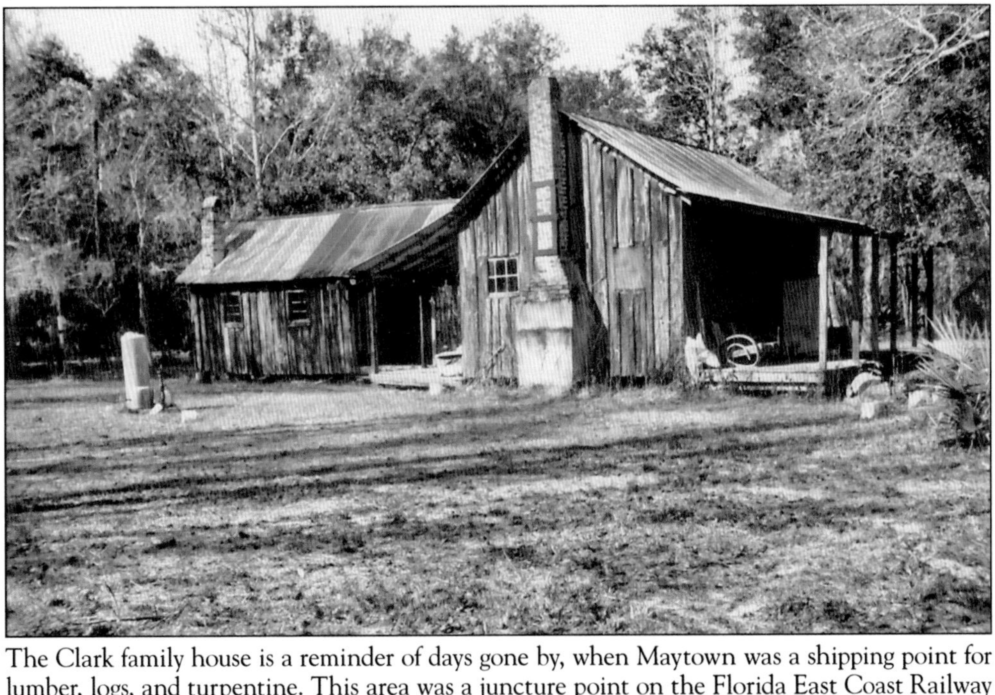

The Clark family house is a reminder of days gone by, when Maytown was a shipping point for lumber, logs, and turpentine. This area was a juncture point on the Florida East Coast Railway (FEC) lines from Titusville to Benson Junction, where they made a tie-in to the Atlantic Coastline Railroad. It was also a juncture point on the FEC branch line connecting Edgewater to Lake Okeechobee. (Courtesy of Edward Clark.)

William Mack Hutchinson and his wife, Minnie Lee Pulham Hutchinson, arrived in Oak Hill from Sparks, Georgia, in 1914. He was a commercial fisherman and loved to sit at the old store and tell yarns. Their 11 children were Colon, Viola, Claude, Howard, Loraine, Ira, Ruth, William Mack Jr., Lester, Arnett, and Leon. Many of their descendants still live in Oak Hill today. (Courtesy of Kathy Bittle.)

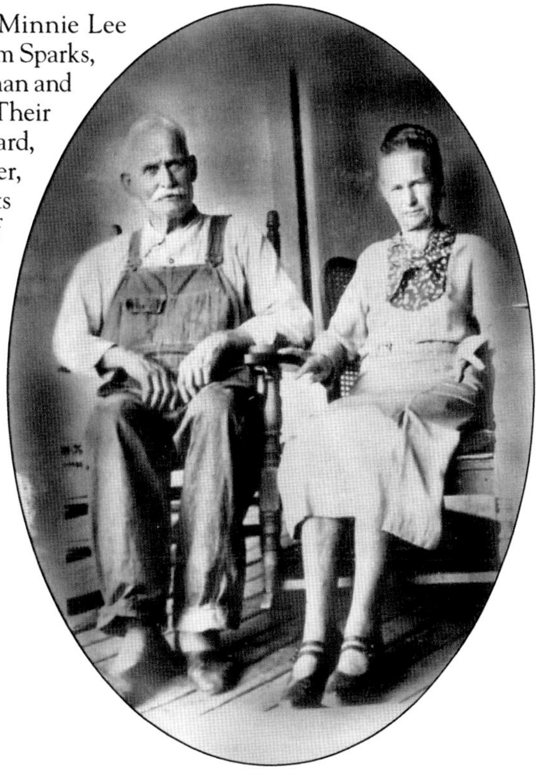

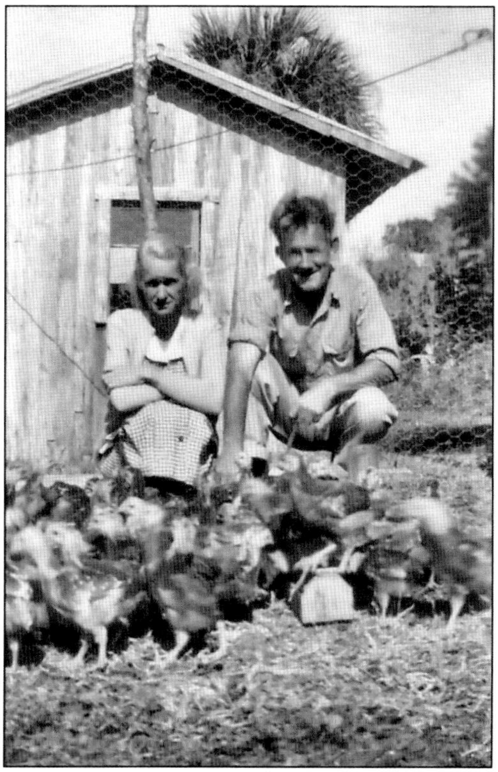

Times were hard, and families depended upon subsistence farming. Garrett and Lorraine Howland were married on August 1, 1920. They always had a family garden and chickens. (Courtesy of Kathy Bittle.)

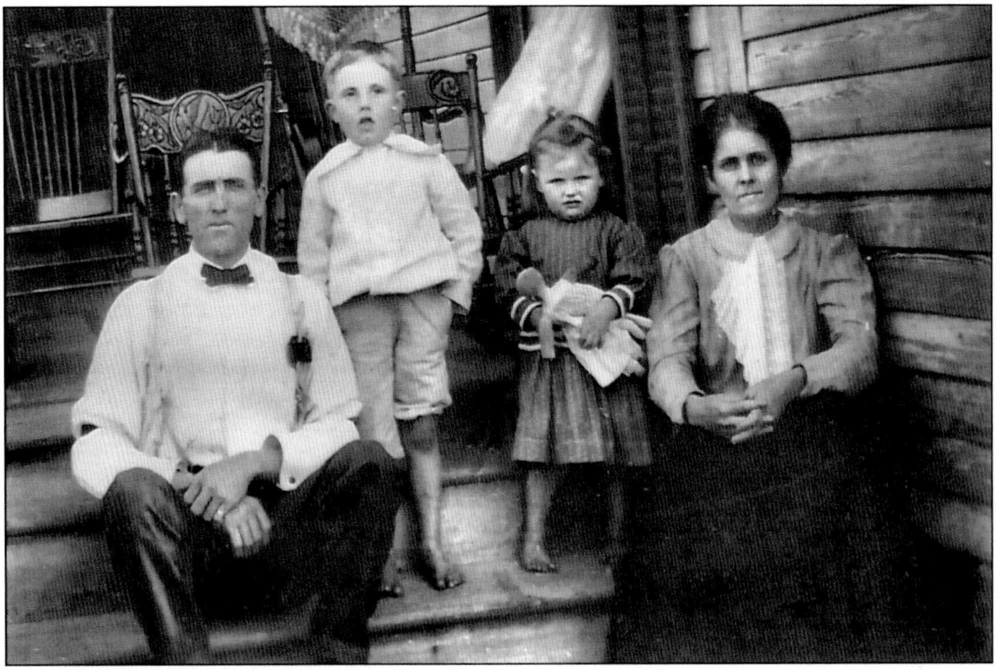

The McGee family moved here from Georgia. Pictured above is William Walter McGee with his children, Clifford and Dovie, and his wife, Mattie. Later Clifford, known by most as "Mac," worked for Hubert J. Magruder in the groves before he became a deputy sheriff and the city building inspector. (Courtesy of Bill McGee.)

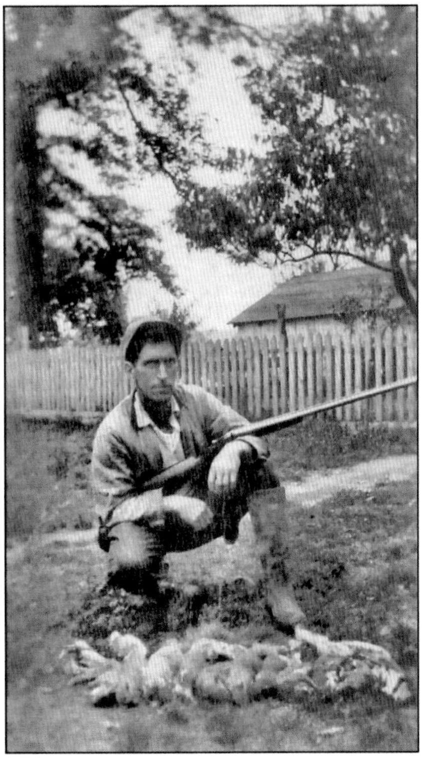

During hard times, men like Jesse Mosby hunted almost daily for meat and ate many squirrels. He and his wife, Amanda, came to this area in 1898 from Berry's Ferry, Kentucky. Their friends, the Taylors, had preceded them in moving to Oak Hill. Jesse was a carpenter, and Amanda was a seamstress.

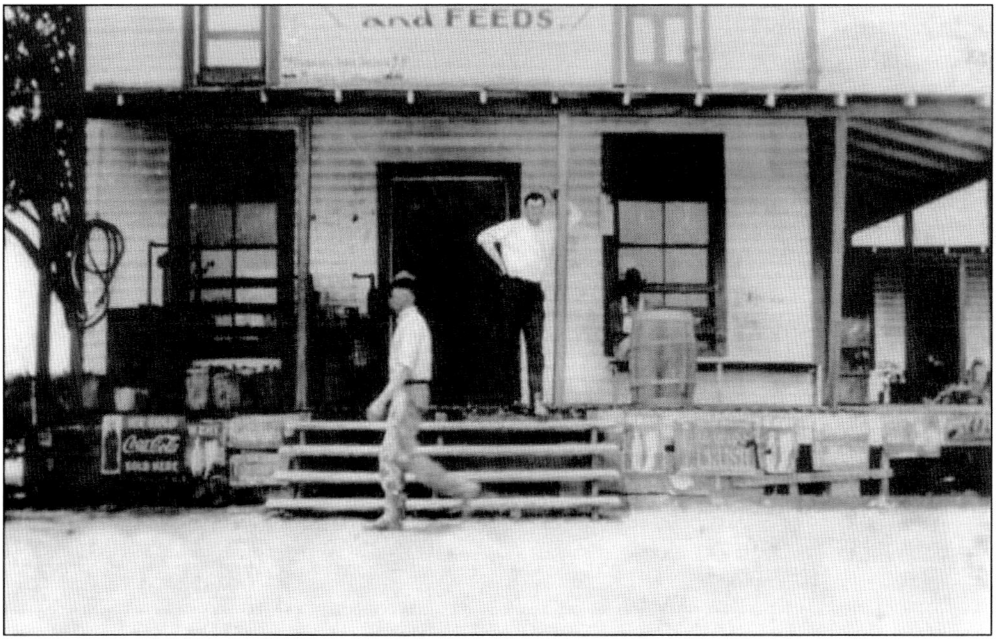

The Axson Goodrich family set up a store in part of their house and served the locals with food and supplies. Store manager H. R. Edwards (father of Marion, Lamar, Evelyn, Milton, Alton, and Lowell) stands on the porch as Clarence Goodrich Sr. walks by. (Courtesy of Ida Goodrich.)

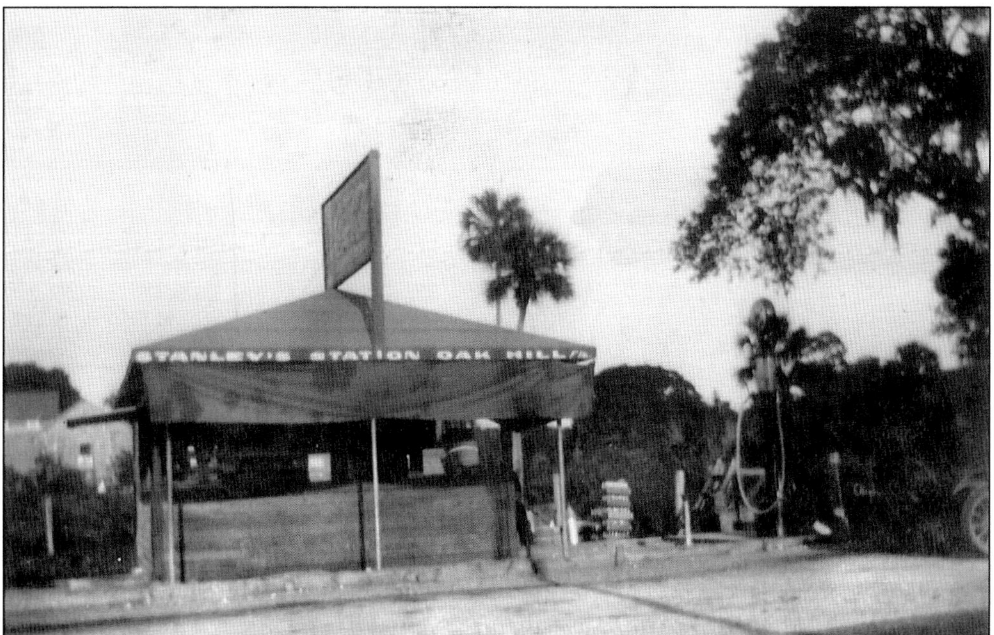

Fred Stanley's first business was established along the old Dixie Highway, conveniently located for travelers to stop for food and beverages. He and his wife, Elizabeth, had twins: a daughter, Dorothy, and son, Walter. Elizabeth died 12 days after giving birth. (Courtesy of Betty Bellamy.)

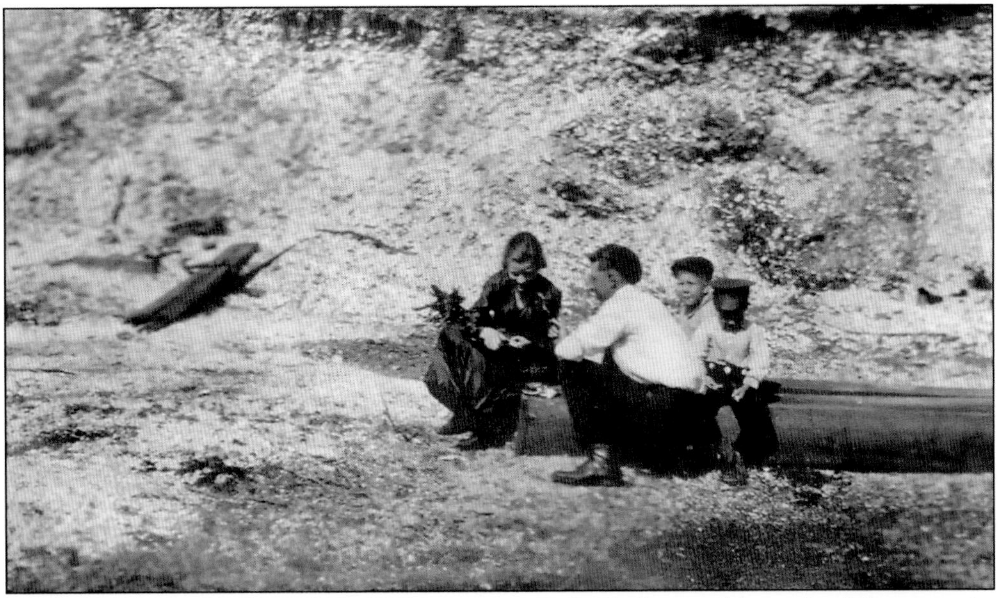

A group of unidentified people looks for artifacts in the shell mound being hauled away to be used for roads. Many protested in concern for the preservation of Native American mounds, while others needed the money and sold the shell on their property without hesitation. The difference in values remains. (Courtesy of Ida Goodrich.)

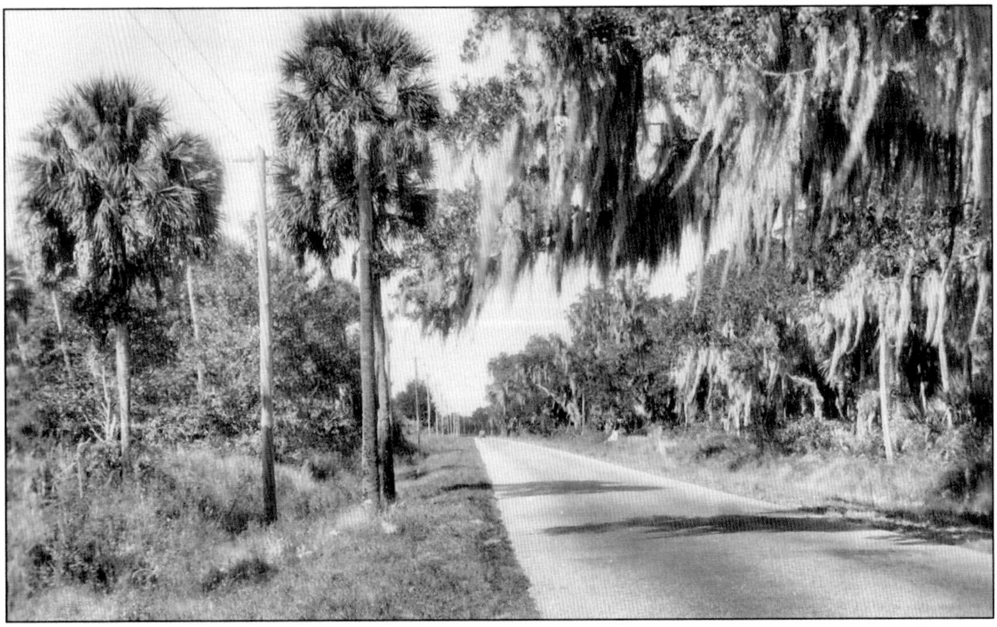

The Old Dixie shell roadway, completed in 1912, became the newly paved U.S. Highway 1 by 1924.

Five

Soldiers and Sacrifice

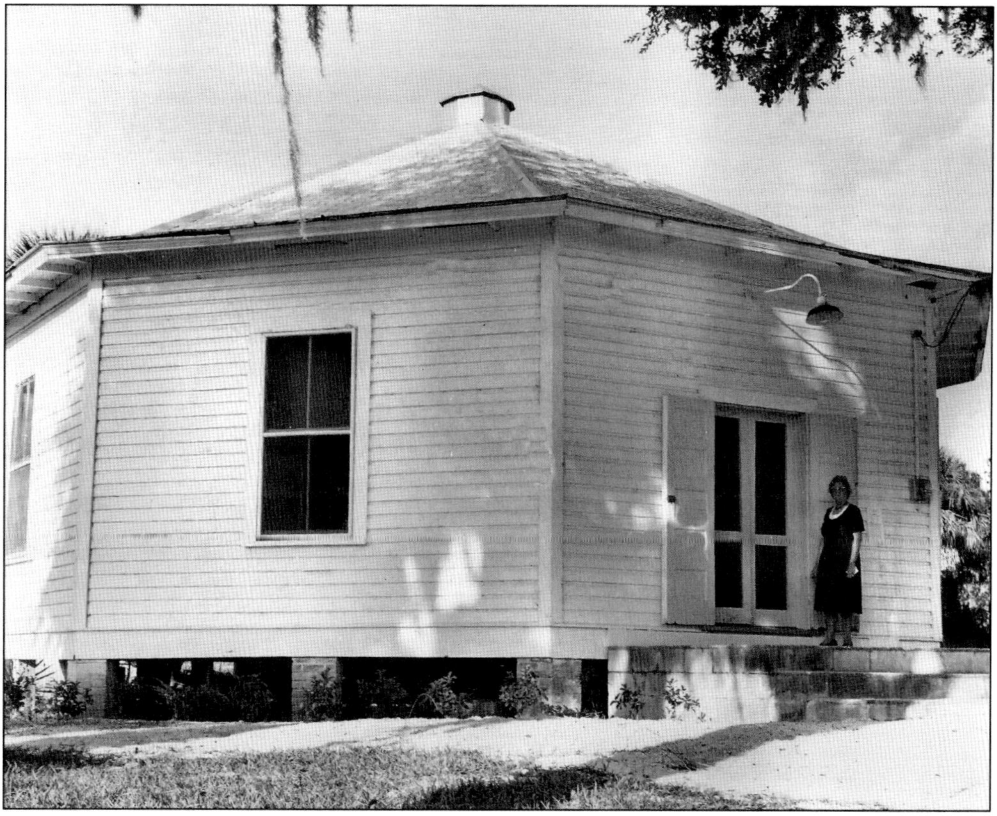

The center of town seemed to be growing, so citizens wanted to move the Village Improvement Association (VIA) Hall closer to the center of activity. In 1917, Joan Howes donated property located at 126 East Halifax Avenue to the Village Improvement Association. This land was deeded to the people of Oak Hill and cannot be sold. In an effort to locate the building closer to the center of town, association members and community volunteers arranged for a team of horses to pull the building on skids to its new location, where it remains today. This building remains the only public historic building in the city, adjacent to Chung Park. A Volusia County ECHO grant and matching funds from Dr. K. T. Chung provided for the total restoration of the building.

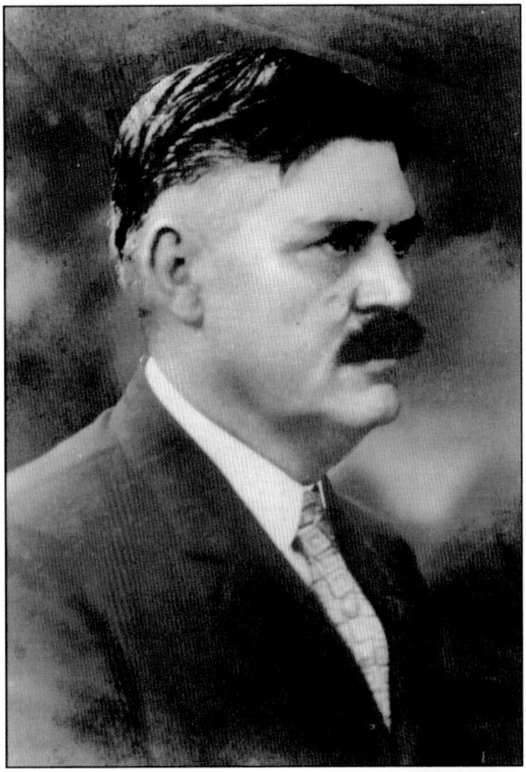

Local leaders petitioned the Florida Legislature in 1927 to become an incorporated city. Once this was granted, Howard Putnam (pictured here) became the first mayor, and commissioners were Clayton McCullough, Leonard Mosby, and W. L. Williams. Howard Putnam also served in the state legislature as a representative and senator. (Courtesy of Betty Bellamy.)

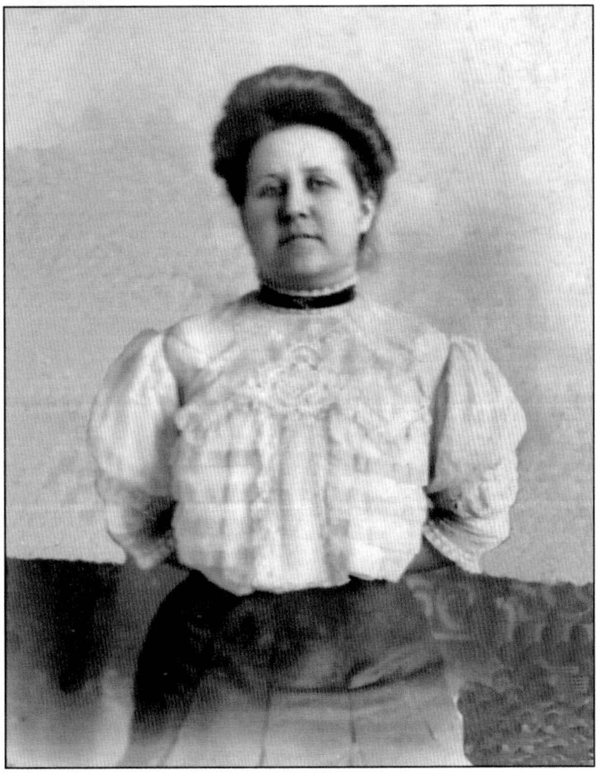

Mary Putnam was the sister of Howard Putnam. She worked hard to take care of her brothers when their parents died. (Courtesy of Bill Dyall.)

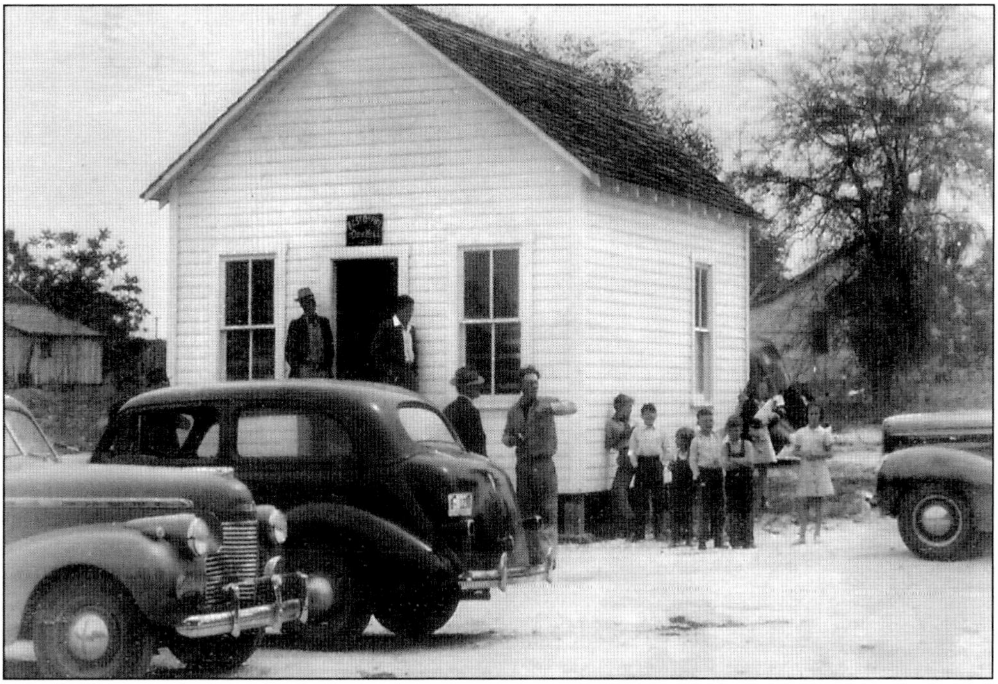

The earlier post office site in 1875 was located in Howes' General Store, and both William Howes and his wife, Joan, served as postmasters until they sold the store to Leonard Mosby in 1908. Mosby served as storekeeper and postmaster until World War I interrupted his life in 1915. Ernest W. McCullough, a local builder, provided this separate post office building while serving as postmaster until 1922. (Courtesy of Ida Goodrich.)

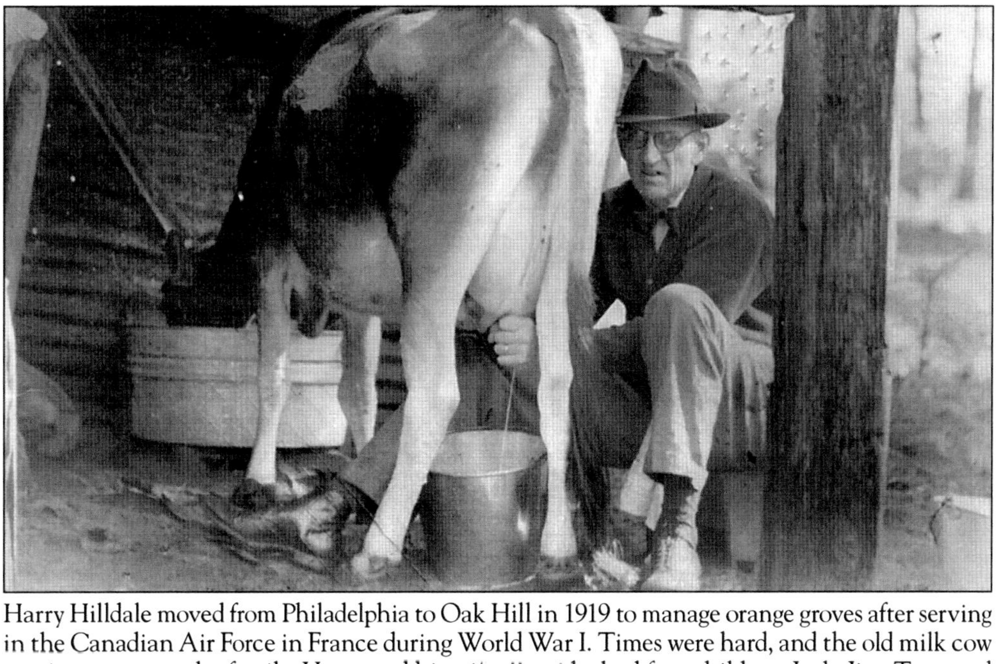

Harry Hilldale moved from Philadelphia to Oak Hill in 1919 to manage orange groves after serving in the Canadian Air Force in France during World War I. Times were hard, and the old milk cow was important to the family. Harry and his wife, Provida, had four children, Jack, Jim, Tom, and Peggy, before she died at the age of 33 from tuberculosis. (Courtesy of JoAnn Blackburn.)

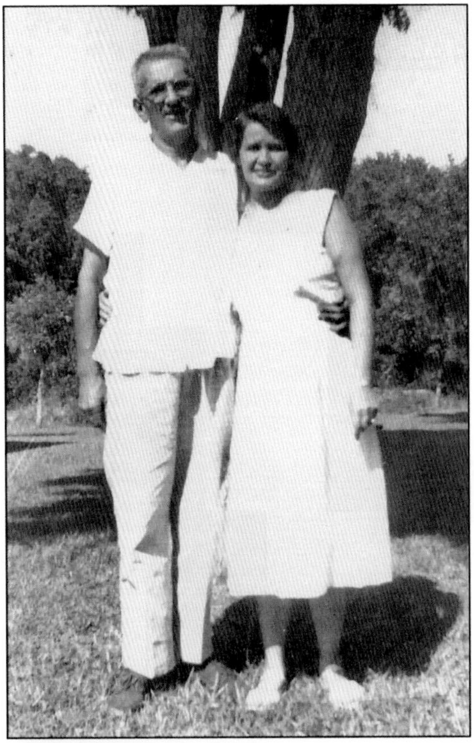

Harry Hilldale raised chickens and sold eggs to a New Smyrna restaurant, where he met Molly, who became his second wife and the mother of Beth, JoAnn, David, and Doug. Harry and Molly Hilldale served in the Oak Hill Post Office from 1922 until 1959, when son David took over for his father, serving as postmaster until 1966. (Courtesy of JoAnn Blackburn.)

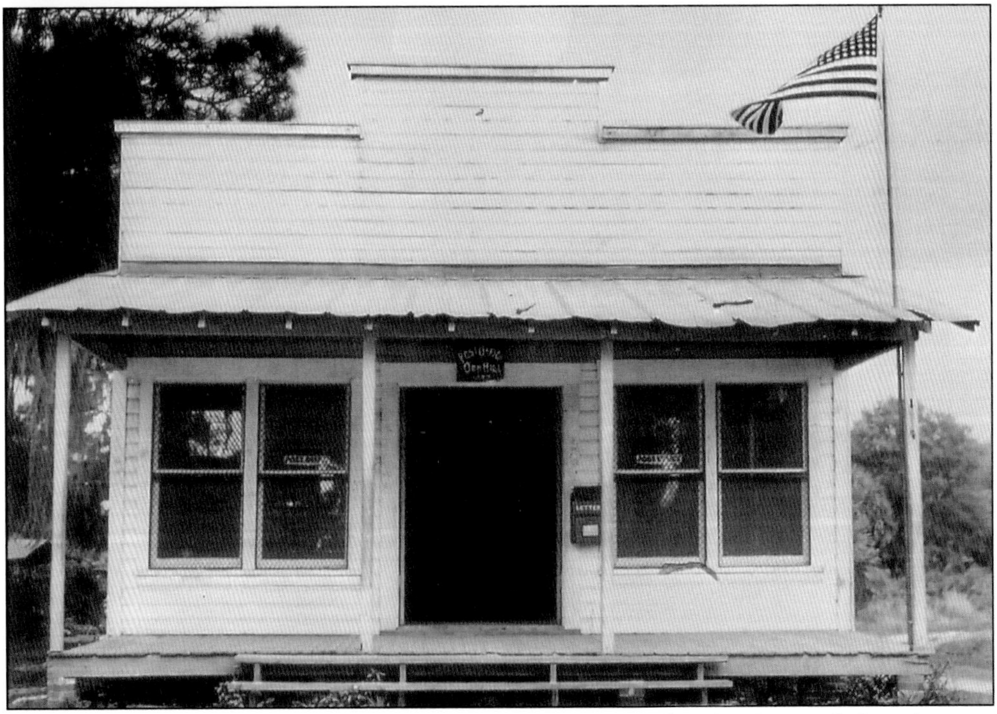

As the population grew, the post office needed more room, so when Jim Putnam's Store became available, the Hilldales moved into that building in the late 1940s, and the post office remained there for the next 20 years. (Courtesy of Betty Bellamy.)

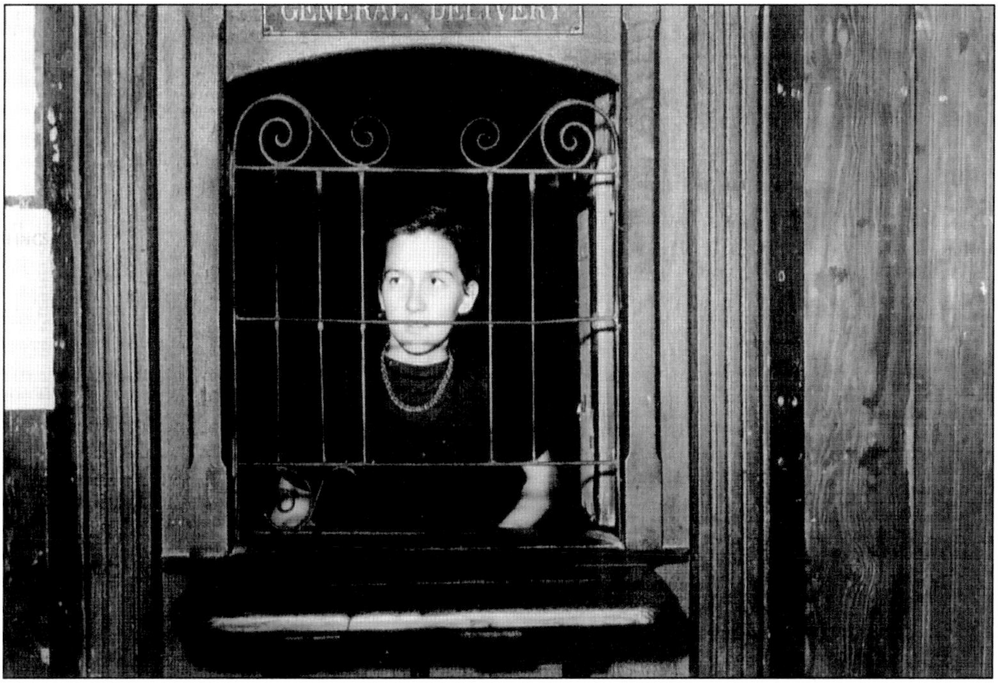

Peggy Hilldale also worked in the post office. She is pictured here at the general delivery window as an unidentified community resident stops by to pick up the mail. (Courtesy of JoAnn Blackburn.)

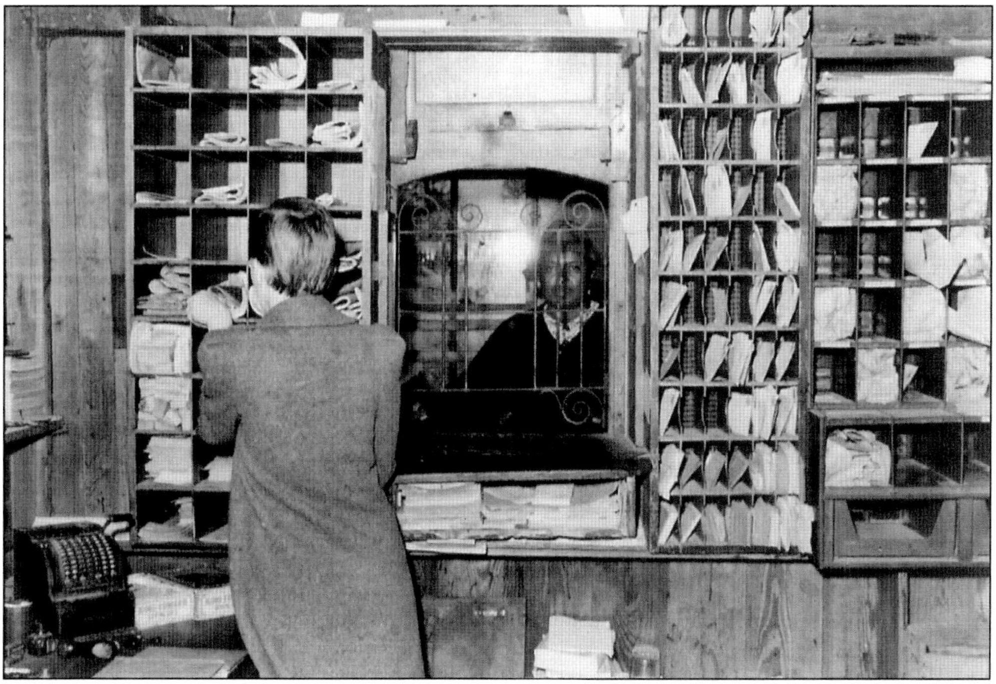

A look behind the lobby wall offers a glimpse of the Hilldales' "postal world," which was rarely seen by citizens. Many locals recall Harry Hilldale raising the general delivery window to hand out a letter, always accompanied by the phrase, "Read 'm and weep!" (Courtesy of JoAnn Blackburn.)

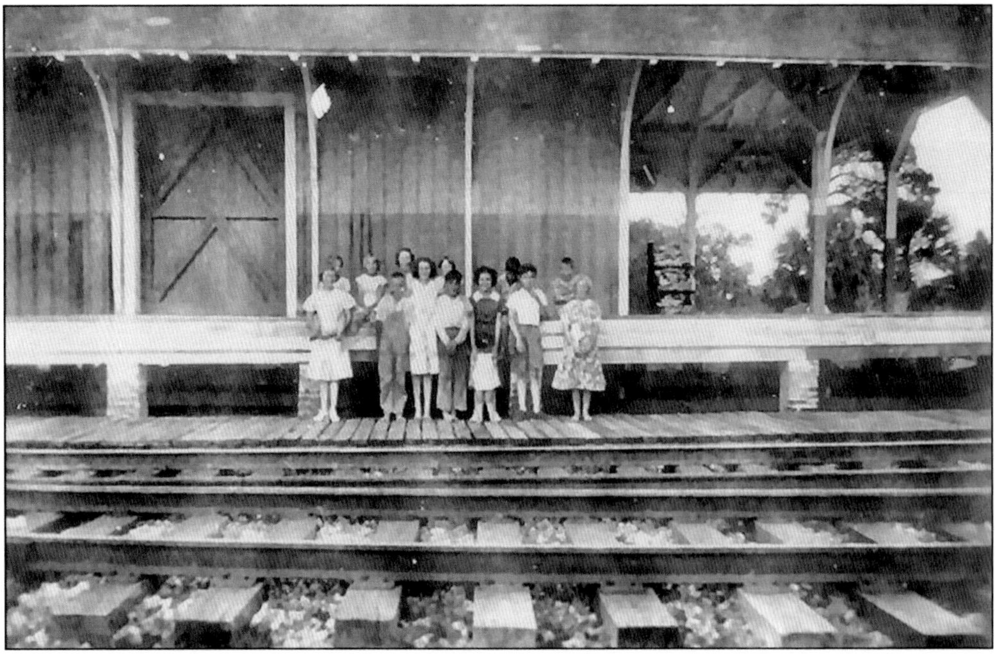

Some unidentified young people wait to catch the train for 10¢ to go to the movies and shopping in New Smyrna. (Courtesy of Marie Goodrich.)

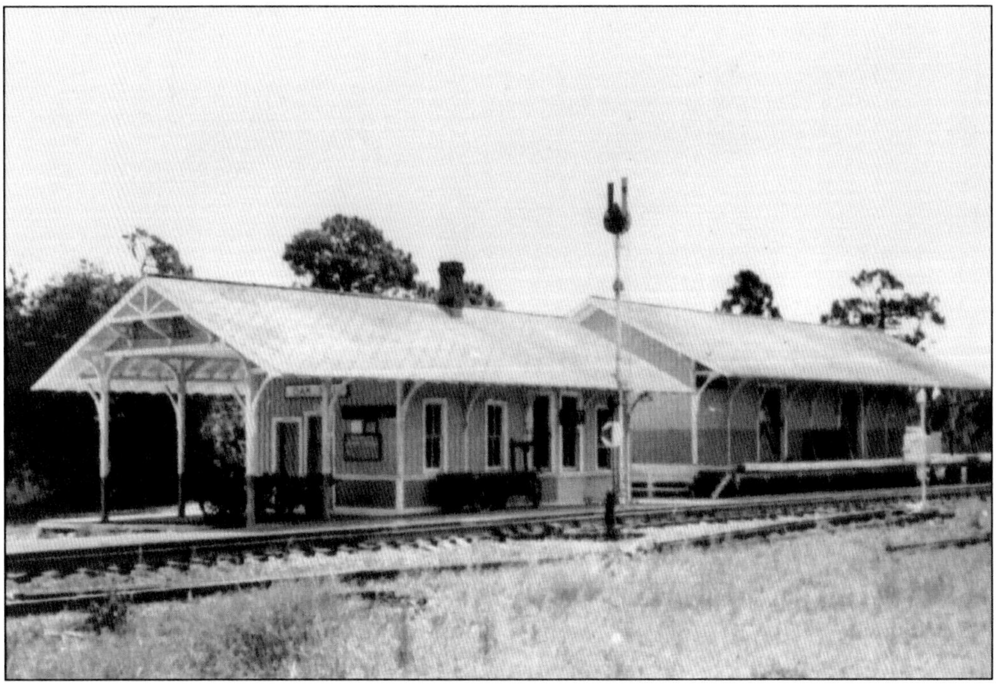

The railroad depot was remodeled and expanded as the town grew and shipping increased. (Courtesy of Ida Goodrich.)

Dorothy Lee and Allen Williams, children of Dorothy and Lee Williams, wait on a rail cart for the next train. The arrival of the train was entertaining and exciting for the local children. (Courtesy of Dorothy Lee Hutchinson.)

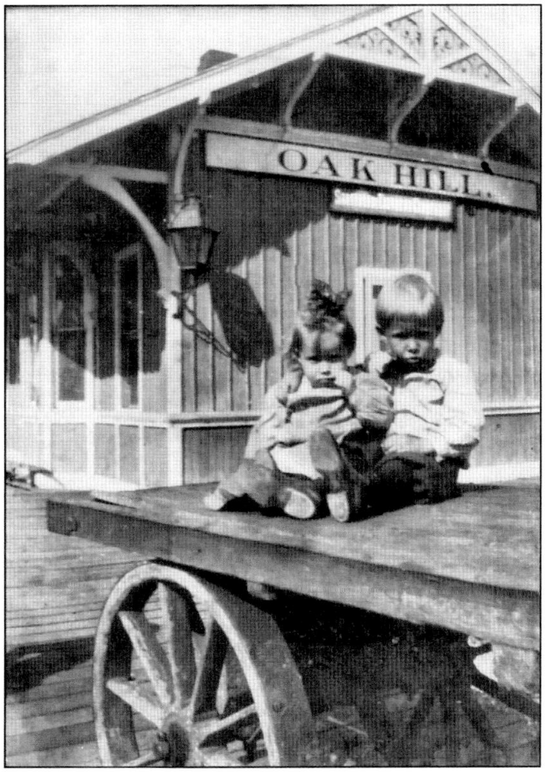

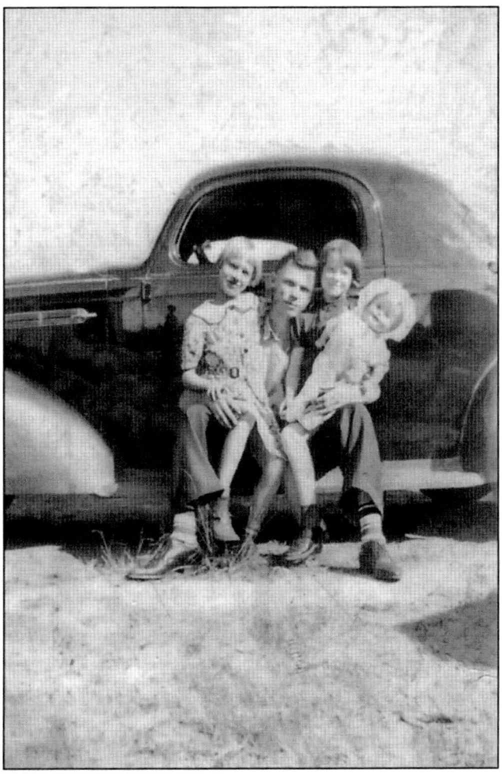

The Treadwell children, Ann (left) and Helena (right), are waiting for the train with their older brother Horace. (Courtesy of Ann Simmons.)

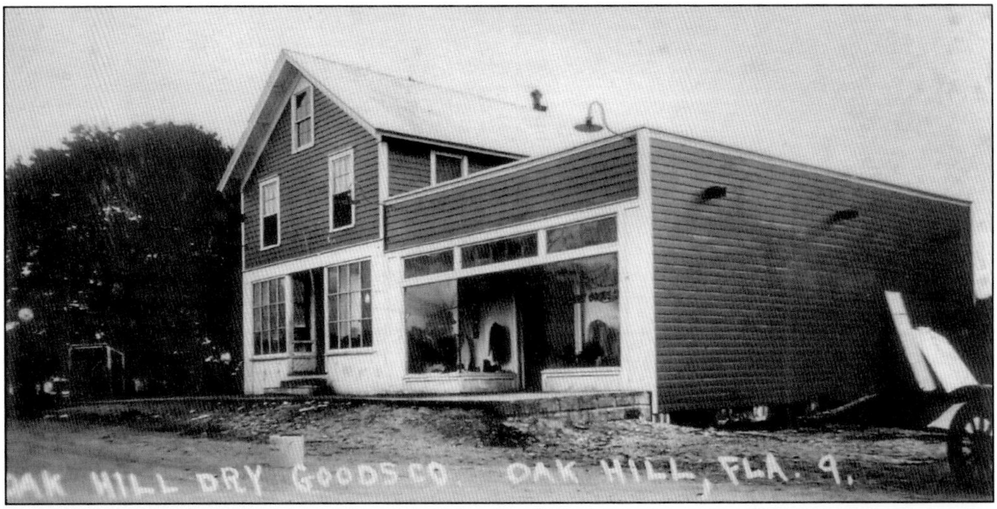

Van Buren Baldwin added a much-needed dry-goods store to the original building, built by the Howes in the late 1800s. Growth and change were coming to Oak Hill. Horses and wagons used to be sent to the river to pick up supplies, including gasoline in 110-gallon drums. Now most supplies came south by railroad from Jacksonville.

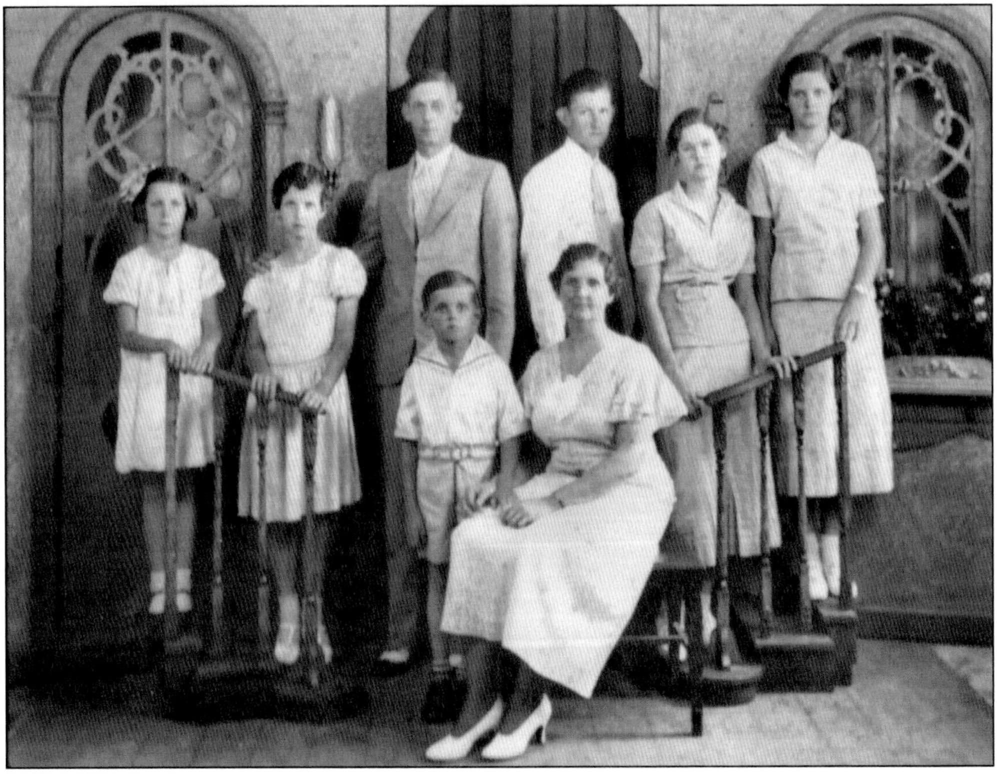

Van Buren Baldwin and his wife, Mary, had six children: from left to right, Vanita, Florence, Charles Wilbur, Van Buren Jr., Jeanne, and Frances. They all lived above the store. On Labor Day in 1935, while the family was enjoying a picnic at the beach, their home and business burned to the ground. Perhaps old wiring was a possible cause, but they never really knew for certain. All they knew was they had lost everything.

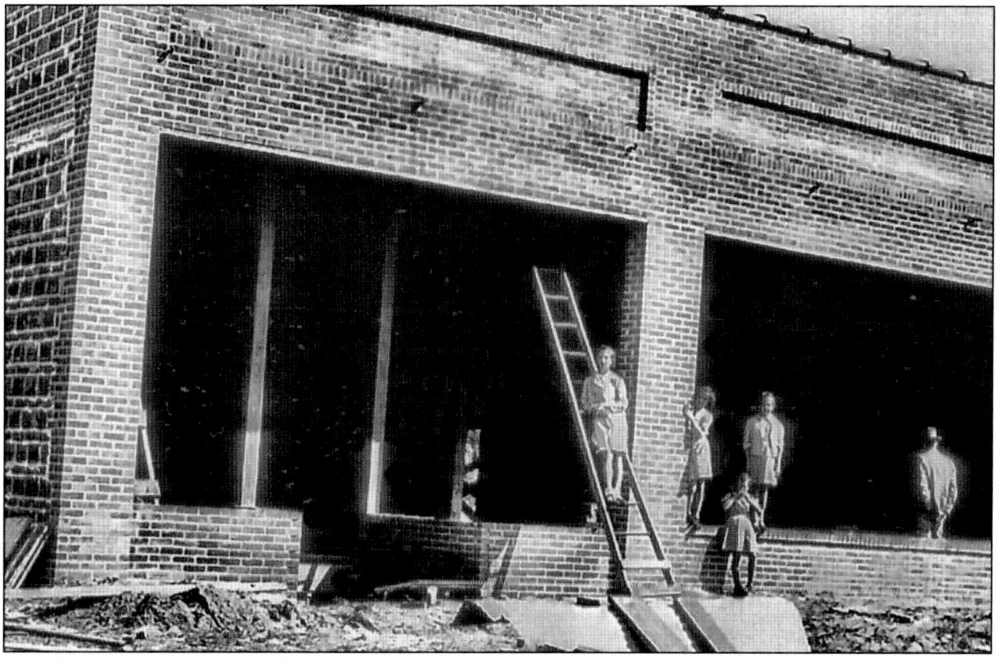

Van Buren Baldwin called the wholesale grocery company in Jacksonville the next day and ordered more supplies, determined to open for business in the VIA Hall "because people here needed food." Since many people had no refrigeration and depended upon the store for food daily, Van Buren felt an urgency to provide for his local customers. There was electricity in the VIA Hall, so he quickly purchased refrigeration and set up a general store "on his good name alone." The family rented rooms in the Woodman Hall, built in 1911, until they purchased the Gordon house on Campton Street By 1935, a New Smyrna contractor named Lopez had completed the new Baldwin Store on U.S. 1, where the building remains today.

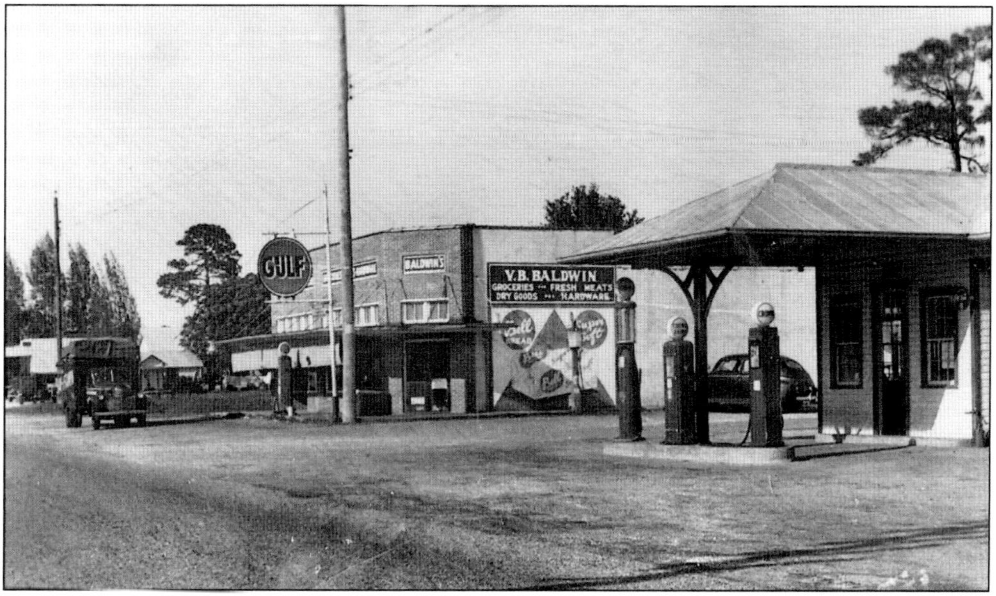

Soon after the Baldwin Store was opened, Fred Stanley built an auto garage and a small café across the street. (Courtesy of Betty Bellamy.)

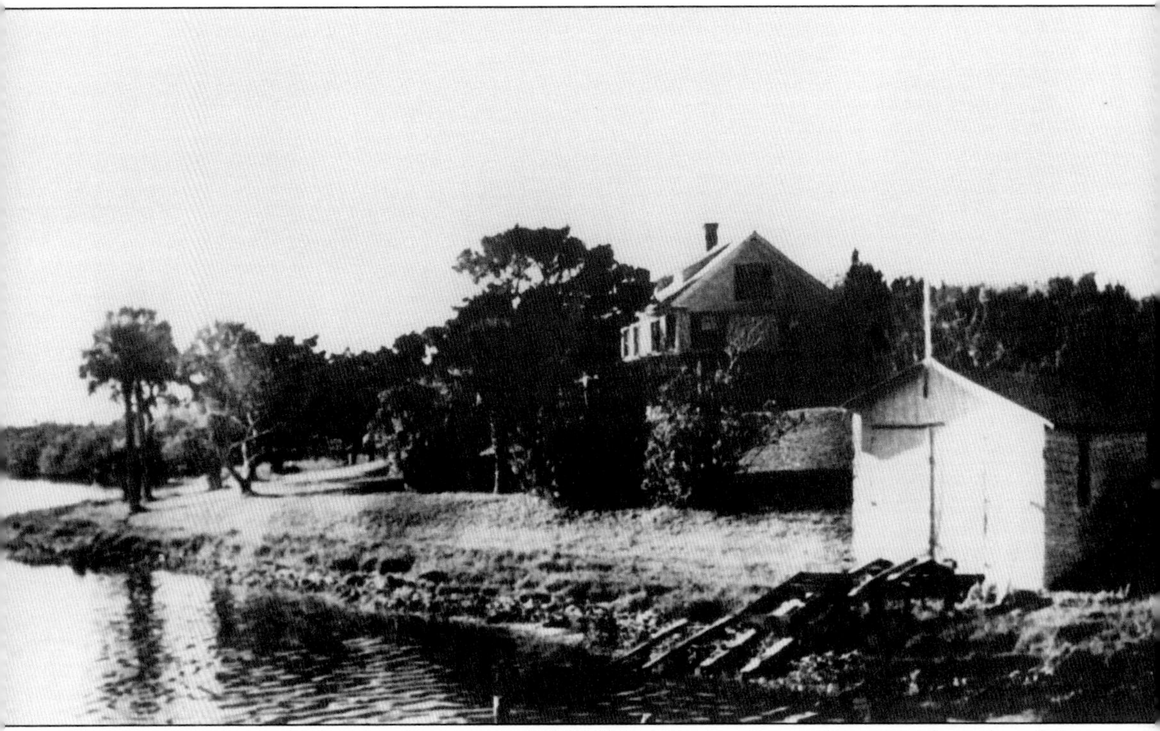

In 1911, Wesley and Clara Snyder came to Oak Hill from Beaver, Pennsylvania, and purchased the Hatton Turnor house, caretaker's house, and 35 acres on the river for only $2,000. Because of the beauty of the houses on the high mounds, Wesley Snyder refused to allow these shell mounds to be sold to build roads. The family named this property Seminole Rest, but locals always referred to it as "Snyder Hill." Lee Williams and his family lived in the caretaker's house, grooming the

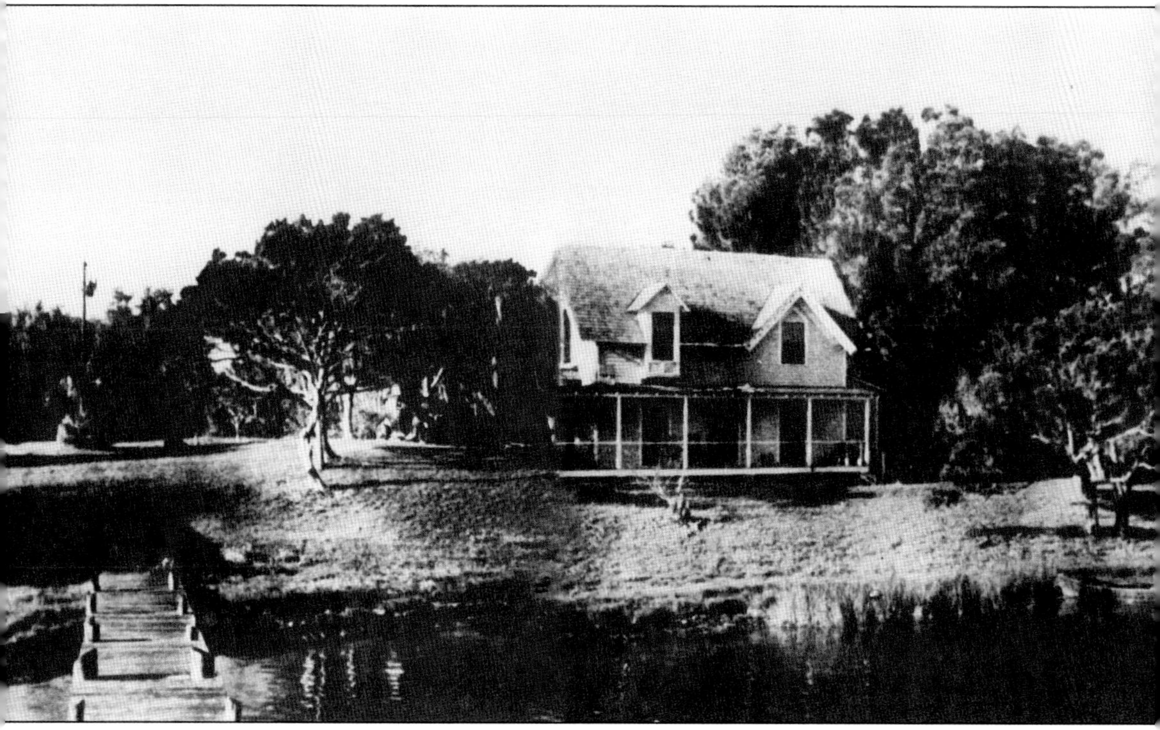

property while the Snyders were away. Wesley and Clara's children were Wesley Carl, Forrest Wall, and Jacqueline, who enjoyed spending winters here. Snyder's son Wes moved to Owensboro, Kentucky, but continued to bring his daughters, Penny (Instone) and Marion (Porta), to Seminole Rest, as he had enjoyed this place as a child. (Courtesy of Marion Porta.)

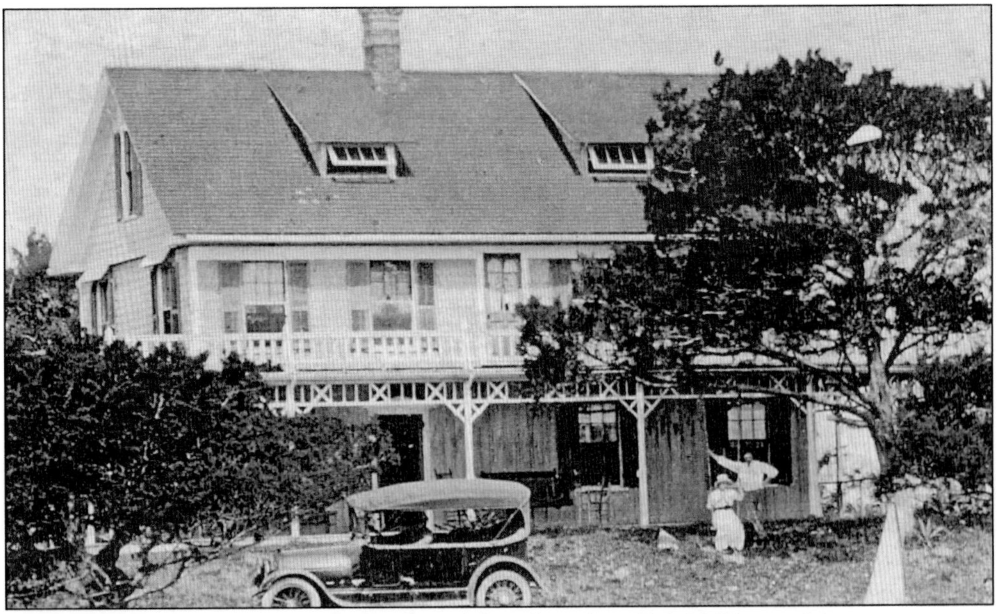

The Snyders enjoyed entertaining family and friends at their Oak Hill home. Many parties were held, and a frequent visitor was John D. Rockefeller. He owned many acres of groves here and added three indoor bathrooms to the Snyder home. (Courtesy of Marion Porta.)

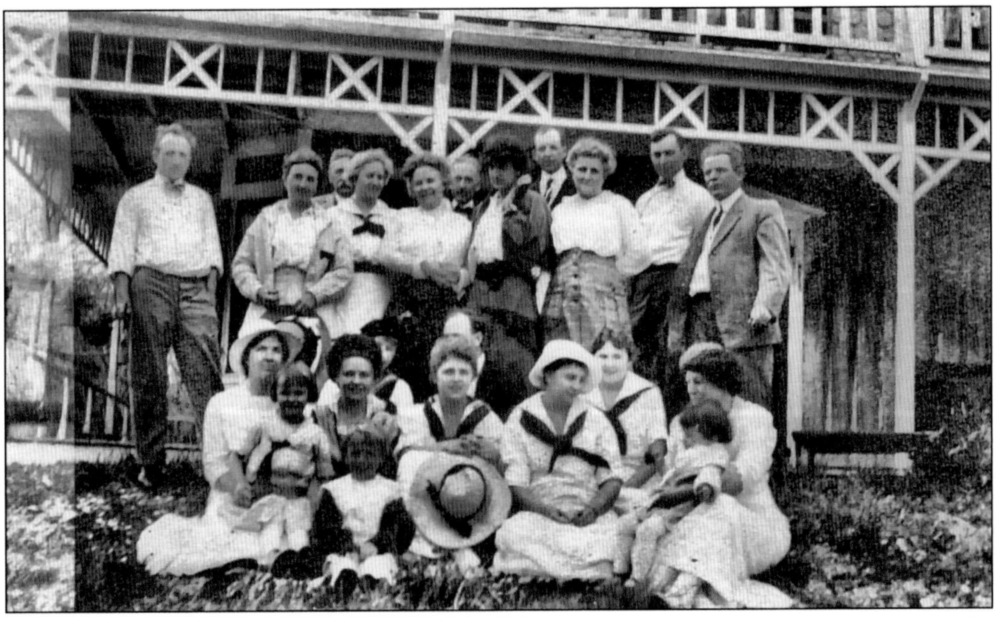

The Wesley Snyder family often gathered with friends at their Seminole Rest home on the riverfront. (Courtesy of Ida Goodrich.)

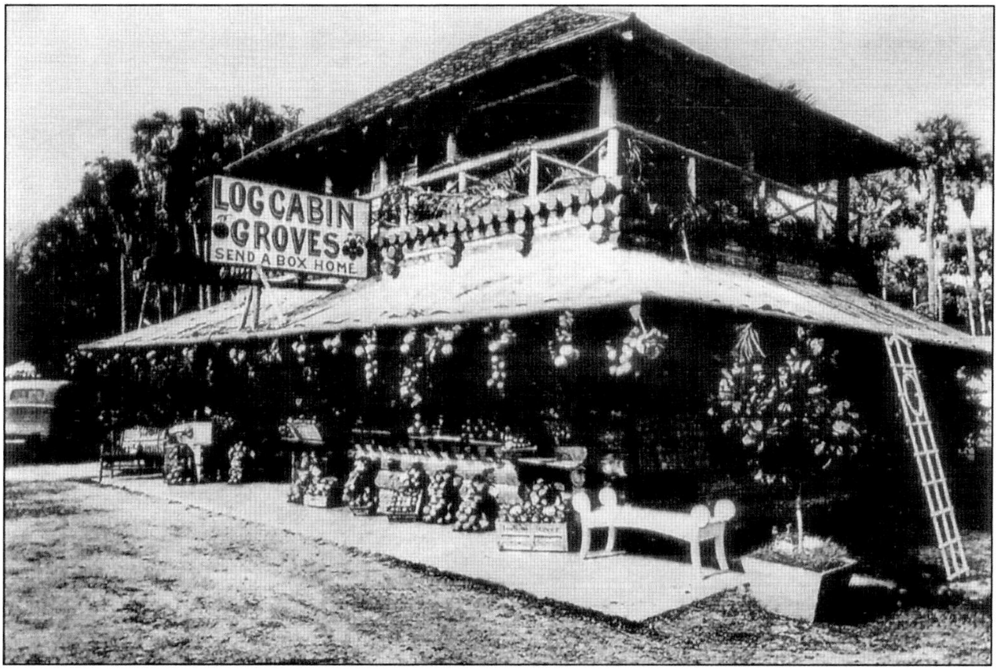

When the land was cleared to plant orange groves in the early 1920s, logs from the clearing were used to build many cabins and buildings. This fruit stand was one of these buildings, giving the area the name Log Cabin Groves. (Courtesy of Marie Goodrich.)

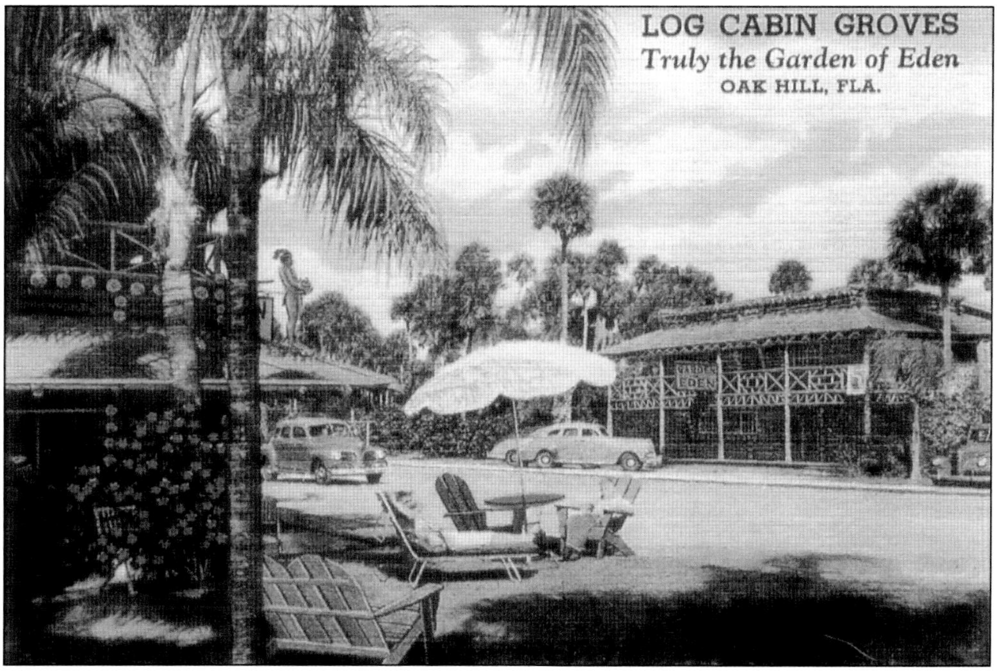

The Log Cabin Groves Fruit Stand and Gardens were a special attraction from the 1920s to the 1940s in Oak Hill. Pearl Law Travis owned this 100-acre grove, and originally, a fruit stand and citrus packinghouse were on the property. (Courtesy of Marie Goodrich.)

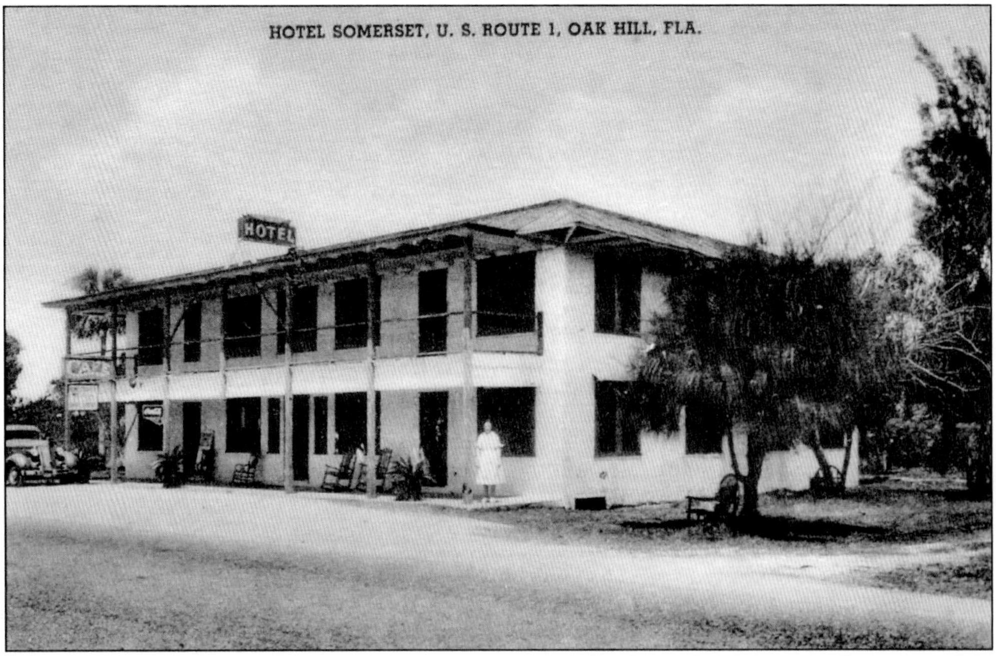

The Somerset Hotel, originally built by John Somerset but leased to A. P. Gordon, was taken back over by the Somerset family. Nancy Dyall (pictured above) managed the hotel restaurant. (Courtesy of Bill Dyall.)

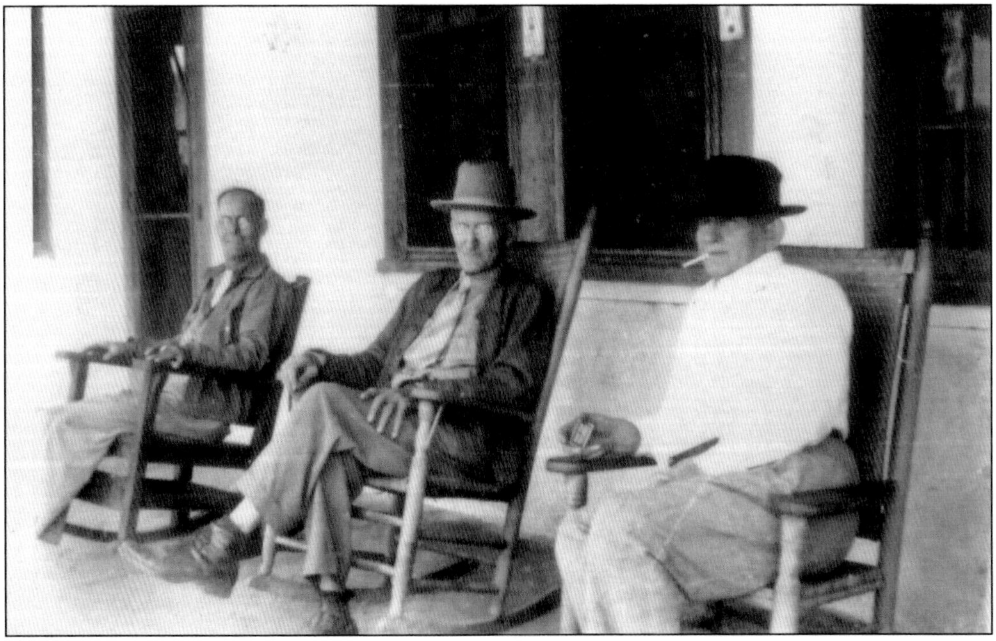

Enjoying a cool breeze on the porch of the Somerset Hotel are, from left to right, Earl Kircher, W. R. Hawkins, and Russell Dyall. The hotel restaurant was open to locals for a great meal. (Courtesy of Bill Dyall.)

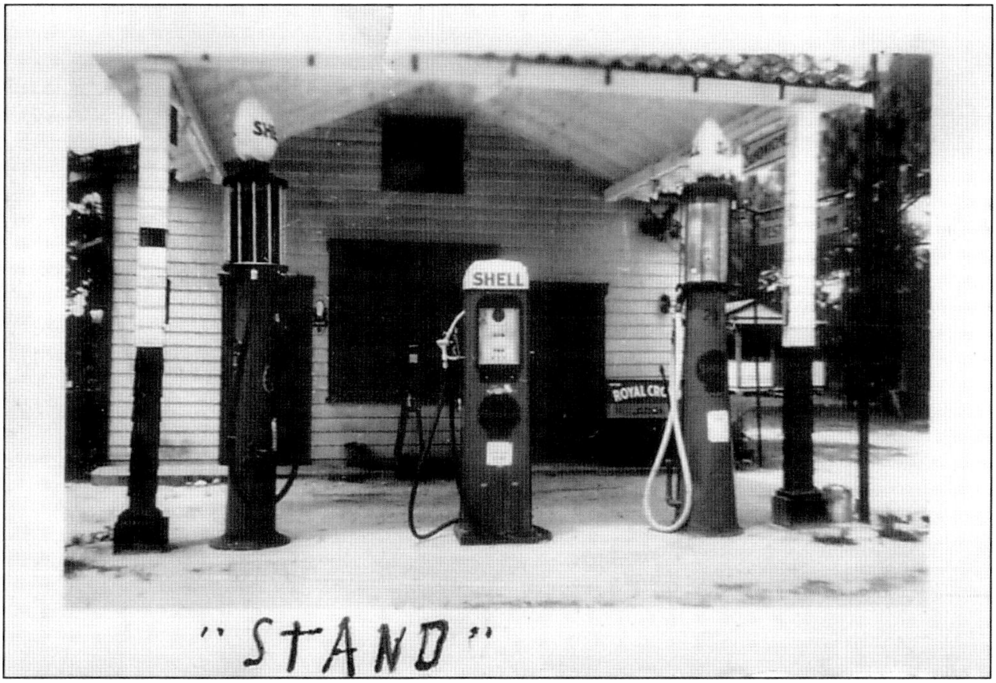

Clifford "Mac" McGee Sr. and his wife, Evelyn, opened a stand just south of the Oak Hill intersection. They sold fruit, juice, snacks, and food. (Courtesy of Bill McGee.)

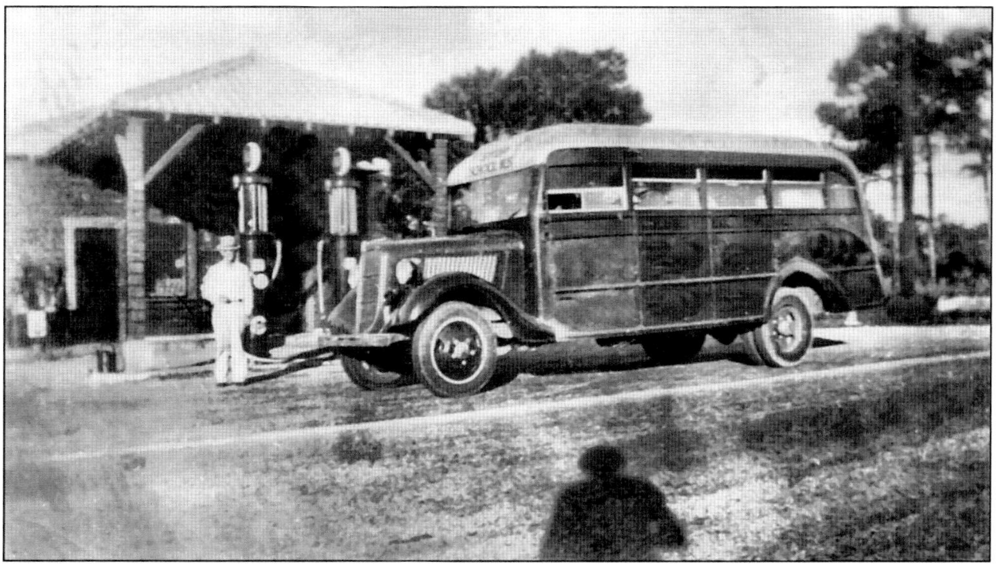

Charlie Simmons, father of Evelyn McGee, stops at Stanley's station to fill up his bus with gasoline. He owned the school bus and drove students to New Smyrna High School between 1930 and 1940. (Courtesy of Bill McGee.)

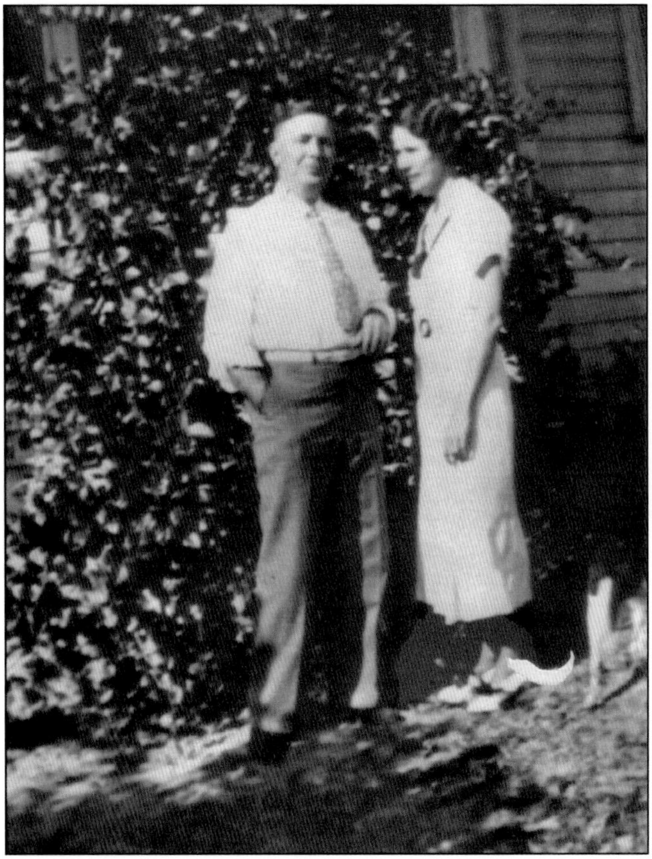

John and Eva Treadwell were active in the church and community. Their children were John, Horace, Raymond, Virginia, Doris, Randall, Helena, and Ann. (Courtesy of Ann Simmons.)

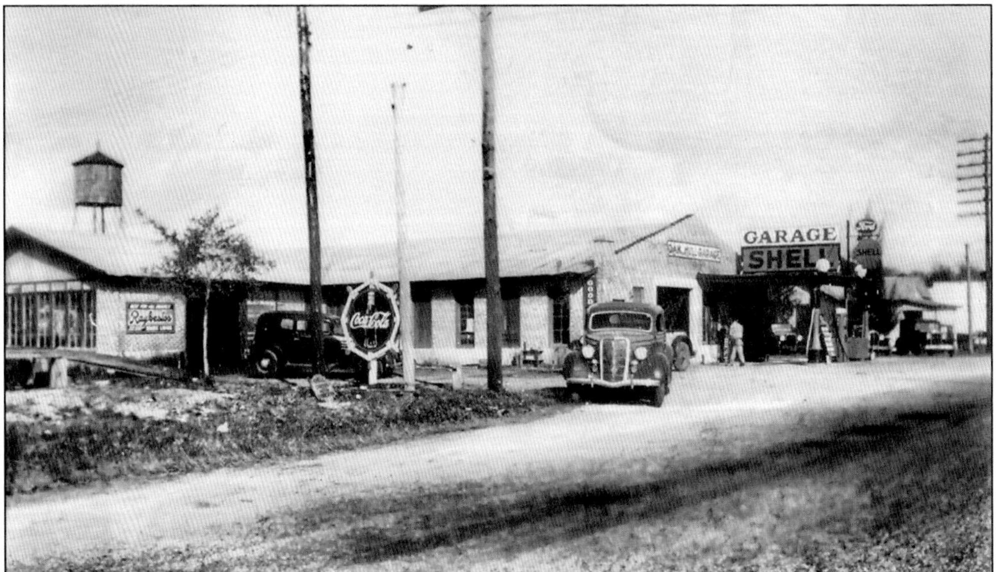

John Treadwell first drove a gas truck for the C. T. Patillo Oil Company. Then in the late 1930s, he built the Treadwell Garage, which he ran for 25 years. Upon his death in 1957, his son Horace took over managing the business. (Courtesy of Ann Simmons.)

Twenty-five-year-old Ollaf Damgaard, son of Ankor and Clara Damgaard, is pictured in a 1935 rodeo competition. He was the local blacksmith and never married. He always said, "Just me, my horse Maude, and my dog . . . that's enough." (Courtesy of Ida Haverly.)

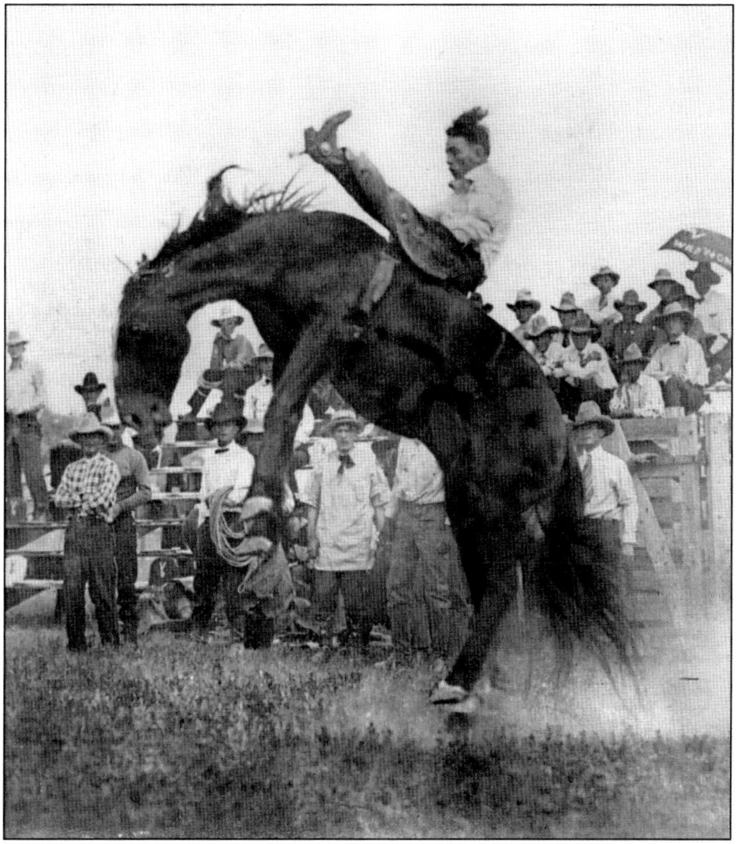

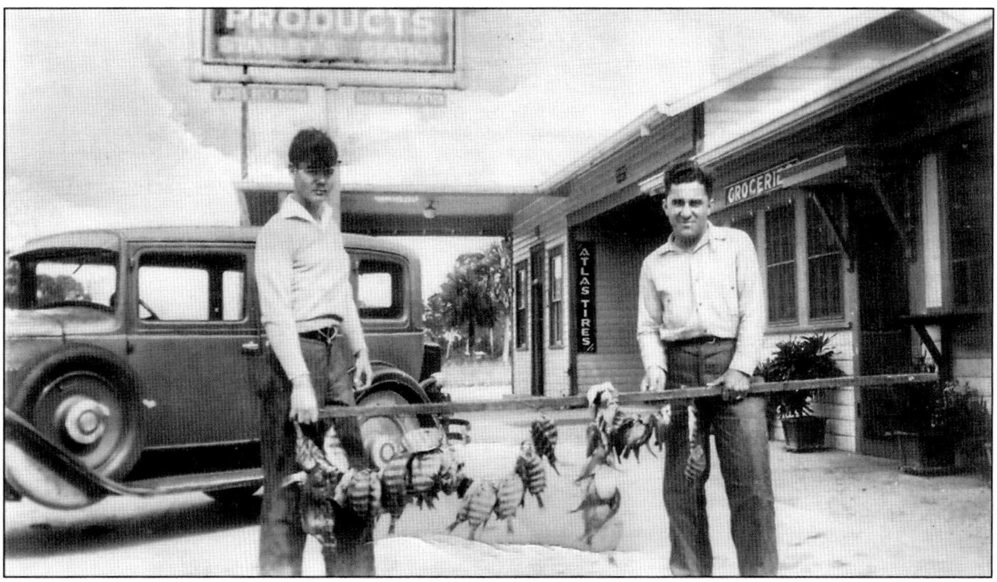

One did not have to be a local fisherman to enjoy a big catch of sheepshead. A winter visitor from Massachusetts, Chris Papouleas (right) and his friend Charlie Panetsos were proud of their afternoon catch. Chris later married local girl Lillian Simmons, and he was a meat cutter at the Baldwin Store. (Courtesy of Ida Goodrich.)

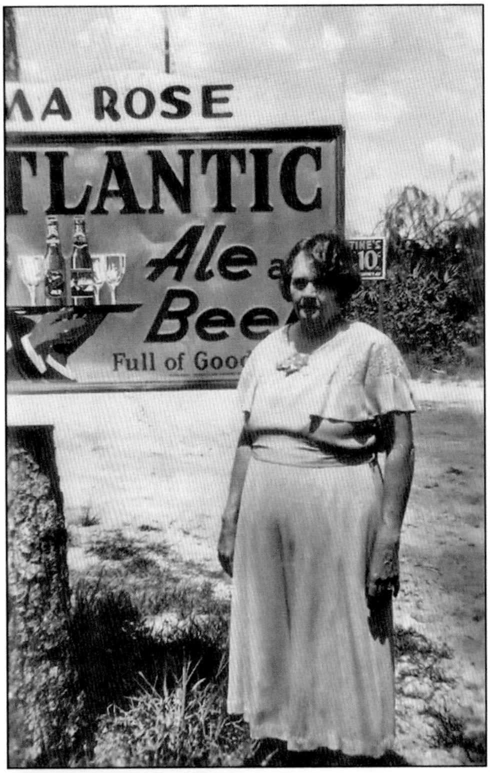

Rose Robinson, known to most as "Ma Rose," stands in front of her sign advertising her business. (Courtesy of Kathy Bittle.)

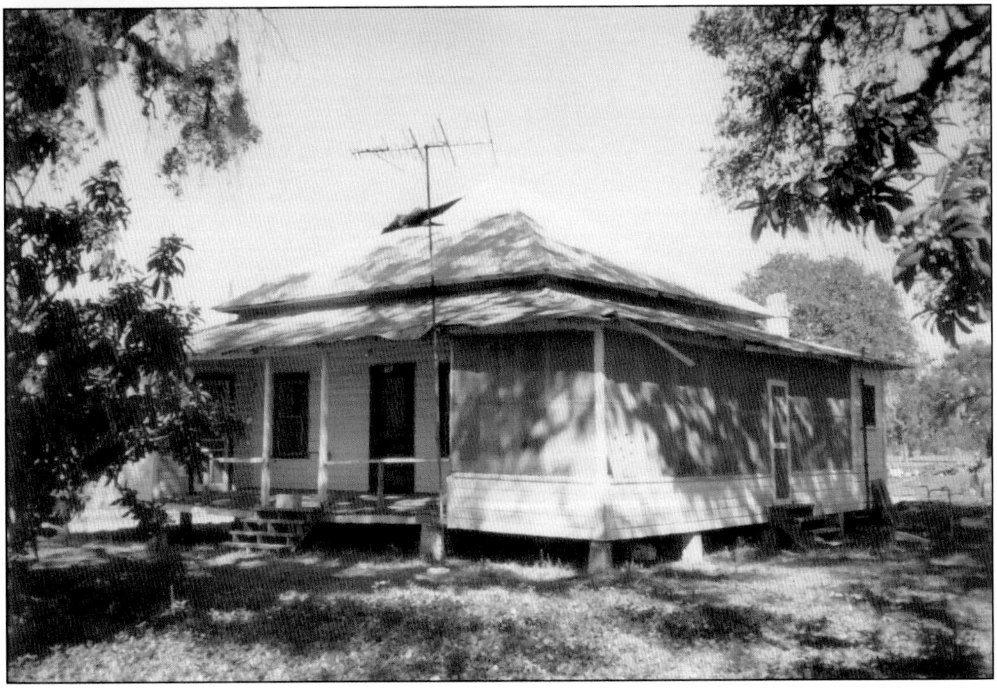

The Eugene and Rose Robinson house, built in 1900, is pictured above. Their children were Carl Eugene, Russell Norman, Davis "Chippy," Fannie Mae, and Eleanor Catherine. (Courtesy of Ida Goodrich.)

Arthur Simmons and Frank Simmons joined the Civilian Conservation Corps (CCC) in the late 1930s. This took them on a trip to California, where they worked in the Sequoia National Park. They helped to develop the park so visitors could safely enjoy the huge trees growing there. Frank Simmons (third from left) is pictured at a CCC camp with unidentified friends. (Courtesy of Ida Goodrich.)

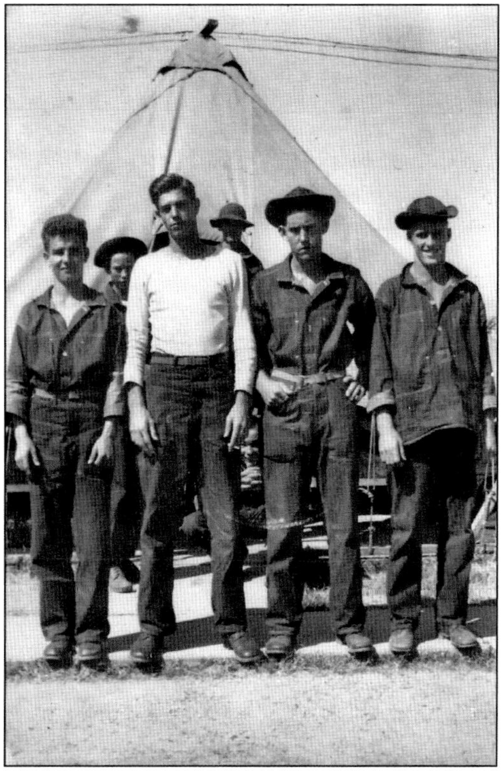

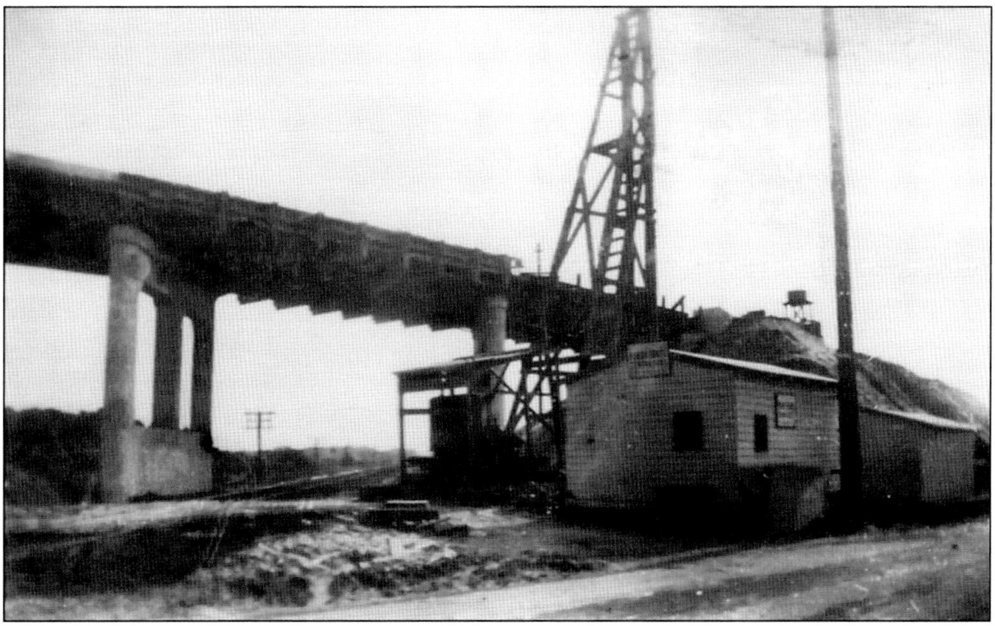

The overhead pass just south of Oak Hill brought workers like Henry and Fred Wheeler, who were looking for jobs in the early 1930s. Fred met Jeanne Baldwin at the local store; they fell in love and married. They had two children, Anita and Richard. The Wheelers later opened an automobile garage and service station in the 1940s. The overhead pass was completed in 1935. (Courtesy of Bill McGee.)

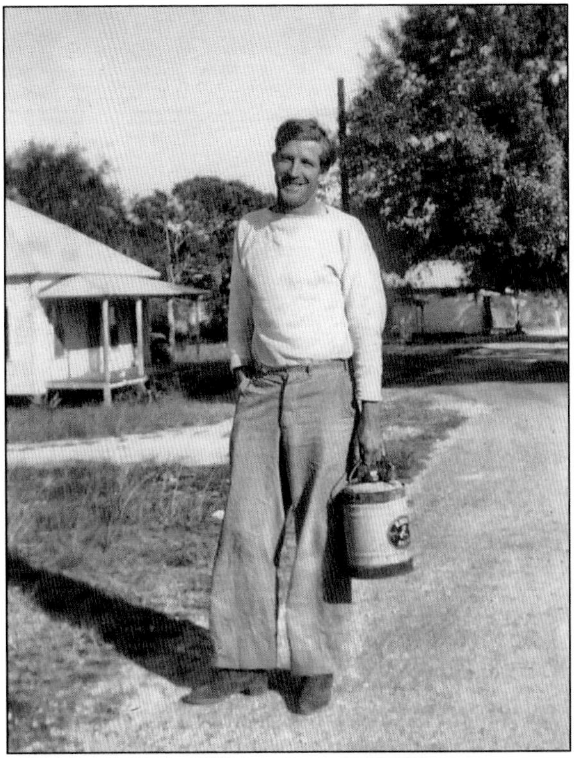

The spotlight is on the kerosene can in this photograph because it was so important to the people of this community during these days. Wyatt Widner walked to a local general store for a refill so the lady of the house could cook supper on the New Perfection Kerosene stove. Children were sometimes sent on this errand and would make a game out of carrying the can—or they would argue over which one would carry the full can back home. (Courtesy of Marie Goodrich.)

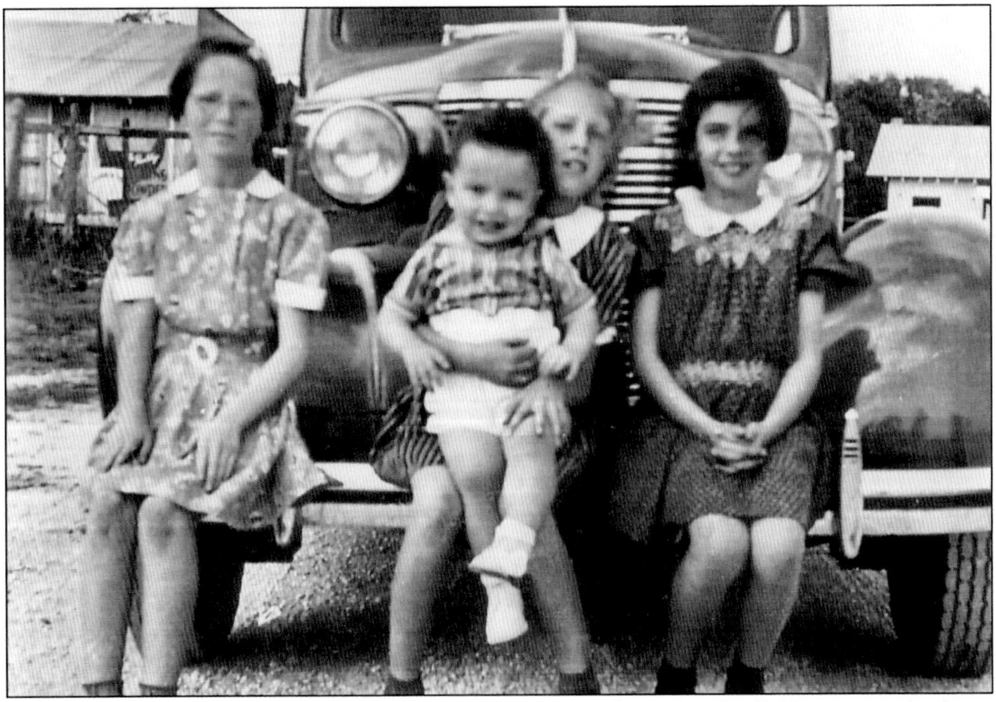

From left to right, Ann Treadwell (Simmons); her sister, Helena Treadwell (Concannon), who is holding Billy Burns; and Betty Burns (Bellamy) pose for a picture at the beach. Ann and Betty still live in Oak Hill and remain good friends. (Courtesy of Betty Bellamy.)

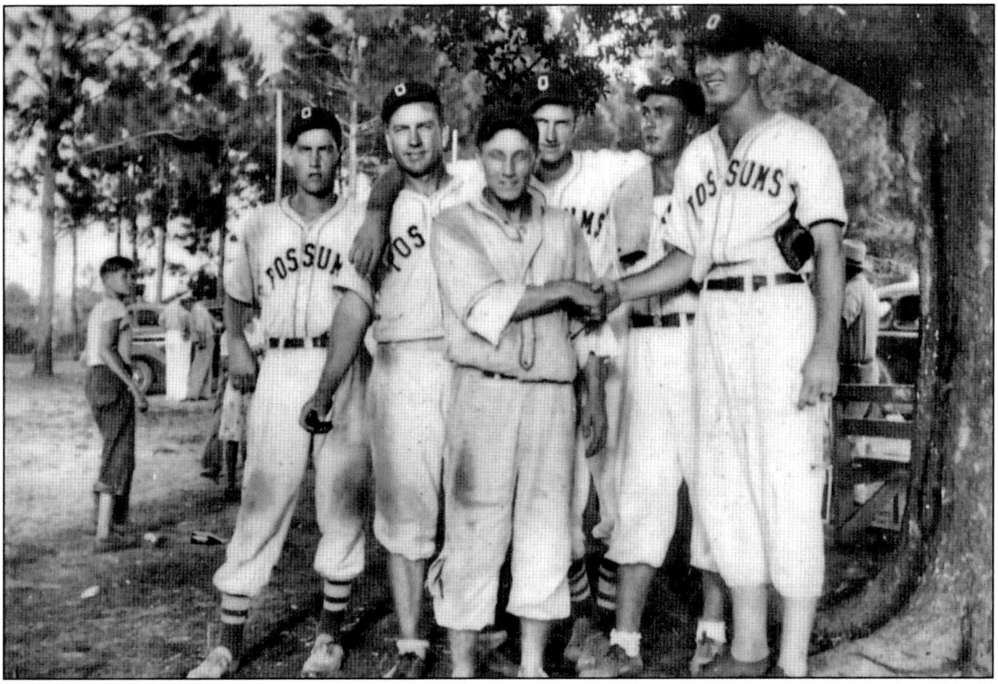

An unidentified baseball fan congratulates pitcher Major Jones (far right) and other teammates, (from left to right), Frank Simmons, Bill Burns, Van Buren "Boo" Baldwin Jr., and June McCullough. The Oak Hill Possums Baseball team won the Central Florida East Coast League Championship over such teams as the New Smyrna Jaycees, Melbourne, Cocoa Indians, Mims, and Titusville Gulls.

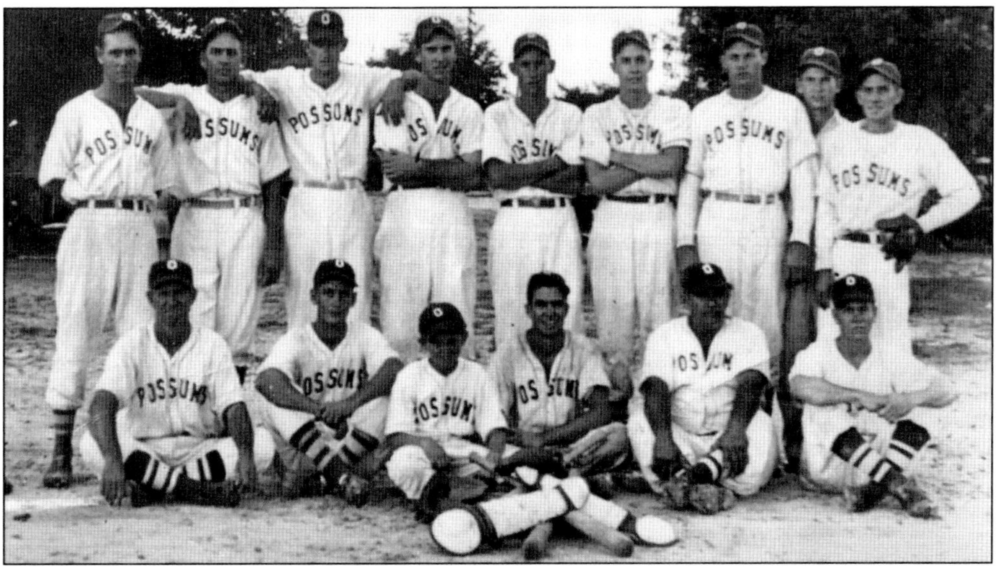

Baseball was a favorite pastime, and these boys drew a crowd of more than 250 on occasion. They played games every Saturday and Thursday, winning the state championship in the late 1930s. Pictured from left to right are (seated) Forte Jones, June McCullough, Charles Wilbur "Boostie" Baldwin, Harry Sargent, Herbie Lopez, and James McKendree; (standing) Major Jones, Bill Burns, Van Buren "Boo" Baldwin Jr., Harold Jones, Frank Simmons, Bob Pattillo, Lamar Edwards, Bill Lopez, and C. W. "Mac" McGee.

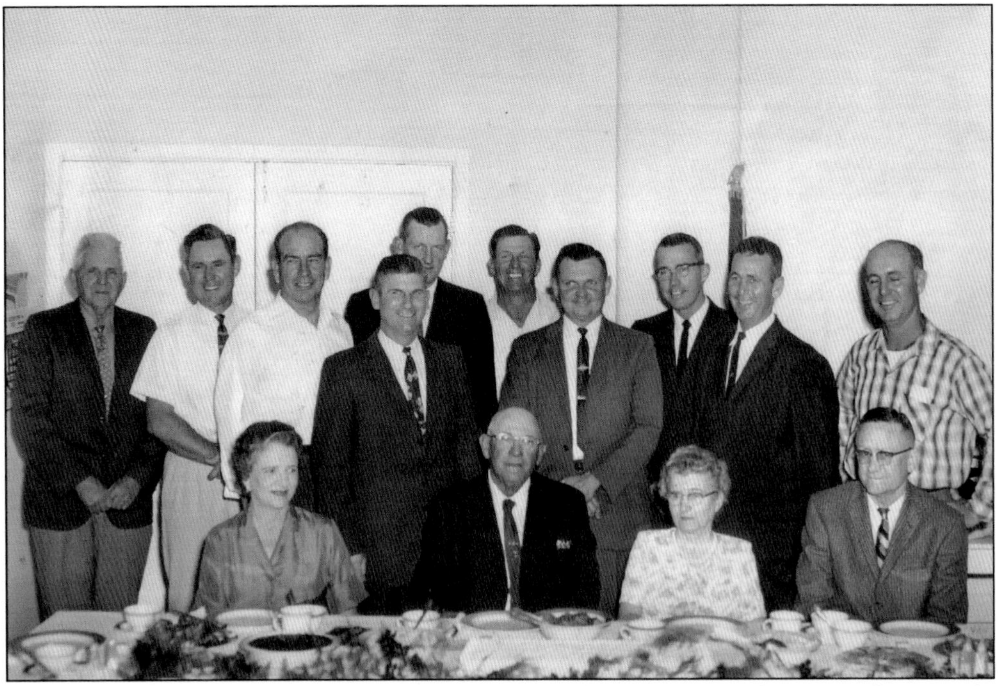

Years later, the baseball players on the Possum team held a reunion honoring their coach, Herbie Lopez. They are, from left to right, (seated) Marge Jones, Herbie and Cora Lopez, and Dr. Carrol D. Jones; (standing) Floyd Jones, Roy Jones, Bill Burns, Bill Lopez, Van Buren "Boo" Baldwin Jr., Lamar Edwards, Charles Wilbur "Boostie" Baldwin, Bob Patillo, June McCullough, and Harold Jones.

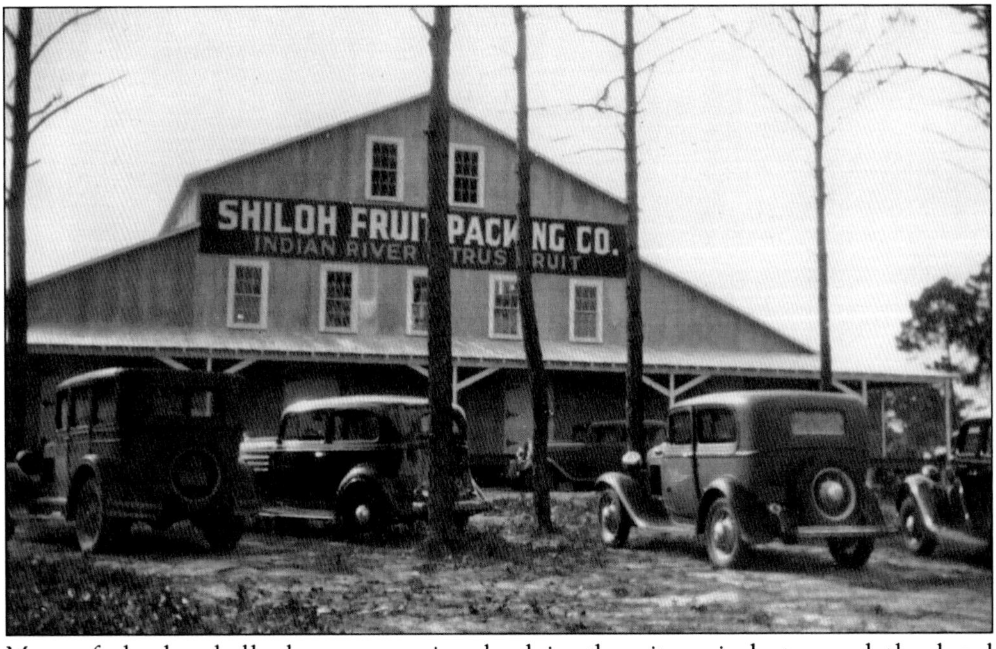

Most of the baseball players were involved in the citrus industry and the local Shiloh packinghouse.

Six

From Prosperity to Another War

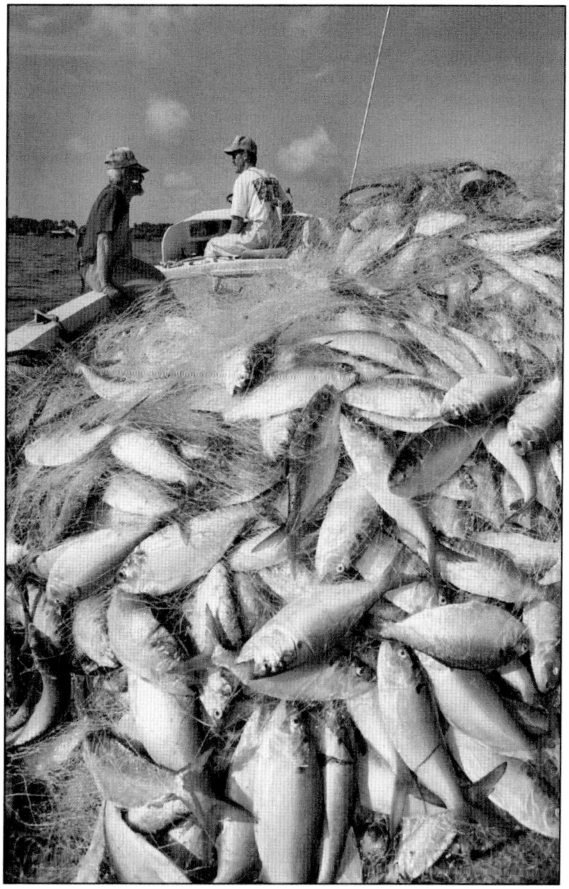

There was always an abundance of mullet, but commercial fishermen worked hard to bring it in to the fish house to sell. In the early days, they would row out at dusk to set the seine nets, large fishing nets made to hang vertically in the water by weights at the lower edge and floats at the top. These were outlawed, and gill nets were used. Gill nets are sized mesh openings that prevent fish from squeezing through as they swim forward. Once in this position, the fish are prevented from backing out as their gills tend to become caught. This effectively traps the fish, which were iced down and carried by wagon to the railroad depot for shipping. Fishermen or their wives would make and repair the nets used to bring in huge catches. Power motors, monofilament nets, and automobiles made significant changes in the fishing industry. Mullet was the staple food. Several generations of families depended upon commercial fishing as their livelihood until the net ban law was passed in the Florida Legislature in 1995. (Courtesy of Ida Goodrich and the *Orlando Sentinel*.)

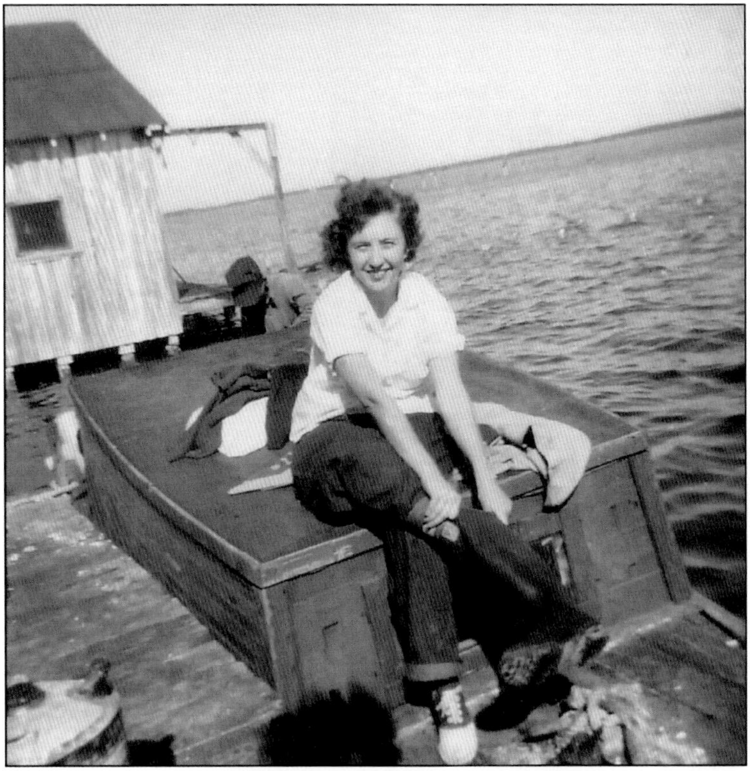

Marie Goodrich was waiting on her father, Harry Simmons, who was a commercial fisherman, to take her for a ride on the launch. (Courtesy of Ida Goodrich.)

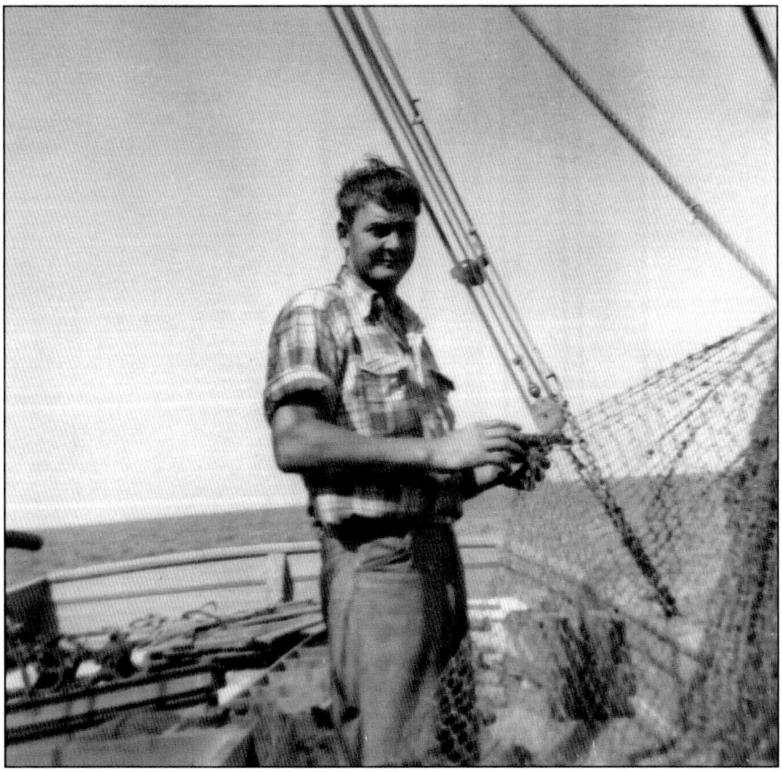

Russell Robinson hangs his nets out to dry after a long night of fishing. (Courtesy of Kathy Bittle.)

In this photograph, Clarence Goodrich Jr. is working for his father, who owned a fish business. Several times a week, he drove a truck to Jacksonville packed with boxes of fish on ice to be sold to markets there. (Courtesy of Ida Goodrich.)

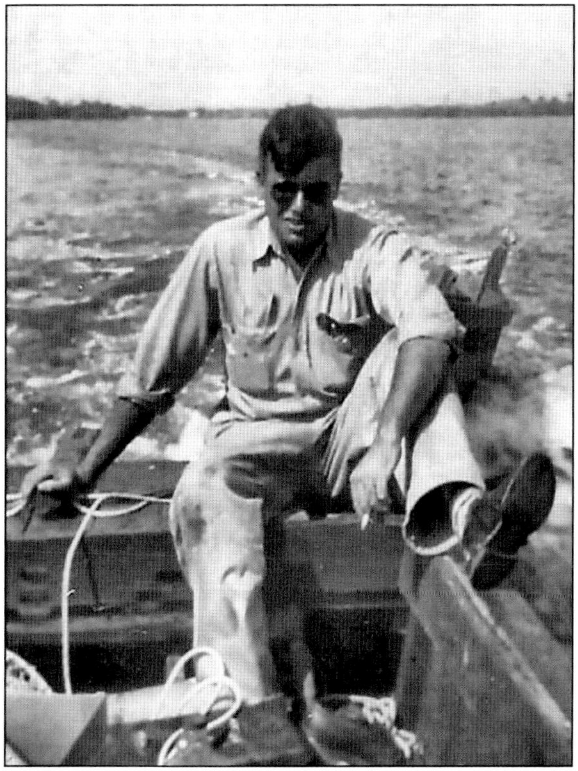

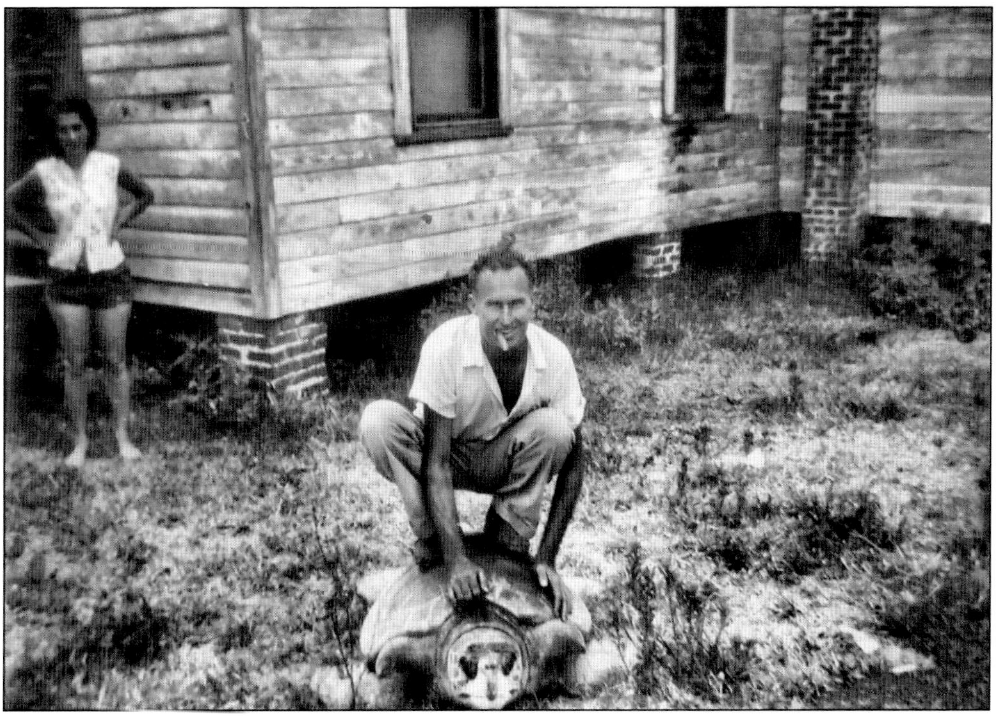

Arnett Hutchinson, also known as "Tiny," was one of many fishermen who caught turtles to sell or feed their families. (Courtesy of Kathy Bittle.)

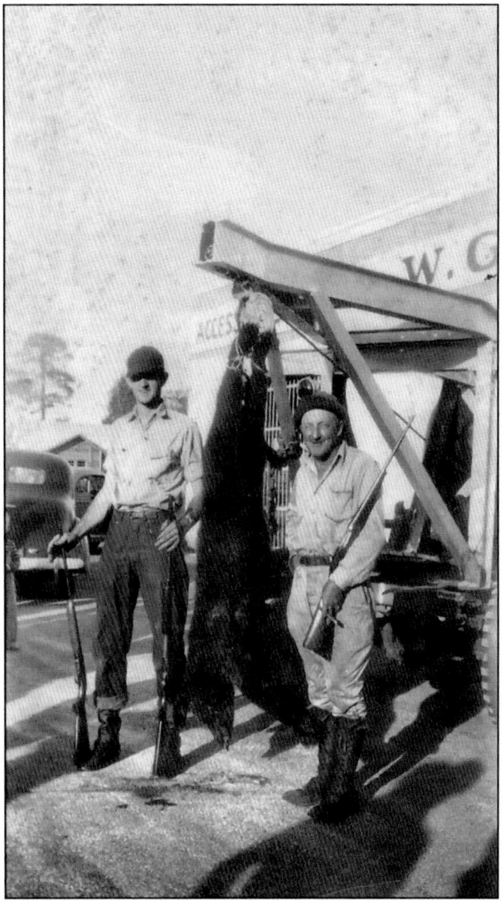

Hunting was for food and sport, but sometimes a hunter was surprised by what he found. Van Buren "Boo" Baldwin Jr. (left) proudly stands with hunting partner Warren Williams after shooting this bear.

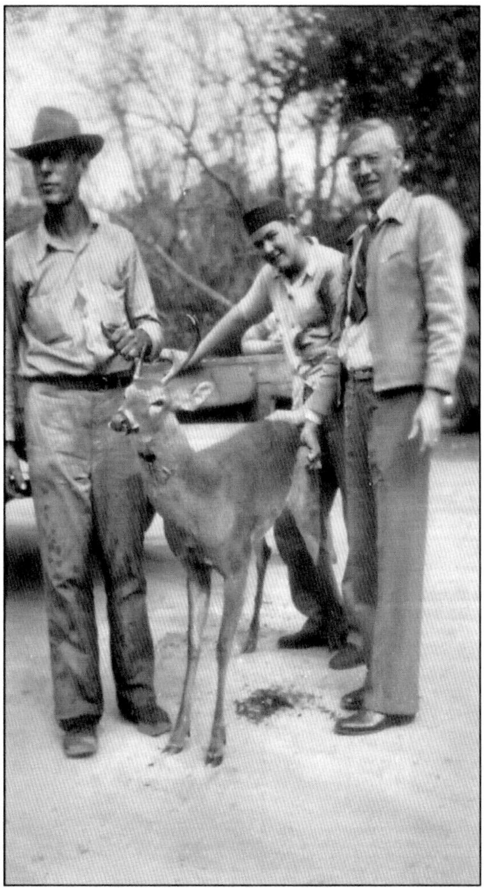

A successful deer hunt was always a welcome meal. From left to right, Harley Cantrell, his son Harley Lee, and Van Buren Baldwin Sr. pose with the deer they shot.

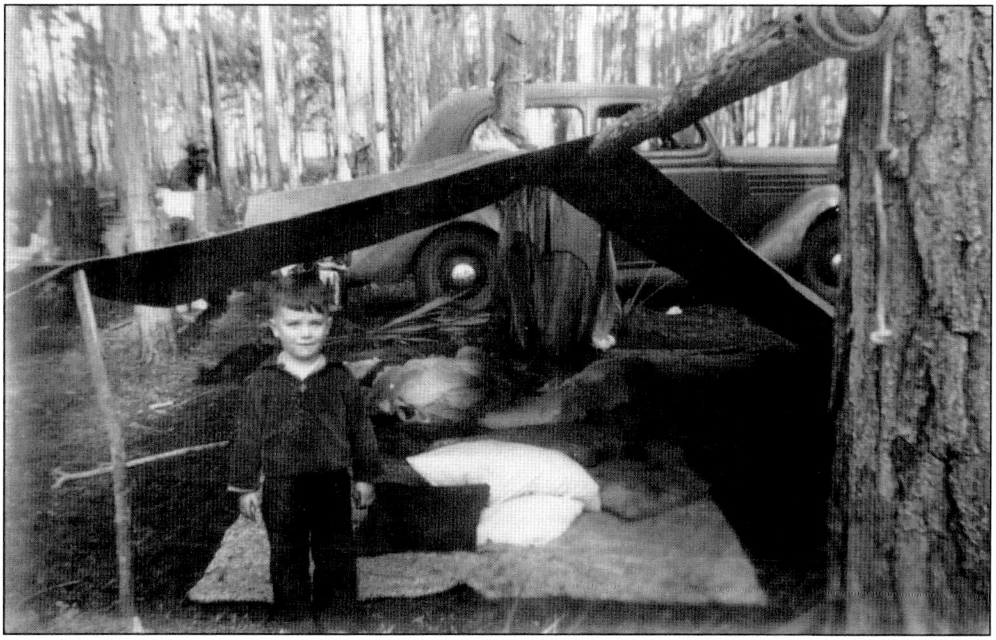

Camping trips in the woods were a favorite weekend treat for families like the McGees. Clifford McGee has his place to sleep all prepared. (Courtesy of Bill McGee.)

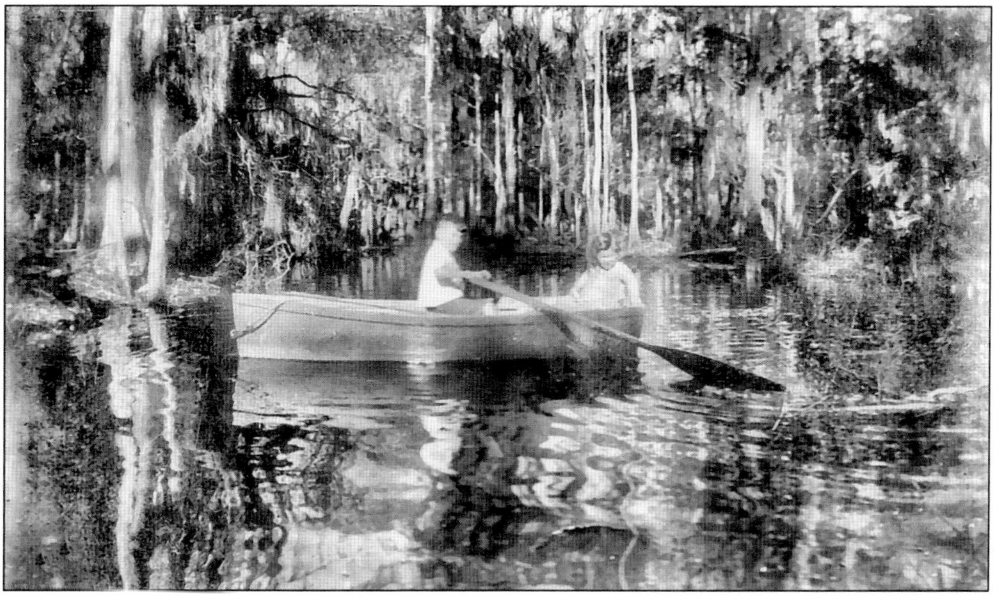

Boating down Cow Creek while on a weekend camping trip was great fun for the McGee family. (Courtesy of Bill McGee.)

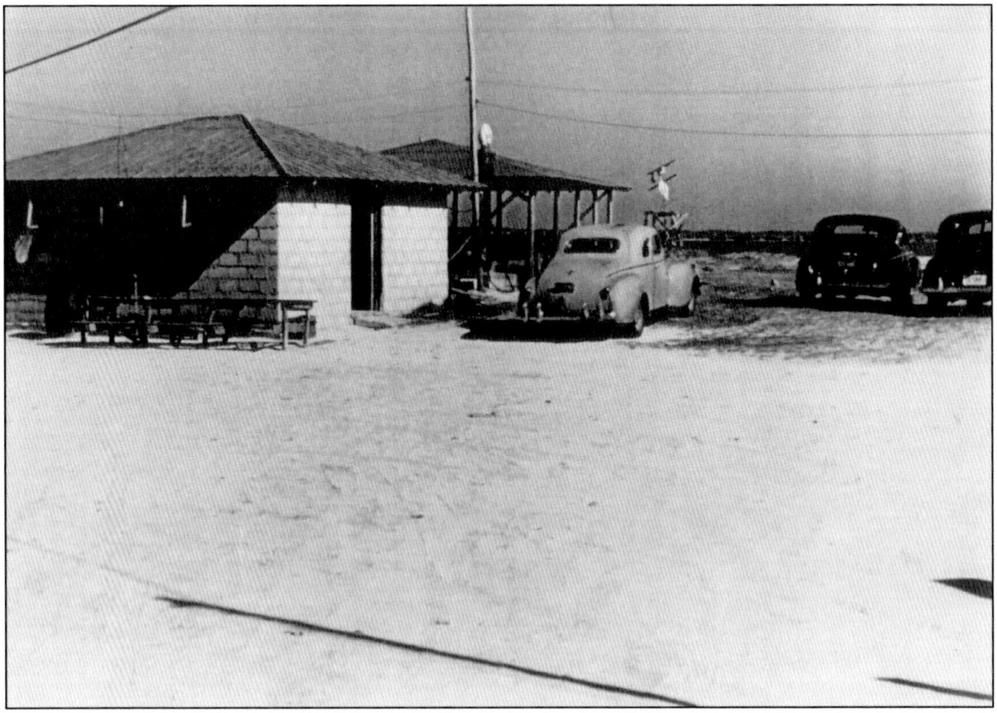

The Lopez Fish Camp, owned and operated first by Herbie Lopez and then by his son Winston, was an important location to launch boats or to fish off the dock. Somerset Beach, just to the right, was the site of end-of-the-year picnics for the students. (Courtesy of Mary Ann Lopez.)

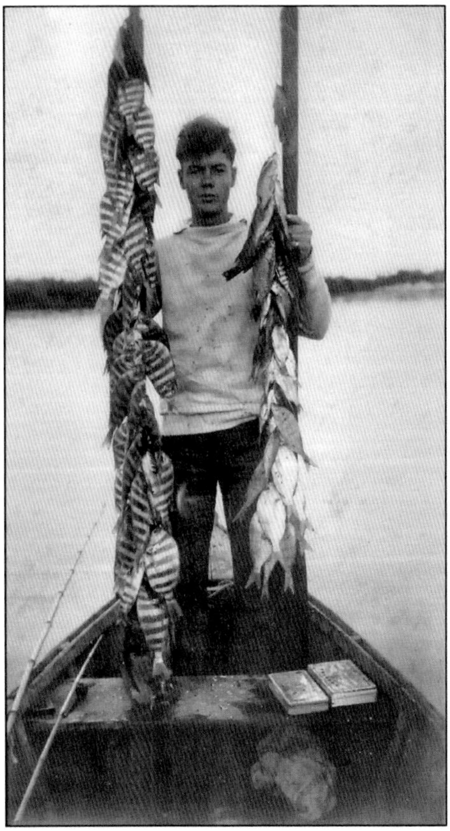

Oak Hill's Mosquito Lagoon was known for its rich harvest of fish. This unidentified man brought in a great catch for his family.

Arthur Simmons joined the navy when the United States entered the war in 1942. He worked in naval intelligence at the U.S. Embassy in Havana, Cuba, and learned to speak fluent Spanish there. (Courtesy of Ida Goodrich.)

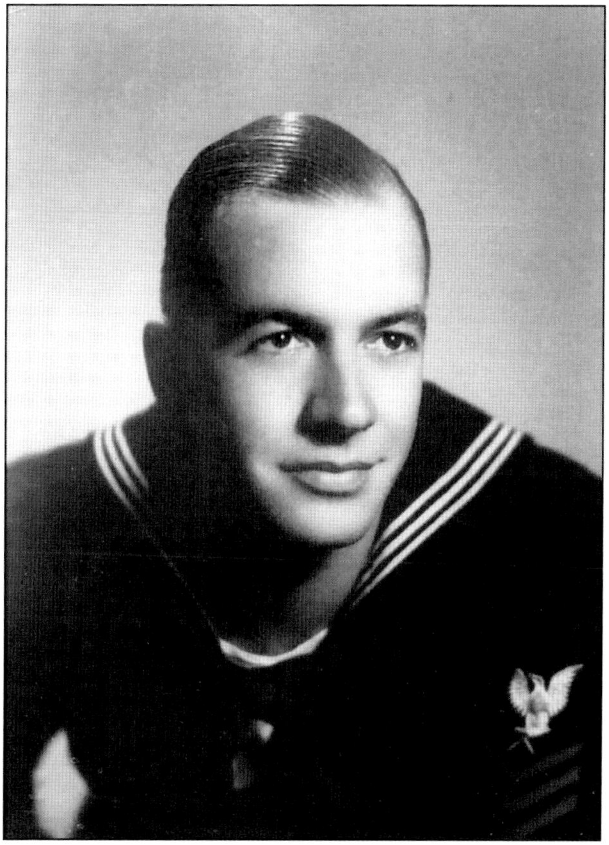

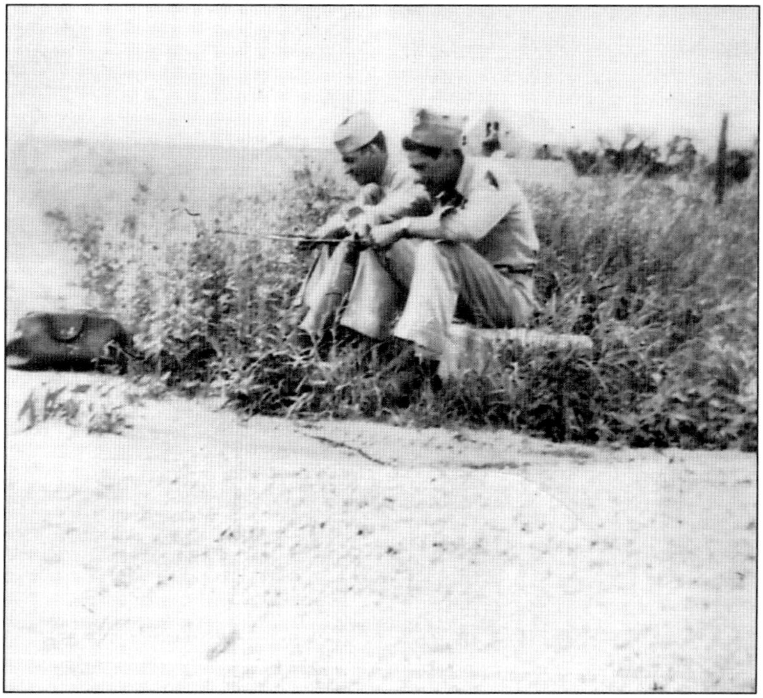

Drafted in 1942, Leonard Mosby Jr. (left) and his unidentified friend wait for the bus to take them to army basic training. When Leonard Jr. returned from the war, he followed his youthful dream into radio and television.

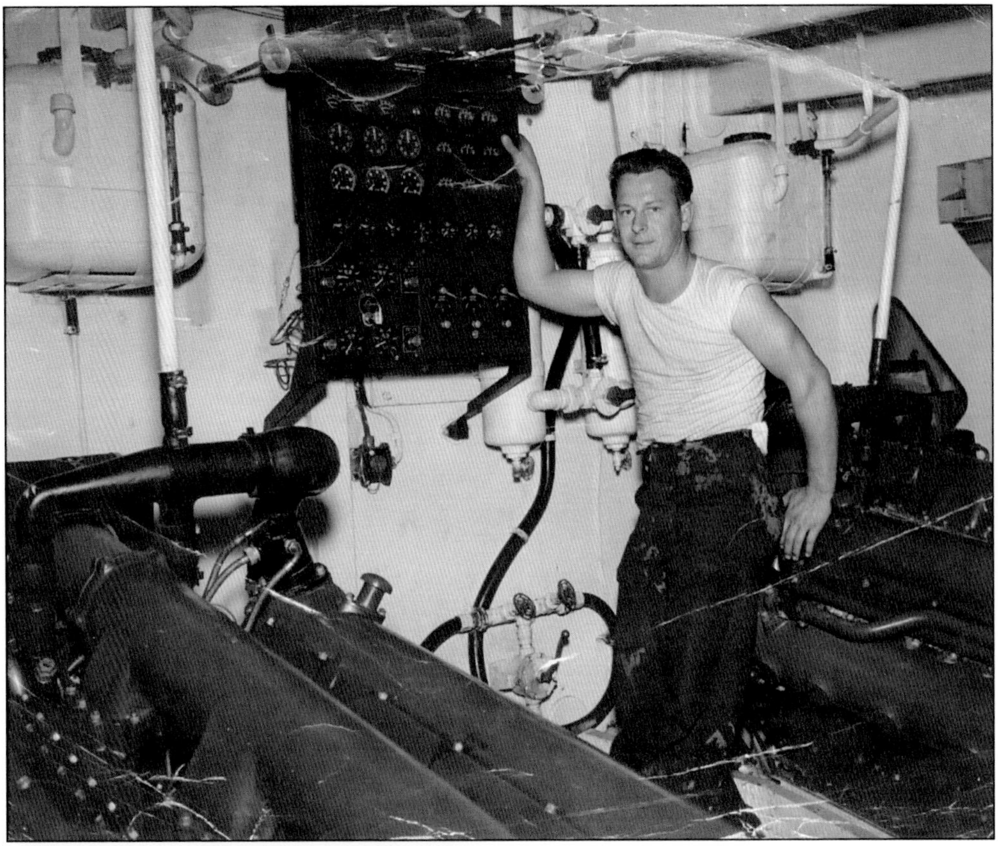

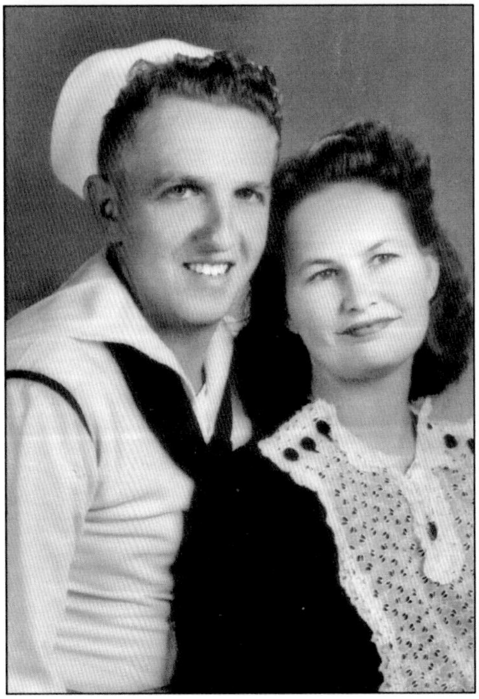

Lamar Robinson served in the U.S. Navy during World War II. (Courtesy of Juanita Robinson.)

Lela Mae Howland, born and raised in Oak Hill, met Jim Avery during the war while he was stationed in New Smyrna with the U.S. Coast Guard. They were married before the armistice was signed and shared their lives for more than 60 years. Their two children are David and Lori. (Courtesy of Kathy Bittle.)

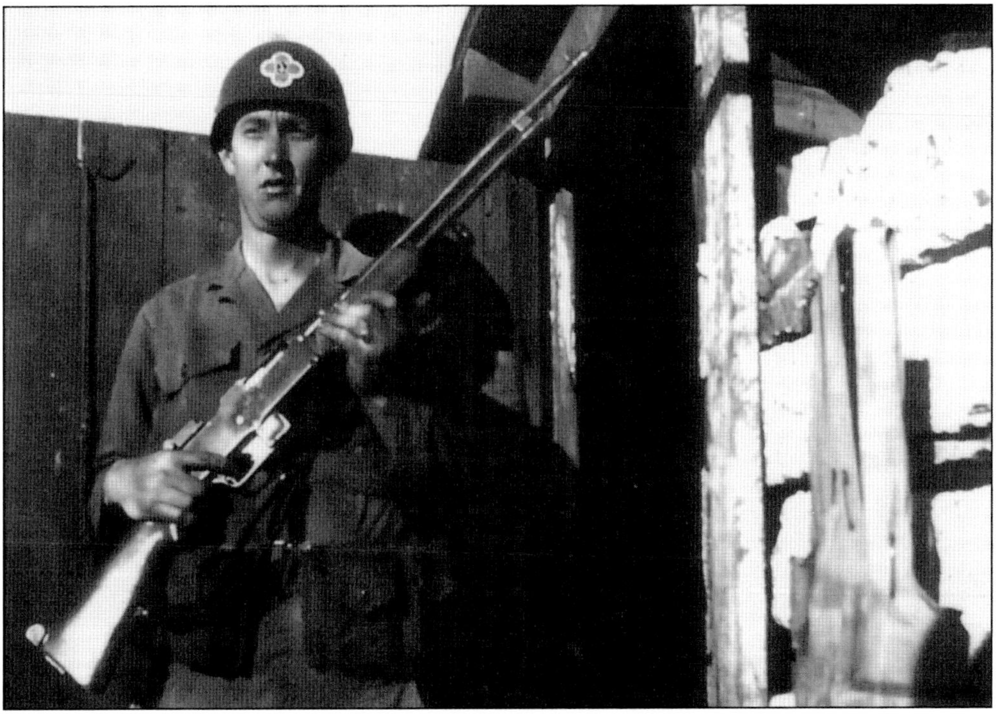

Albert Simmons, U.S. Army infantry, is pictured presenting a weapons lesson on the Browning Automatic Rifle (BAR) in 1947 to his men in Trieste, Italy. He fought in the Battle of the Bulge, and during his tour of duty in Europe, he recalled how his feet and ears froze as they marched long days through freezing temperatures. (Courtesy of Ann Simmons.)

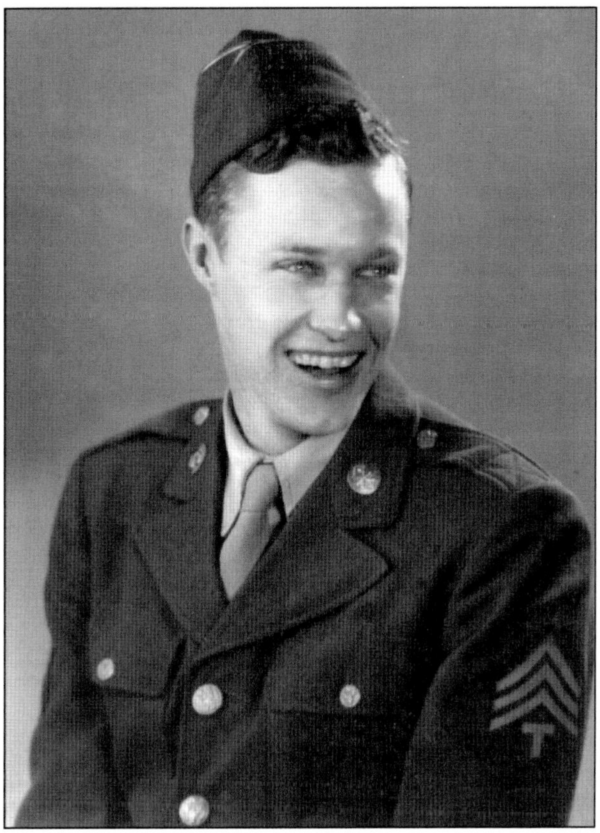

Wilfred Goodrich proudly served in the U.S. Army in Europe during World War II, spending more than three years in England with the signal corps and returning home to a career in banking. (Courtesy of Marie Goodrich.)

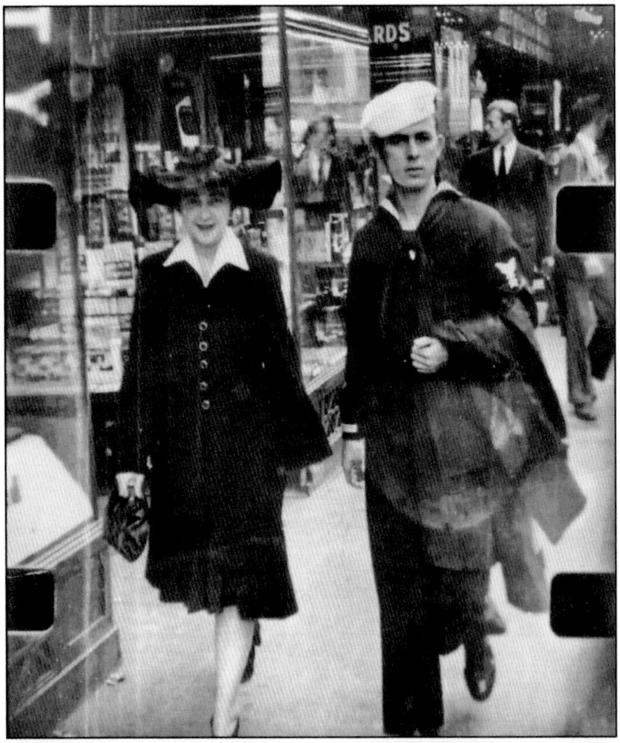

Aleph Somerset and her son James are shown walking down a Washington, D.C., street in 1942. James was visiting his mother before leaving to serve in the U.S. Navy. She left her hotel in Oak Hill during the war to run the Senate Dining Hall. (Courtesy of Dorothy Somerset.)

The citrus industry expanded, and so did the Oak Hill packinghouse, started in 1924 by Howard Putnam, M. W. Ashton, George Fullerton, and others. This aerial view (below) shows how extensive it had grown by the 1940s. (Courtesy of Ida Goodrich.)

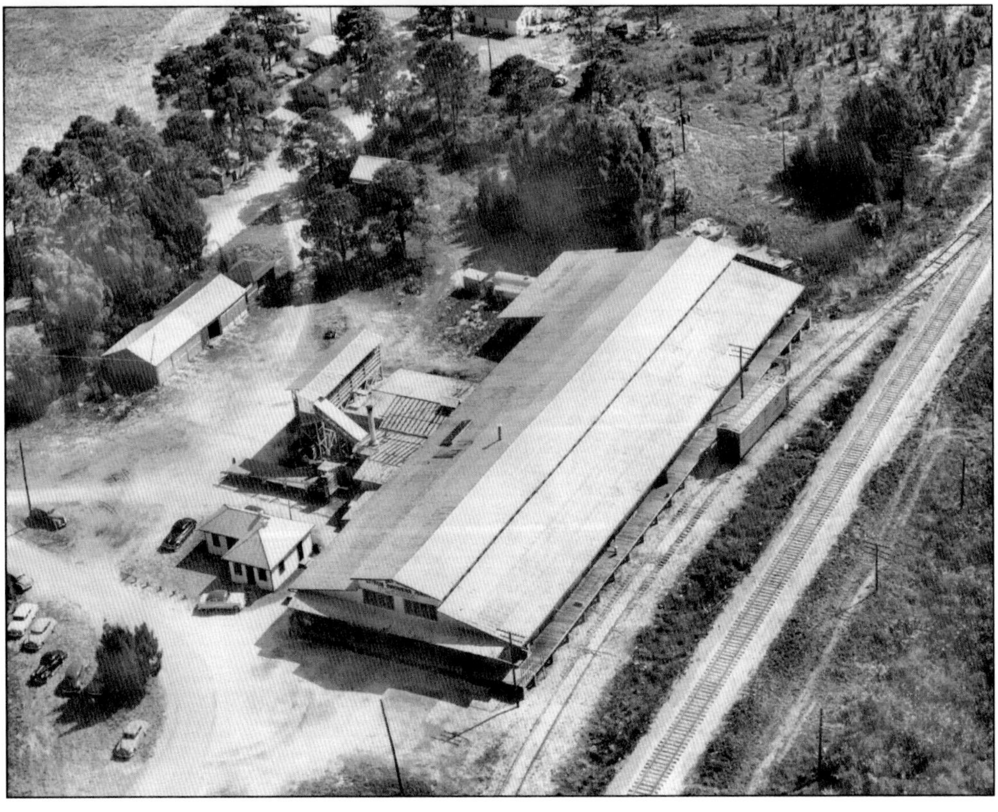

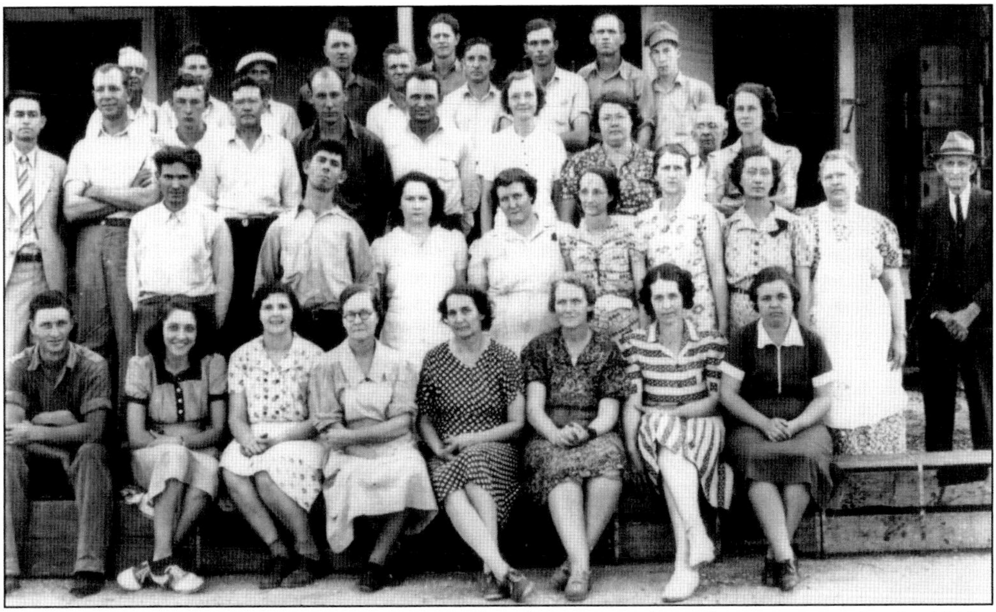

The Oak Hill Citrus Growers Association employed many people in the community by the 1940s. They are, from left to right, (first row) Lester Lamb, Iva Lee Ash, Merle Godwin, Mary Simmons, Gertrude Threlkeld, Eva Jones, Lottie Norman, and Arlou O'Neal; (second row) Lee Willis, Reuben Jones, Mrs. Lester Lamb, Avis Godwin, Mrs. ? Booth, Mrs. Lee Willis, Mrs. ? Mahan, Mrs. Fred Carter, and James Taylor; (third row) Aaron Taylor, Lester Cantress, Charles Glenn, Fred Carter, Carl Cantrell, Emory Ash, Thelma Miller, Lela Carter Booth, Frank Keubler, and Eva Taylor; (fourth row) Ben Keubler, Lawrence ?, C. B. Jones, Walt Davenport, Forte Jones, Clyde Davenport, Ralph Miller, Lonnie Godwin, Sam Norman, and Frank Willis. (Courtesy of Betty Bellamy.)

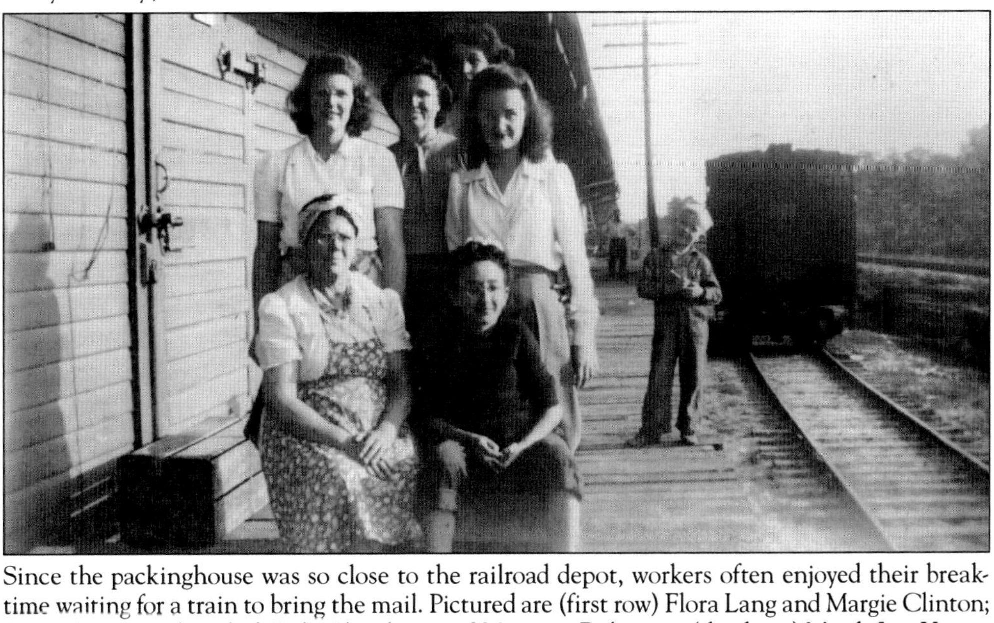

Since the packinghouse was so close to the railroad depot, workers often enjoyed their break-time waiting for a train to bring the mail. Pictured are (first row) Flora Lang and Margie Clinton; (second row) unidentified, Ruby Slaughter, and Margaret Robinson; (third row) Myrtle Lee Harris. (Courtesy of Kathy Bittle.)

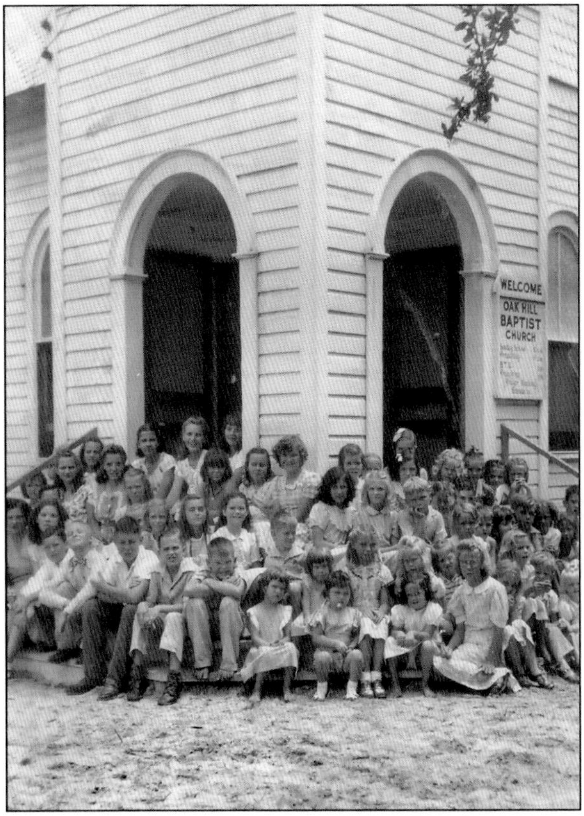

Children pose on the steps at the First Baptist Church after vacation Bible school. It was held for two weeks in June, when school was out for the summer. The children were involved with activities from 8:30 a.m. until noon. (Courtesy of Jodi Wheeler.)

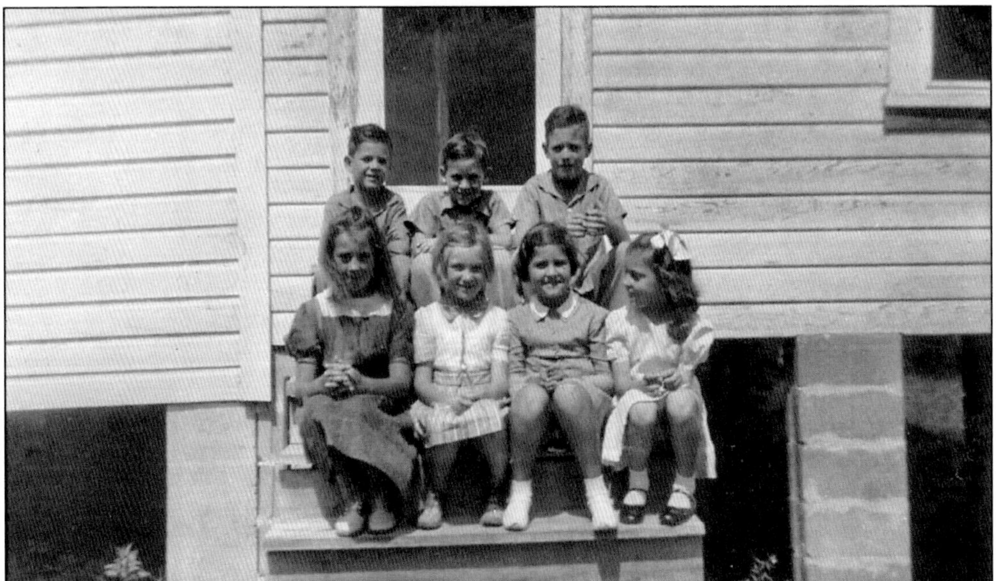

Children paused for this picture at the First Baptist Church between Sunday school and the worship service. Those pictured from left to right are (first row) Evelyn Harris, Jean Goodrich, Julia Jean Stewart, and Barbara Jean Bennett; (second row) Joel Simmons, Hal Edwards, and Ronnie Simmons. (Courtesy of Marie Goodrich.)

Fred and Jeanne Baldwin Wheeler built the B&W Garage in 1946 and worked there for more than 30 years. They were joined by their son, Richard, after he returned from service in the U.S. Air Force. (Courtesy of Jody Wheeler.)

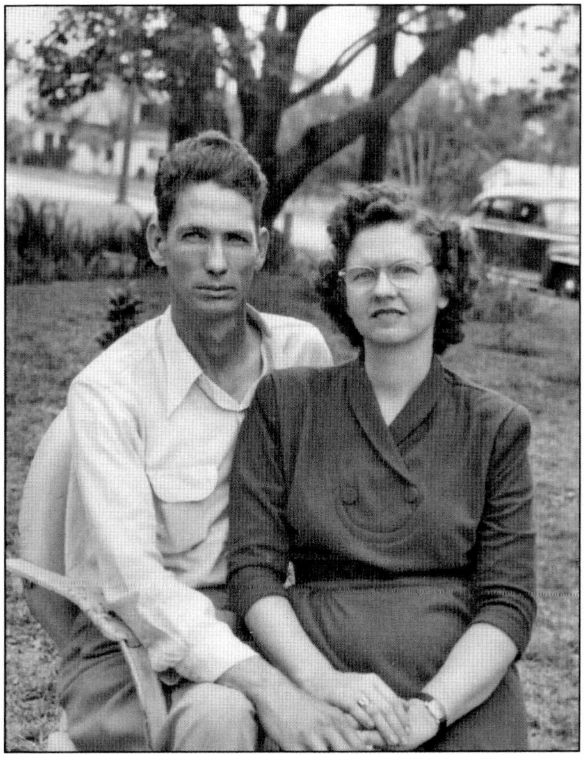

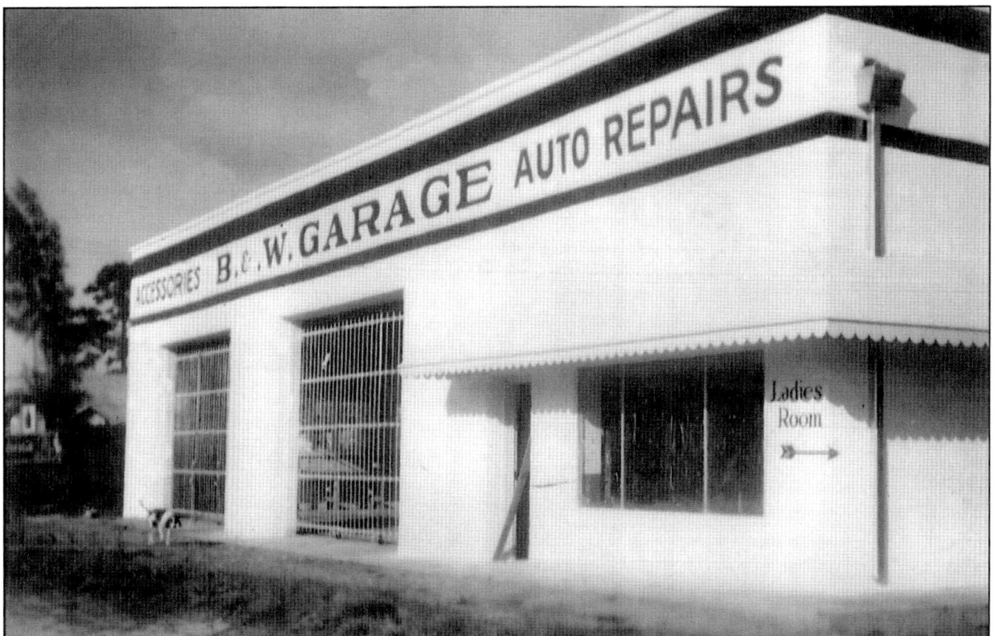

This was an automotive garage, but with Fred Wheeler as the chief mechanic, anything could be fixed. He even built a tractor for Mac McGee, which he needed to work the groves. The B&W stood for Bennett and Wheeler, but soon after opening, Fred and Jeanne owned and operated the business themselves. (Courtesy of Jody Wheeler.)

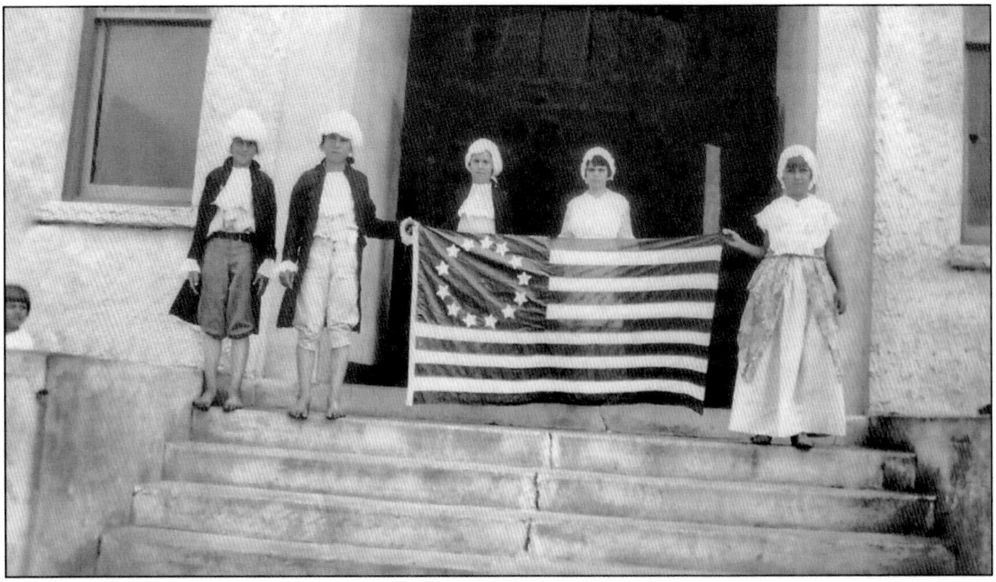

This school play is typical of the Friday assemblies at Oak Hill School in the early days. Different classes were responsible for presenting a program, and students looked forward to participating when it was their class's turn to present. (Courtesy of Bill Dyall.)

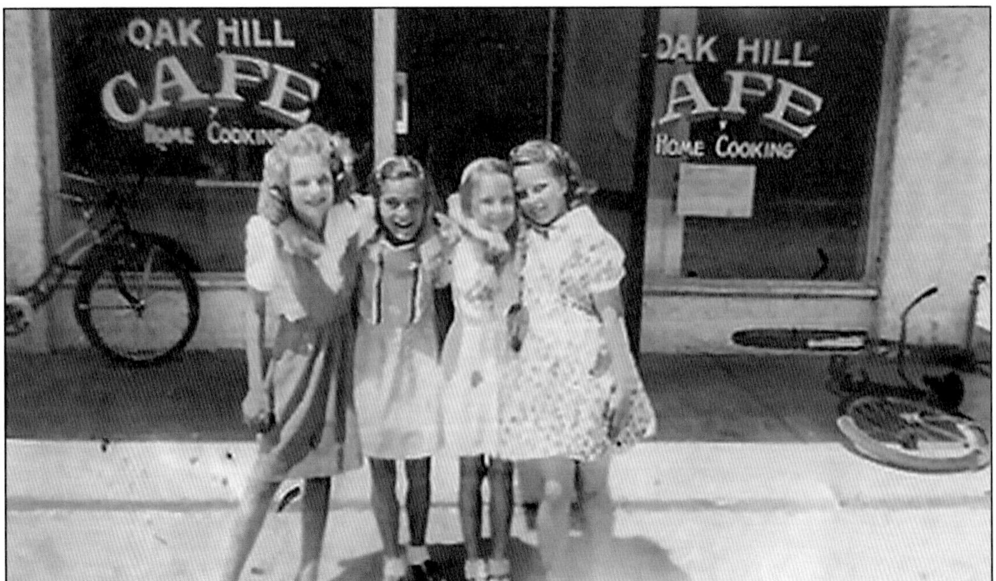

From left to right, Dot Goodrich (Burch), Joyce Butler, Shirley Alderman (Sullivan), and Pat Goodrich (Stever) hang out in front of Mila and Nelson's Café. Mila was Shirley's older sister, who later married Nelson Crawford. (Courtesy of Euda Mary Alderman.)

Mamie Alderman gives instructions to her son, Dan, at their store on Highway U.S. 1. The Aldermans bought the business from Foster Bennett in 1943. They owned and operated the family business until 1955 when Highway U.S. 1 was expanded to four lanes, taking the property where their store stood. (Courtesy of Euda Mary Alderman.)

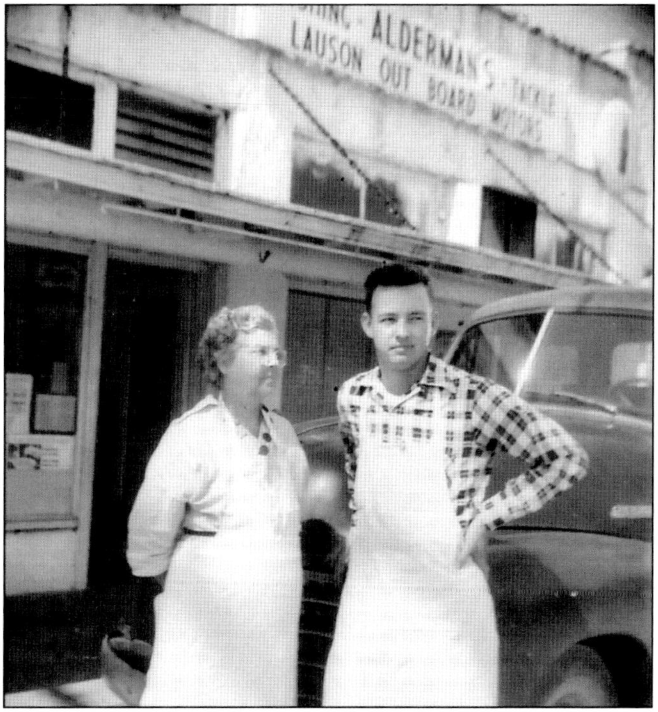

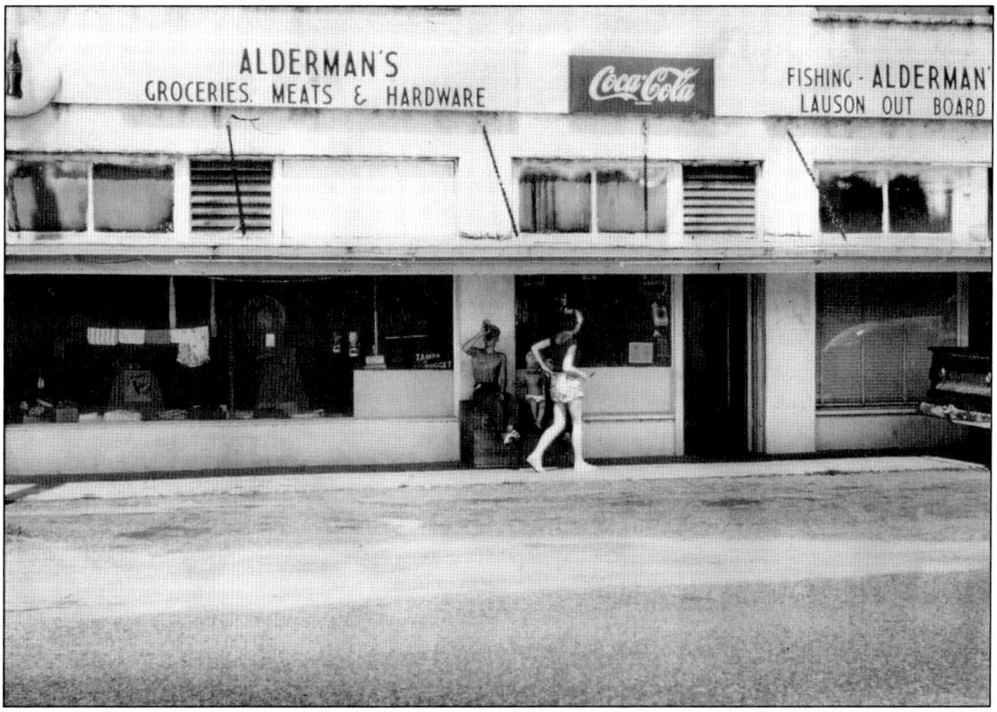

John Johnson (left) and Buren Alderman are sitting on a bread box in front of the Alderman Store in 1954. Shirley Alderman is walking by. The store provided fresh meats and groceries, dry goods, and hardware. When the new air-cooled Lawson outboard motors came out, Oscar Alderman added them to his inventory.

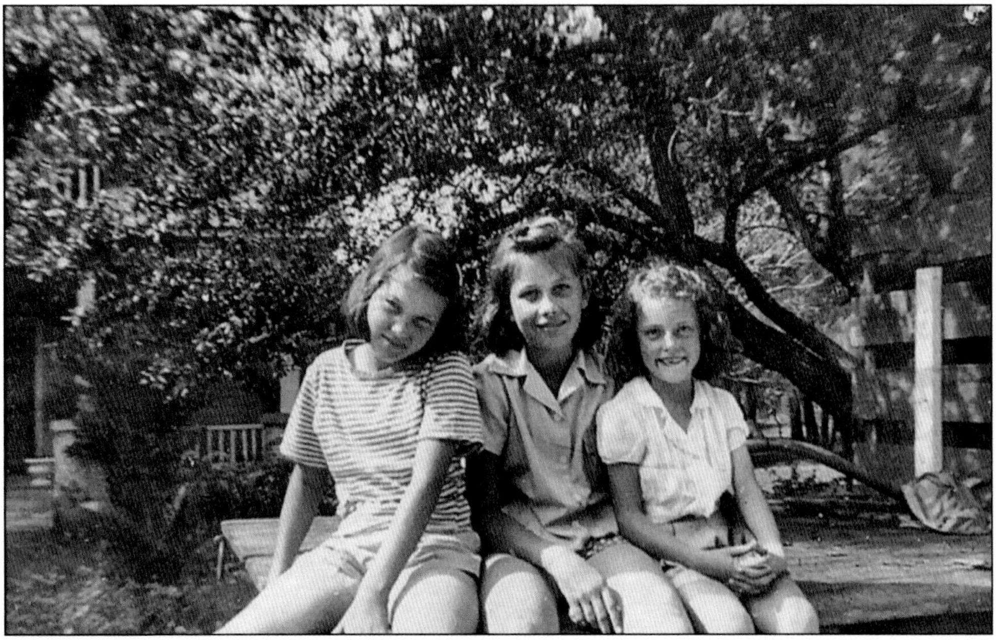

This was an era of friends, when spending time and building lasting relationships mattered. Barbara Bennett (right) and Sue Bennett (left) sit on each side of their friend Ida Simmons; they remained friends their entire lives. (Courtesy of Ida Goodrich.)

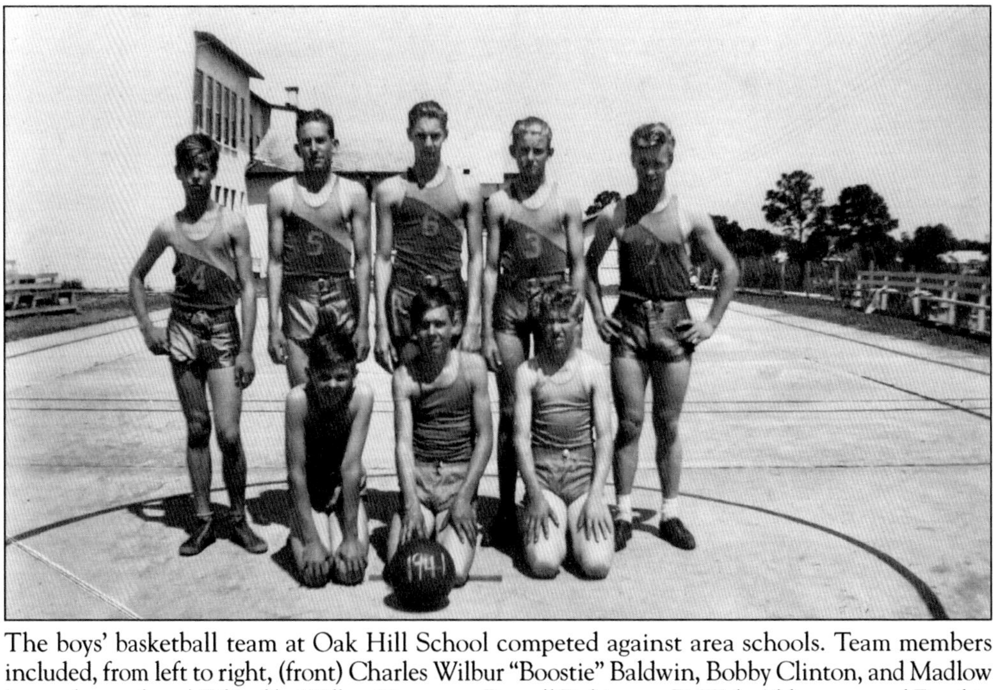

The boys' basketball team at Oak Hill School competed against area schools. Team members included, from left to right, (front) Charles Wilbur "Boostie" Baldwin, Bobby Clinton, and Madlow Jones; (second row) Ed Lefils, Wilbur Simmons, Russell Robinson, DeWalt Alderman, and Frankie LeFils. (Courtesy of Marie Goodrich.)

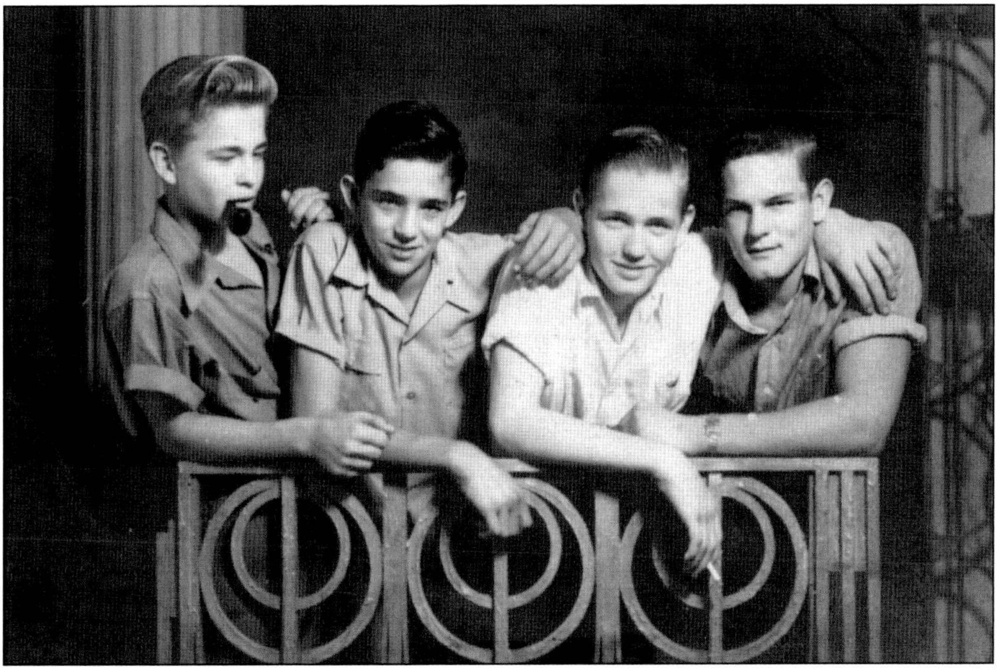

From left to right, Thomas Futch, Jack Bellamy, Edward Futch, and Jamie Robinson were good friends during their childhood and posed together for a traveling photographer. (Courtesy of Kathy Bittle.)

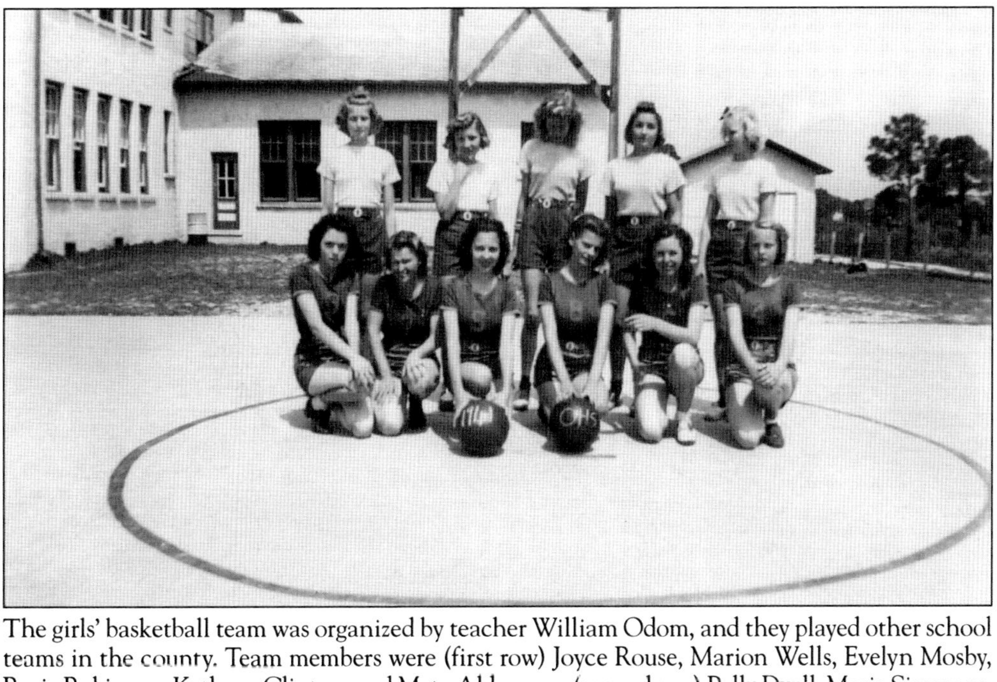

The girls' basketball team was organized by teacher William Odom, and they played other school teams in the county. Team members were (first row) Joyce Rouse, Marion Wells, Evelyn Mosby, Rosie Robinson, Kathryn Clinton, and Meta Alderman; (second row) Polly Dyall, Marie Simmons, Dorothy Hutchinson, Mary Alderman, and Wilma Miller. (Courtesy of Marie Goodrich.)

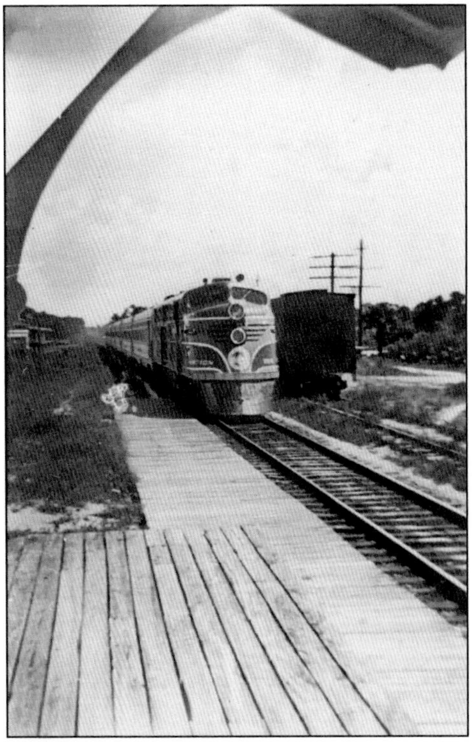

When the *Champion* Streamliner train whizzed through Oak Hill in the 1940s, it was a special event. The school let out, and all the students were brought to the railroad depot to see it pass. (Courtesy of Betty Bellamy.)

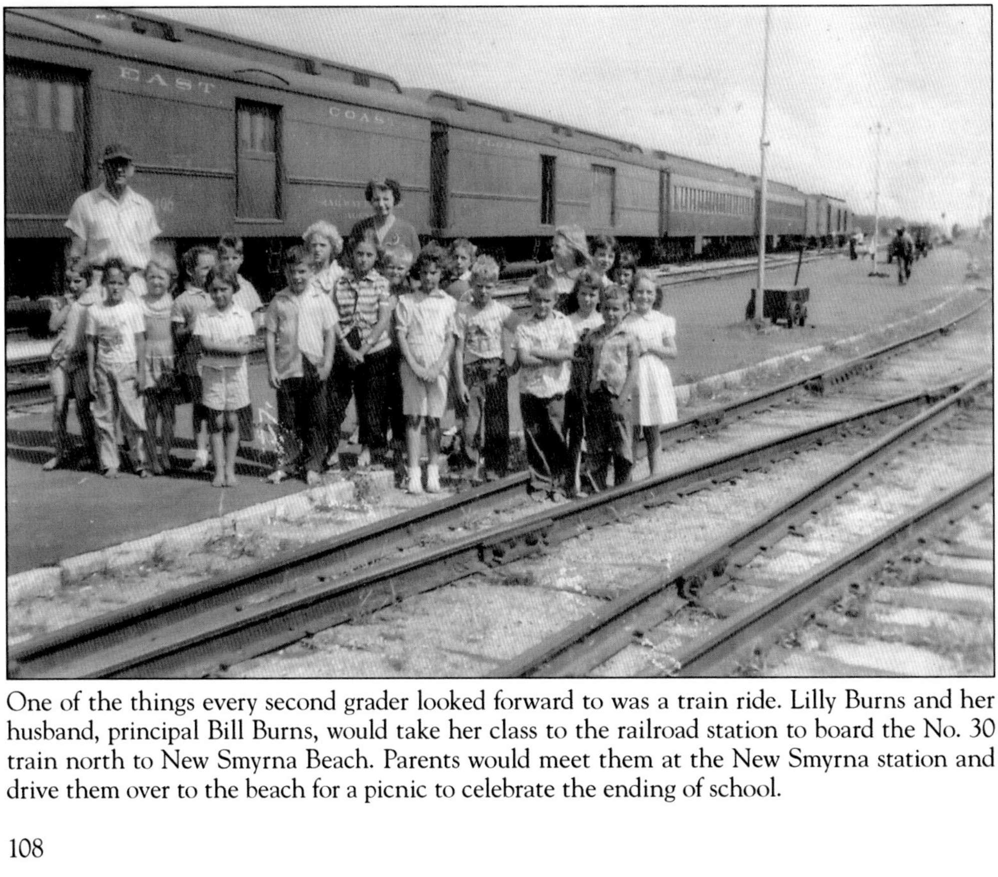

One of the things every second grader looked forward to was a train ride. Lilly Burns and her husband, principal Bill Burns, would take her class to the railroad station to board the No. 30 train north to New Smyrna Beach. Parents would meet them at the New Smyrna station and drive them over to the beach for a picnic to celebrate the ending of school.

Seven

Reactivation and Revitalization of the City

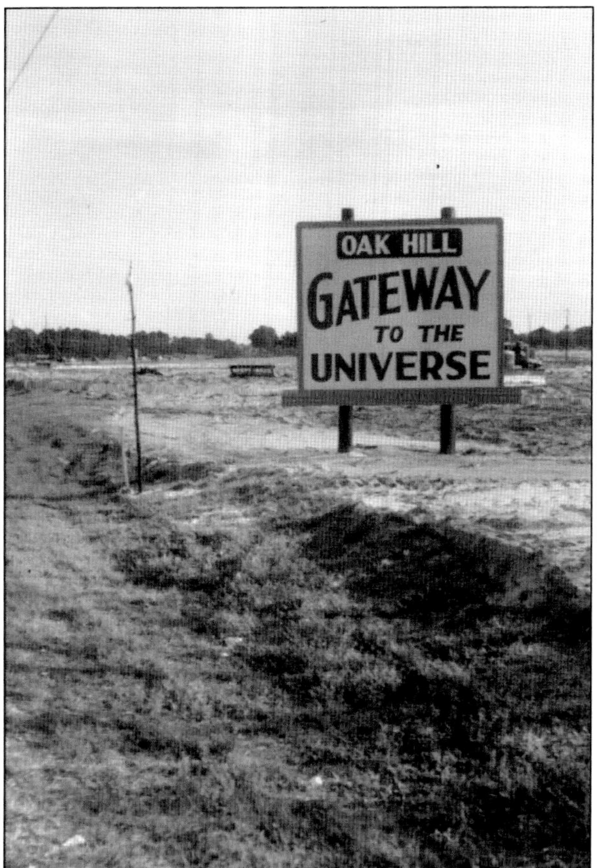

When the National Aeronautics and Space Administration (NASA) purchased property in the late 1950s just south of Oak Hill, speculators believed this little sleepy fishing village was the place to watch. The sign, "Gateway to the Universe," was placed at the north entrance to the town. Citizens were anxious about the projected growth that would result from the development of the space program. This also included many new jobs and opportunities, for which the locals are still thankful.

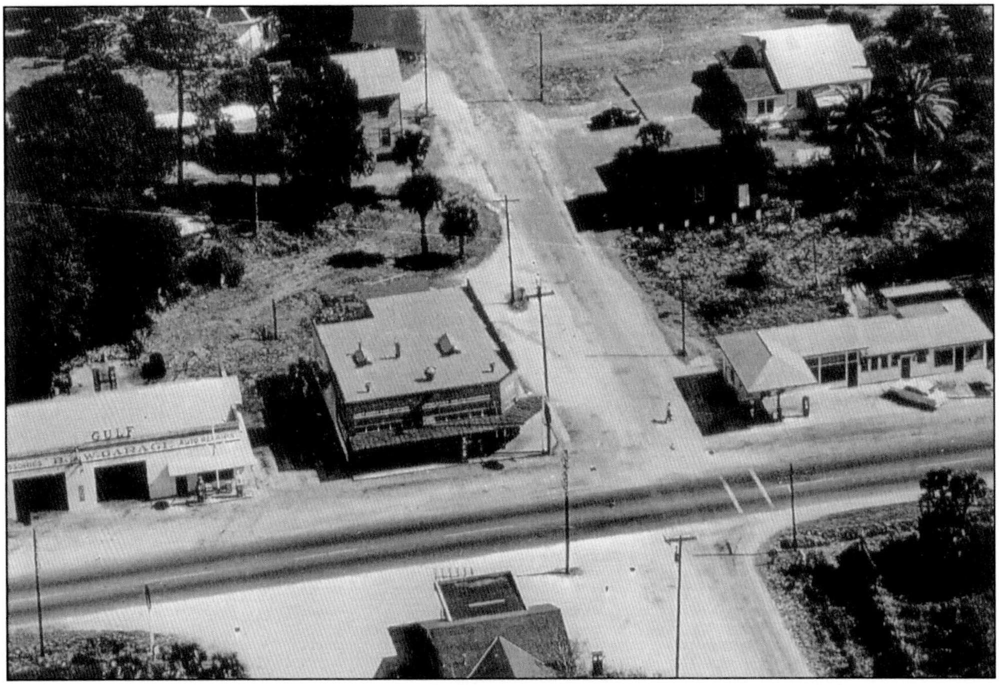

The look of the town began to change. This aerial view gives the location of the town's main buildings in the 1950s and 1960s. (Courtesy of Betty Bellamy.)

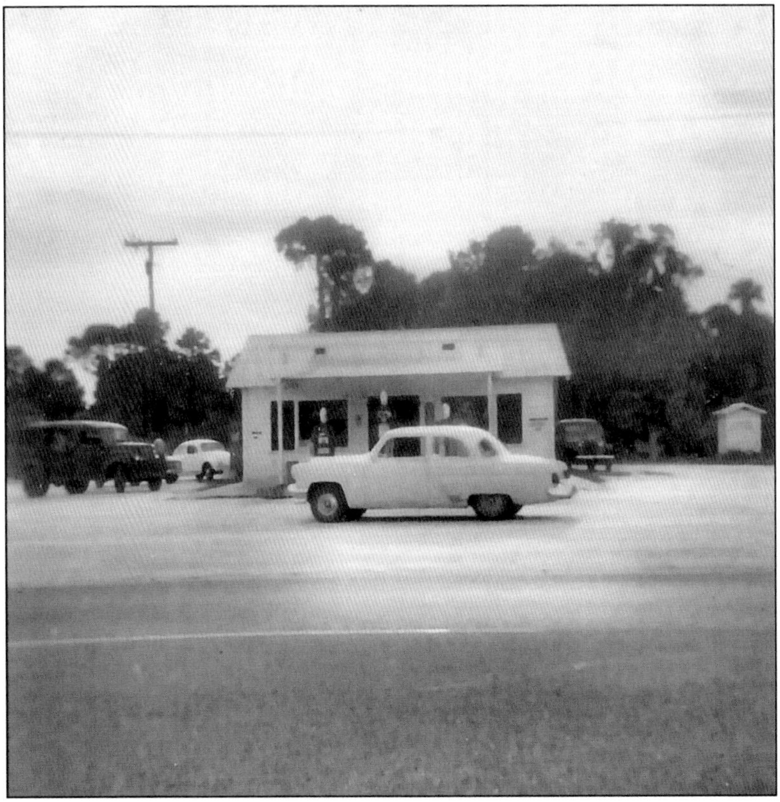

Warren Williams owned this gas station on Highway U.S. 1 at the intersection of Halifax Avenue in the 1940s. (Courtesy of Karen Papouleas.)

Like many other local boys, Vance Jones left his family and job at Baldwin's Store to serve in the Korean War. (Courtesy of Kathy Bittle.)

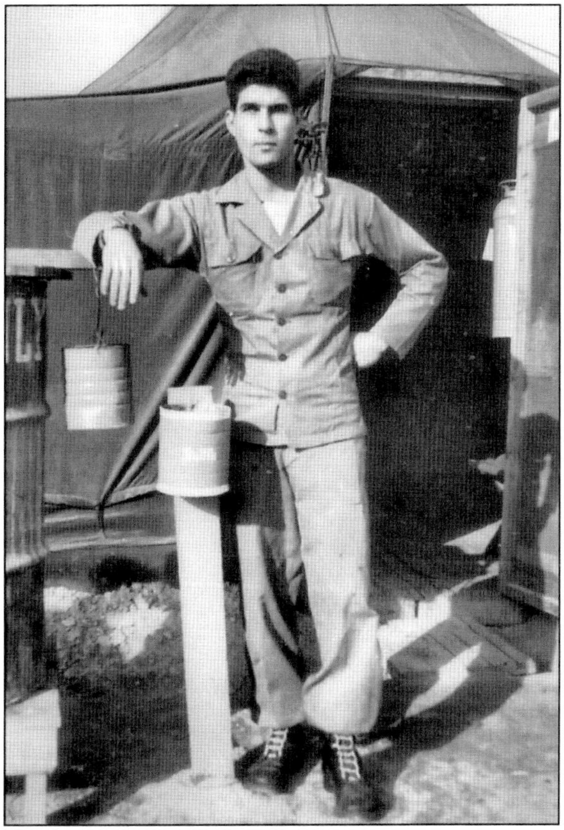

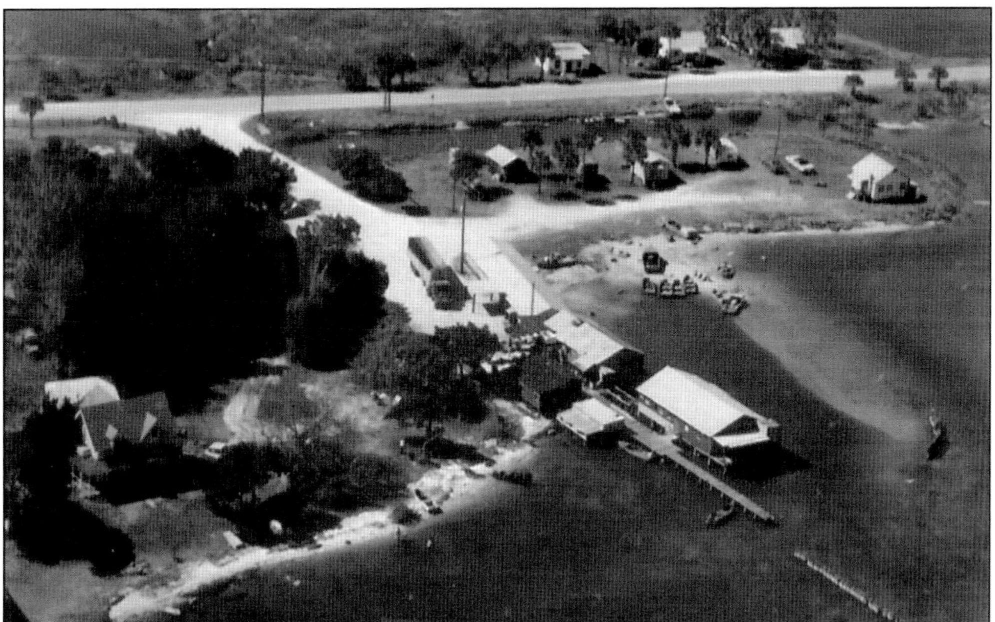

This aerial view of the Oak Hill riverfront is one that locals take with them in their memory anytime they must leave home. (Courtesy of Kathy Bittle.)

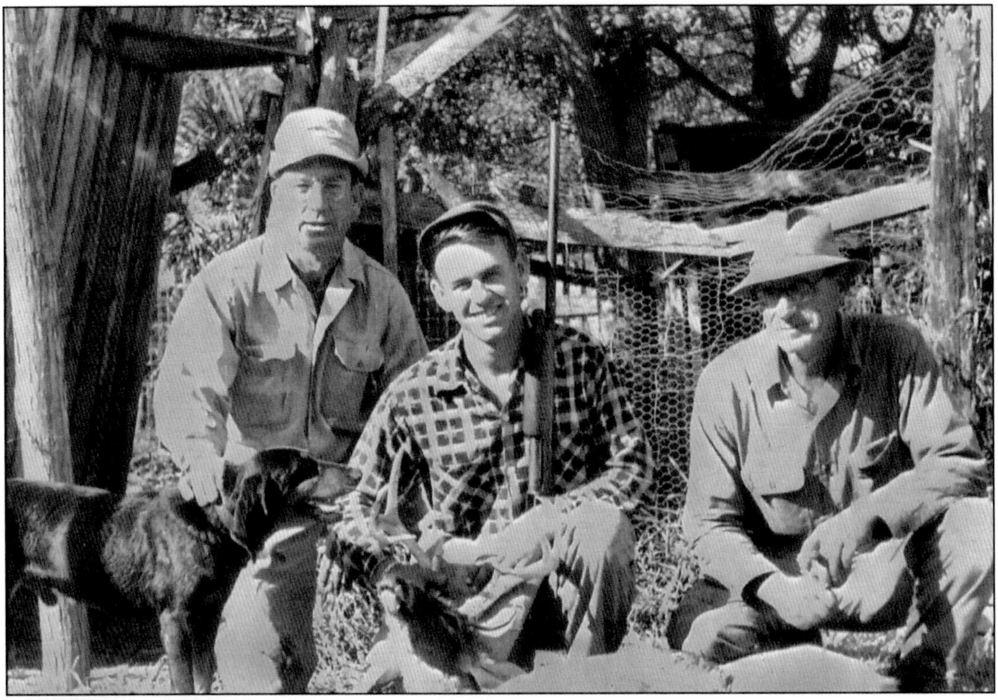

From left to right, Bill Burns, Vernon Goodrich, and Vernon's father, Elmer, proudly pose with the results of their hunt. (Courtesy of Vernon Goodrich.)

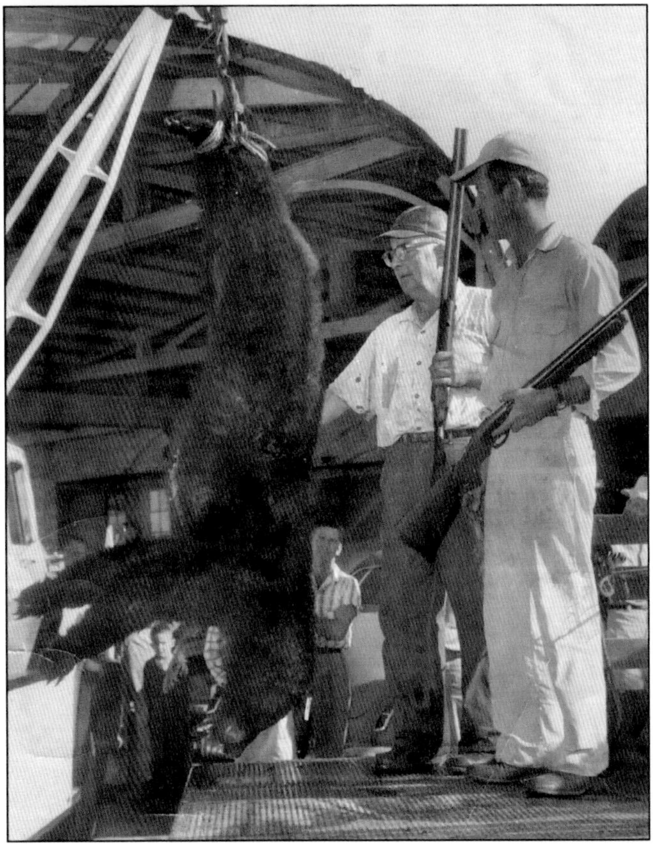

Oscar Alderman (left) and his friend Conrad Cramer decided to put an end to the thief that was taking honey from his beehives. They caught this bear on the second night and killed it, ending a major challenge. (Courtesy of Euda Mary Alderman.)

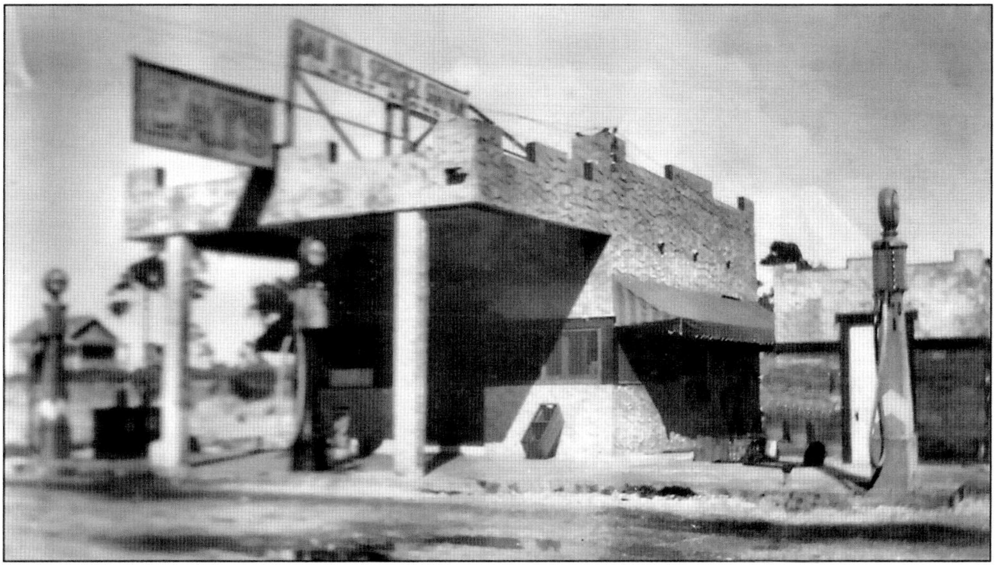

Lopez Service Station was originally built by Herbie Lopez. A weekend favorite outing for many was dancing at his Palmetto Dance Hall. He later sold this business to his son, Bennett, who operated it until 1990. (Courtesy of Mary Ann Lopez.)

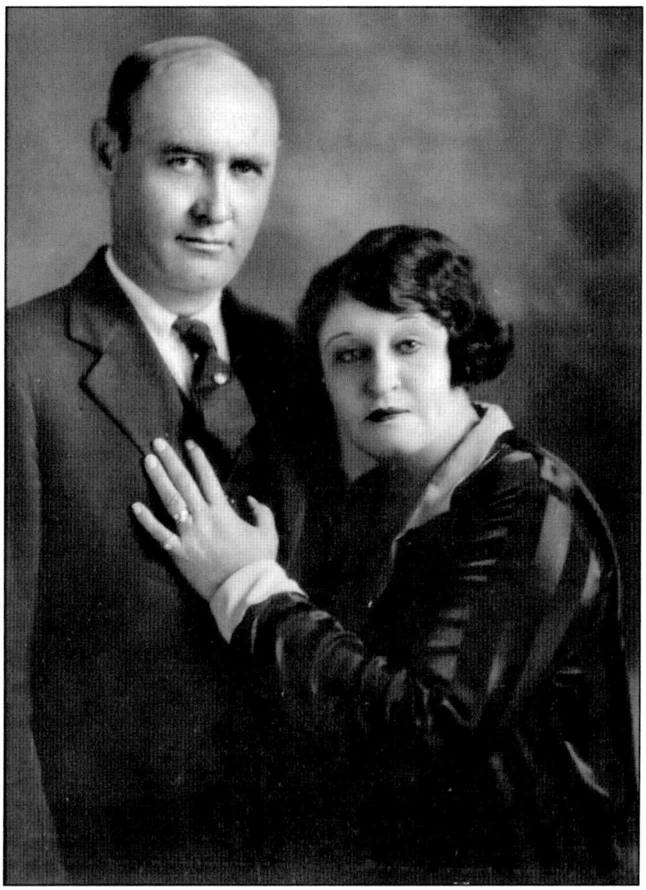

George I. Fullerton and his wife, Mildred, were among those citizens who were concerned Oak Hill would be "swallowed up" by growing neighboring towns if they did not take steps to reactivate the city's charter. George Fullerton, a local attorney, citrus businessman, and state representative, had drawn up the original request in 1927 and wrote the amendments in 1929, which were approved by the Florida Legislature, creating a city. In 1962, it was Fullerton who led the struggle to reactivate the charter, hiring the law firm of Gillespie and Gillespie to take on the challenge. (Courtesy of Eddie Smith.)

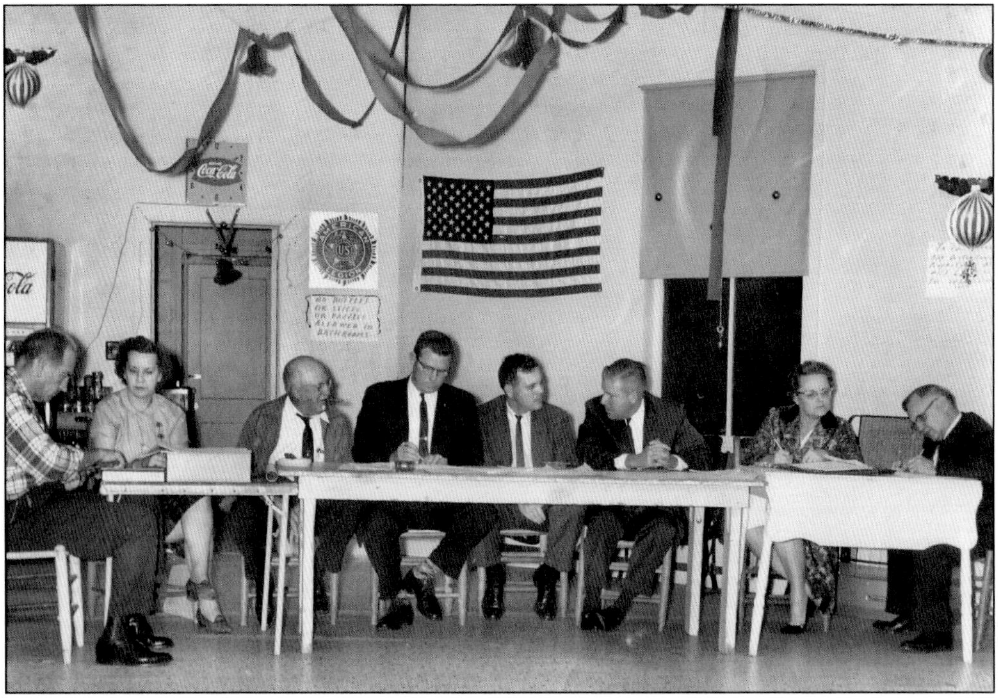

By 1963, an election was held following the state legislature's ruling for Oak Hill to reactivate the city charter. This photograph shows those involved in the first city election since 1929. They are, from left to right, Bill Burns, Ruth Treadwell, Warren Williams, Horace Treadwell, Bill Gillespie, Clarence Goodrich Jr., county supervisor of elections Catherine Odham, and J. U. Gillespie. Clarence Goodrich Jr., James Burch, and Horace Treadwell were elected. Since Clarence Goodrich received the most votes, he was selected to be mayor. (Courtesy of Ida Goodrich.)

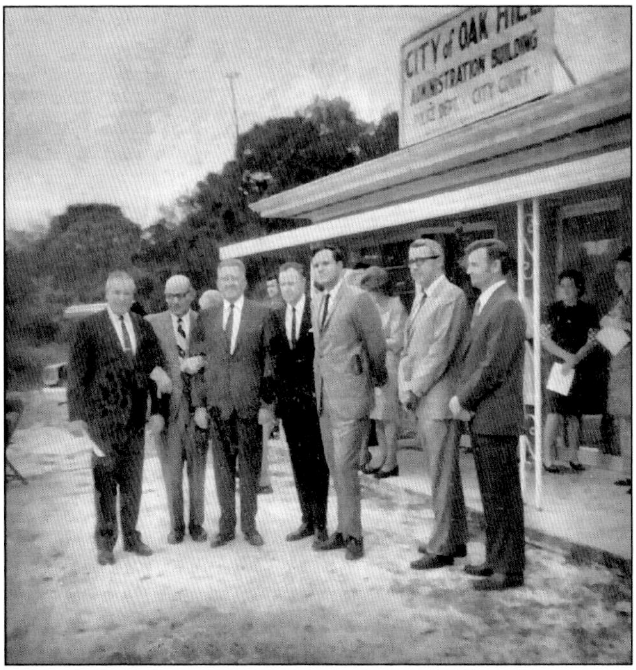

Those attending the dedication of Oak Hill's new city hall were, from left to right, Mayor Clarence Goodrich Jr., Jake Lodico, unidentified, Wilfred Goodrich, Bill Gillespie, Robert Pattillo, and Dan Alderman. (Courtesy of Ida Goodrich.)

Looking west on East Halifax Avenue, the view begins to change, as the Woodman Hall on the right is torn down. The road was paved, and more buildings, including a new post office and library, were built.

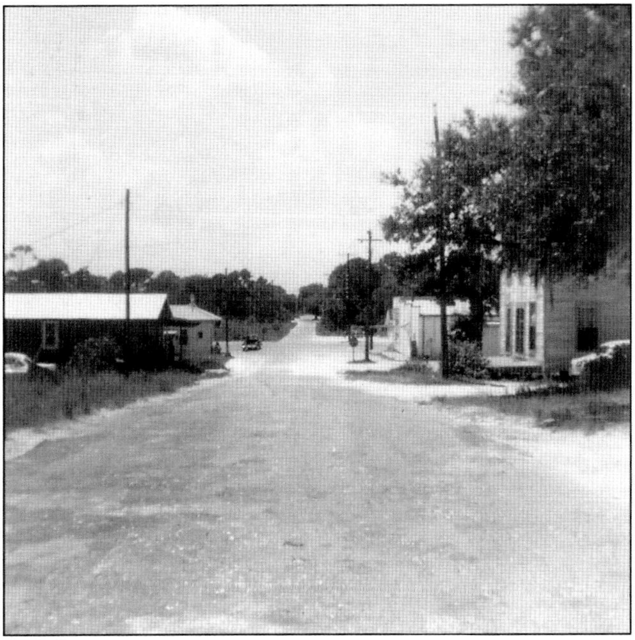

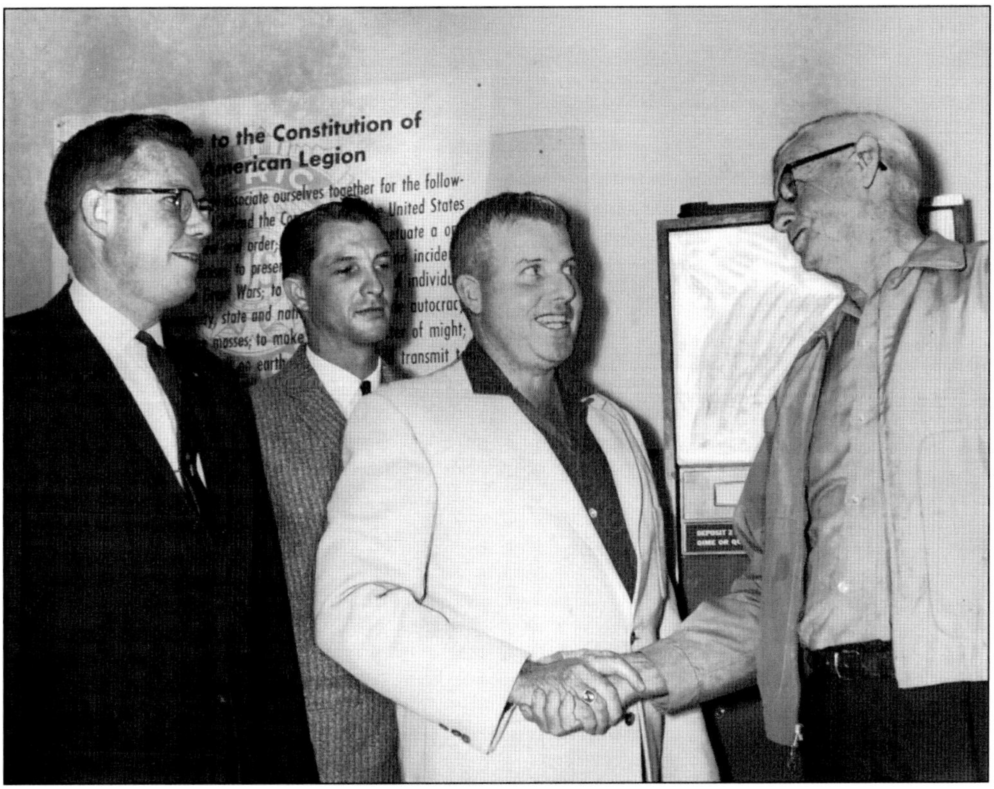

Congratulations went out to newly elected officials from Van Buren Baldwin Sr. (far right). In 1962, Mayor Clarence Goodrich Jr. (third from left), James Burch (second from left), and Horace Treadwell (far left) served as the first mayor and commissioners of the City of Oak Hill since 1930. (Courtesy of Ida Goodrich.)

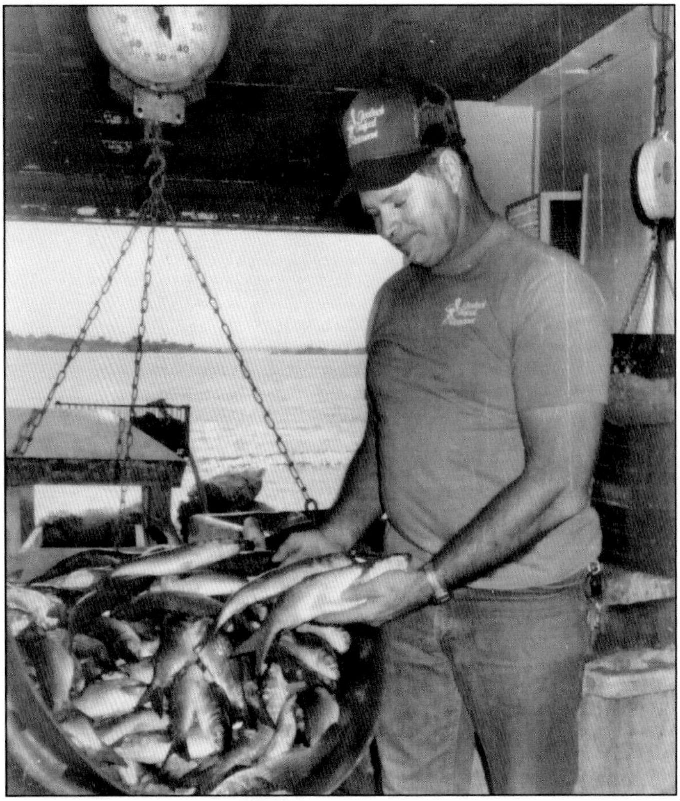

Third-generation commercial fisherman and owner of the Goodrich Fish House, Cecil Goodrich prepares mullet for the Annual Seafood Festival, which was held every October for 10 years. (Courtesy of Ida Goodrich.)

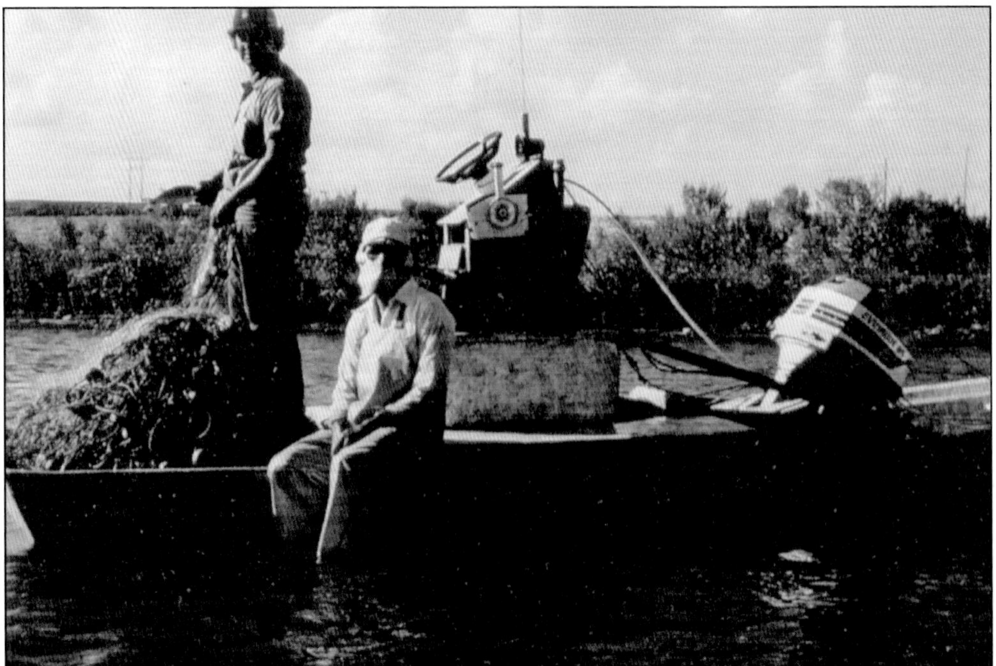

Billy Burns (standing) and Jack "Mullet Man" Bellamy are headed out to catch some fish. Bellamy is wearing a mask to protect his skin from the sun. (Courtesy of Betty Bellamy.)

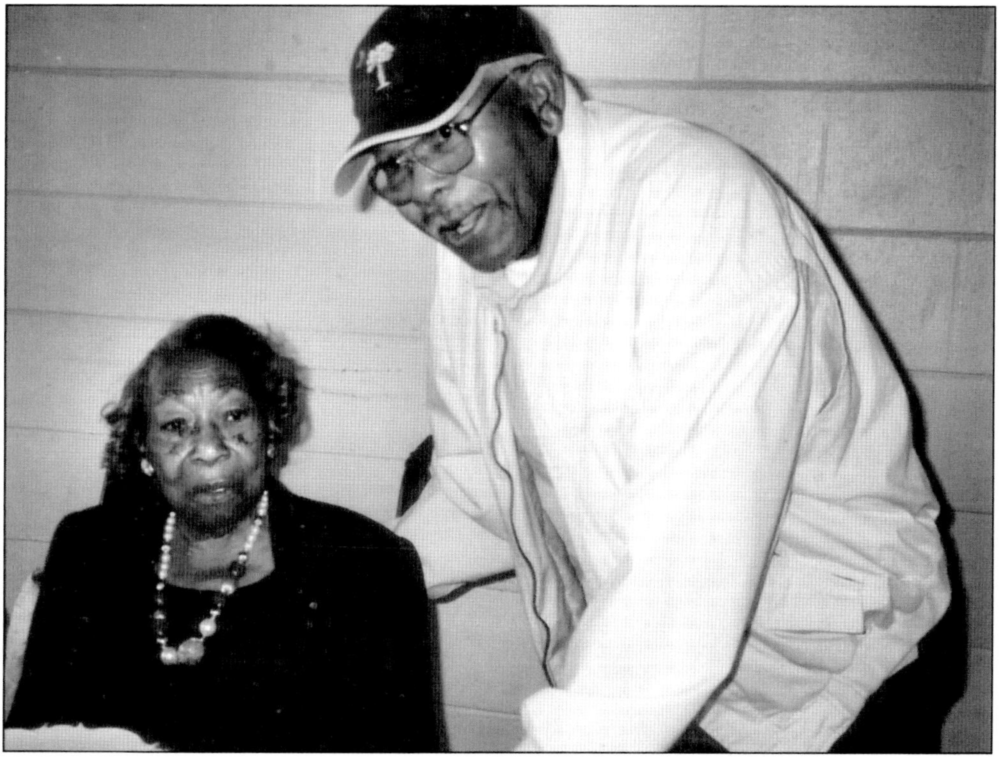

Nancy Cummings, an educator for more than 30 years in Oak Hill, chats with Matthew Wood, a former city policeman and local businessman. (Courtesy of Cathy Bittle.)

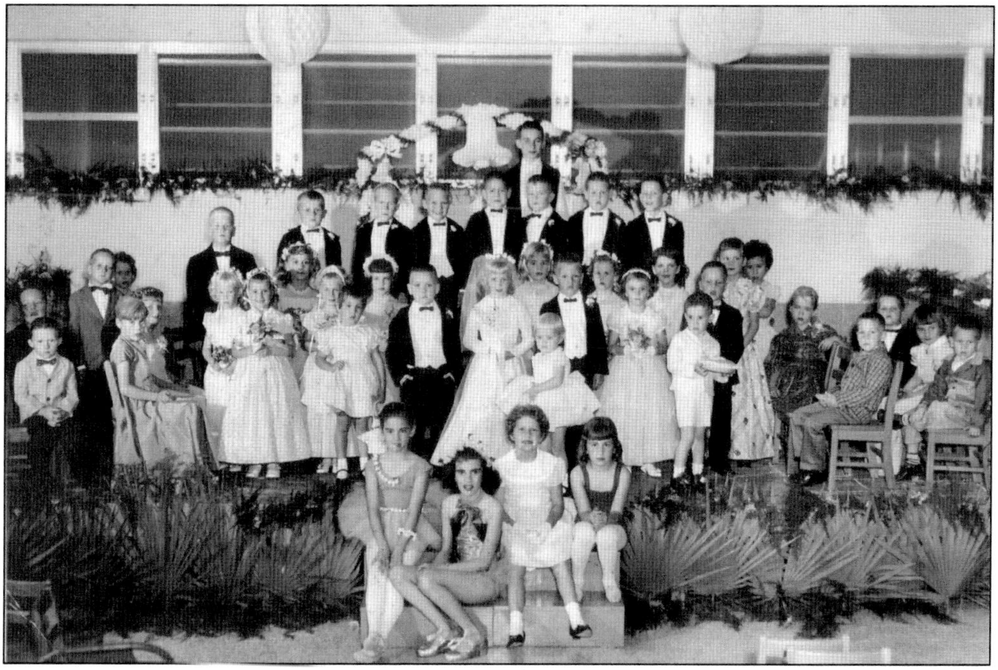

The most successful Parent Teacher Association fund-raiser in the 1960s was the Tom Thumb Wedding, with Billy Mead officiating the ceremony. (Courtesy of Euda Mary Alderman.)

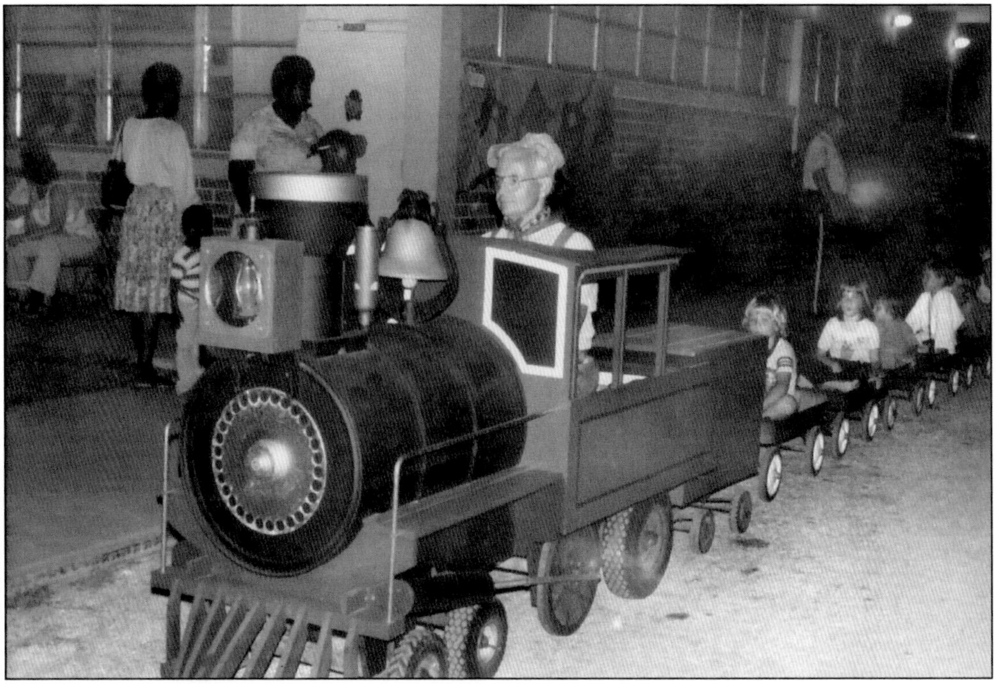

Dan Alderman built a train engine to fit over his riding lawn mower and then attached children's wagons to it so he could give "train rides" around the block during the annual school carnival. Children waited in line for "Mr. Dan's" ride, which became the most popular attraction for 20 years. (Courtesy of Euda Mary Alderman.)

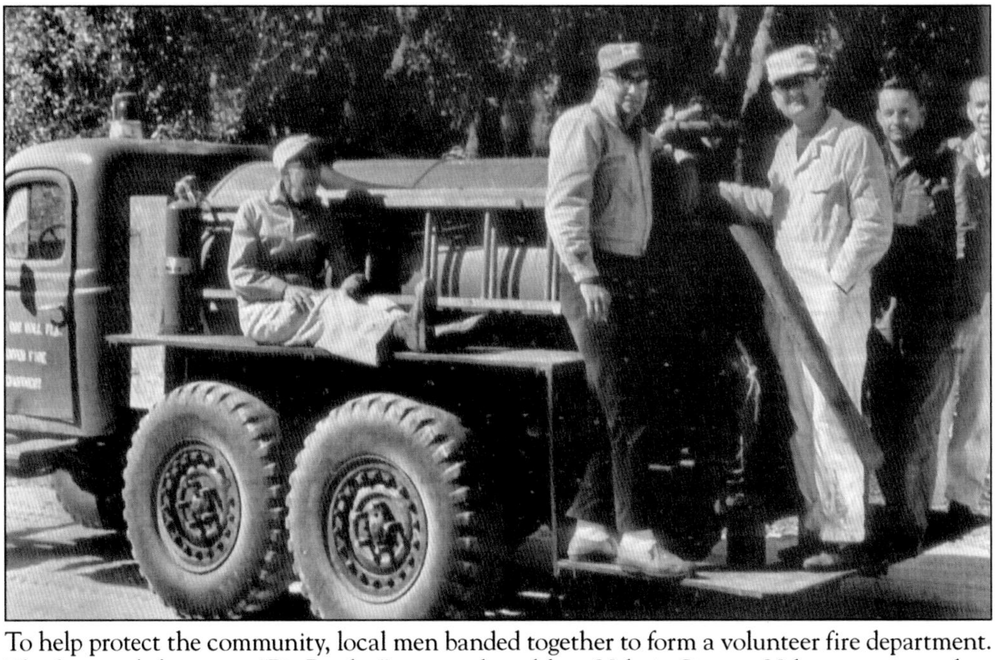

To help protect the community, local men banded together to form a volunteer fire department. The first truck, known as "Big Bertha," was purchased from Volusia County. Volunteers pictured on the truck are, from left to right, Harold Hicks (seated), Joe Kennard, Felix Zeigler, Dan Alderman, and Vernon Goodrich. (Courtesy of Euda Mary Alderman.)

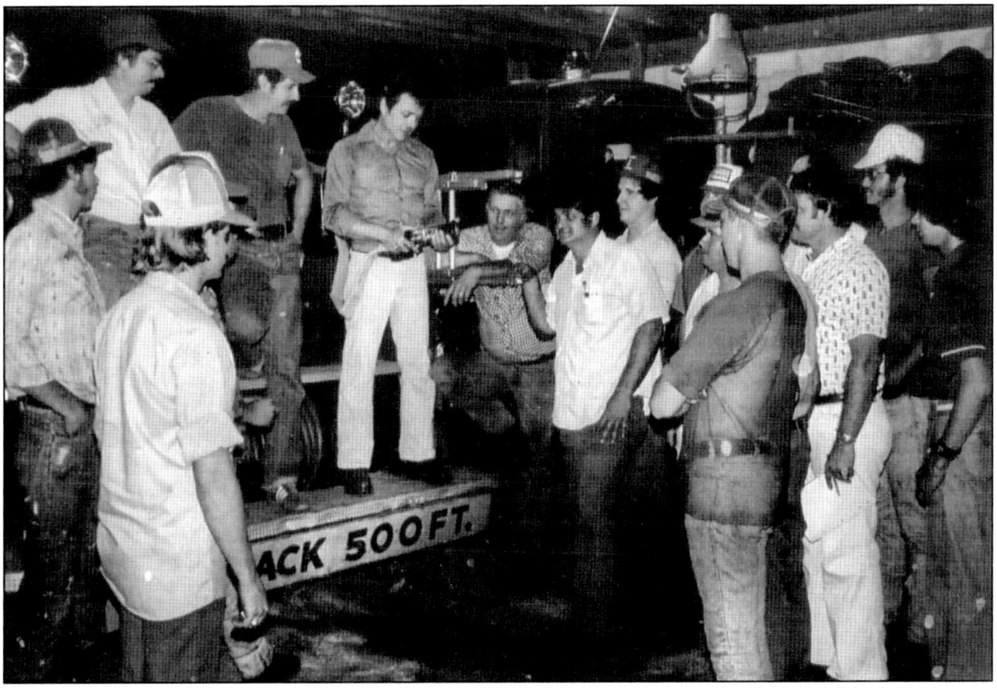

During the early days of the volunteer fire department, there were no funds available for training classes, so once a month, a state-certified fire instructor would travel to Oak Hill and train volunteers. (Courtesy of Kathy Bittle.)

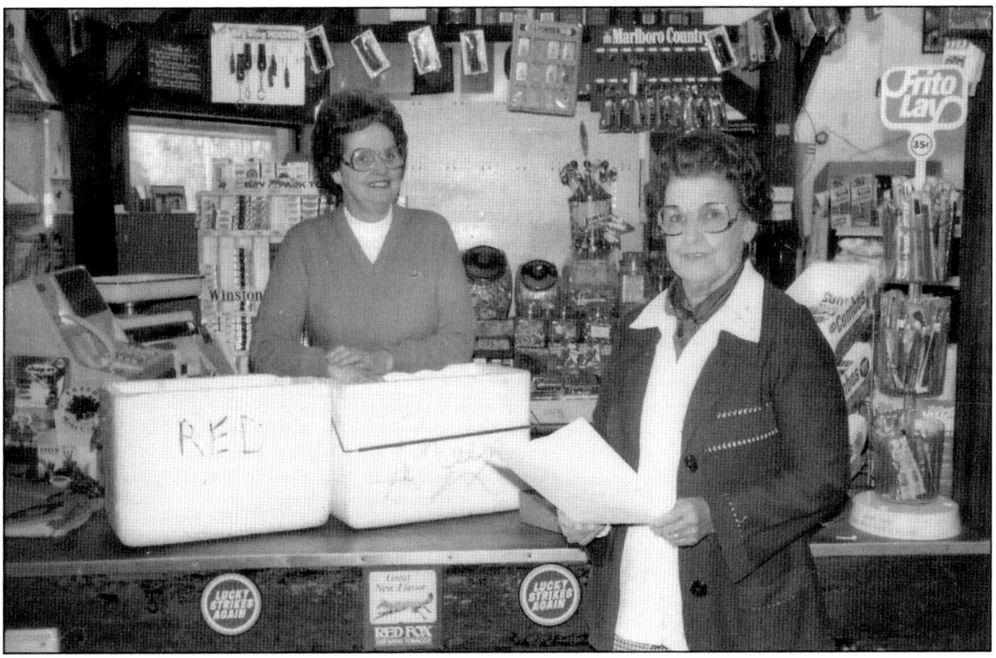

Volunteers from New Smyrna delivered Meals On Wheels to the Baldwin Store each day. Frances Johnson and her sister-in-law Arley Baldwin then delivered the hot meals to local elderly shut-ins. Johnson worked in this store for more than 40 years. The store was first owned by her father, then her brother, and then her niece.

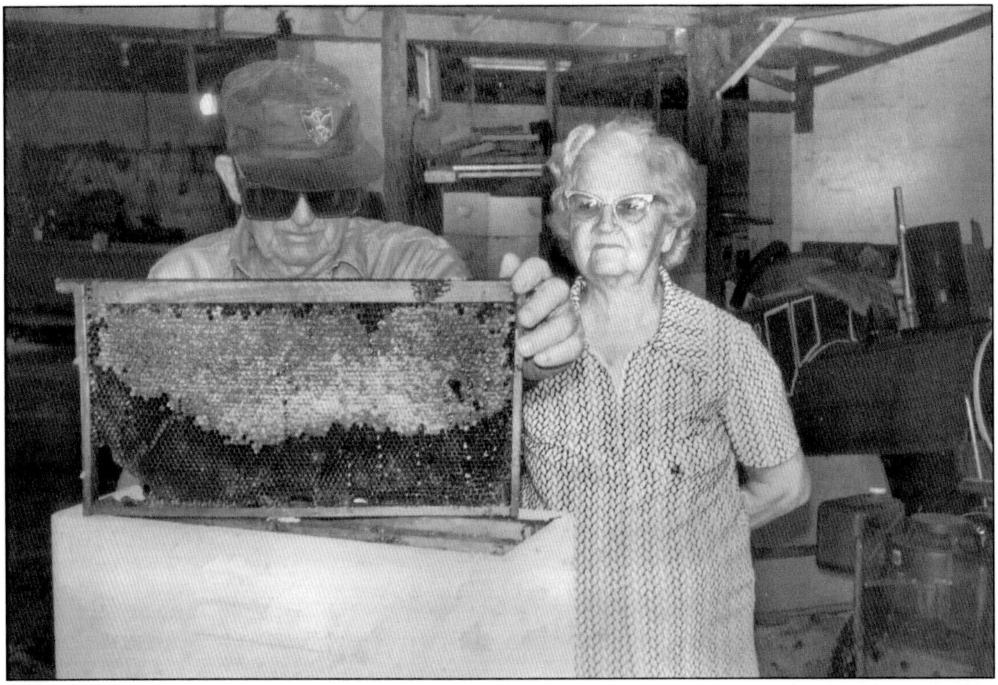

Oscar and Mamie Alderman's hobby was beekeeping, beginning with three hives. However, during World War II when sugar was scarce and rationed, people used honey as a sweetener. Through the years, their business expanded to 555 hives, which became their primary source of income in later years. (Courtesy of Euda Mary Alderman.)

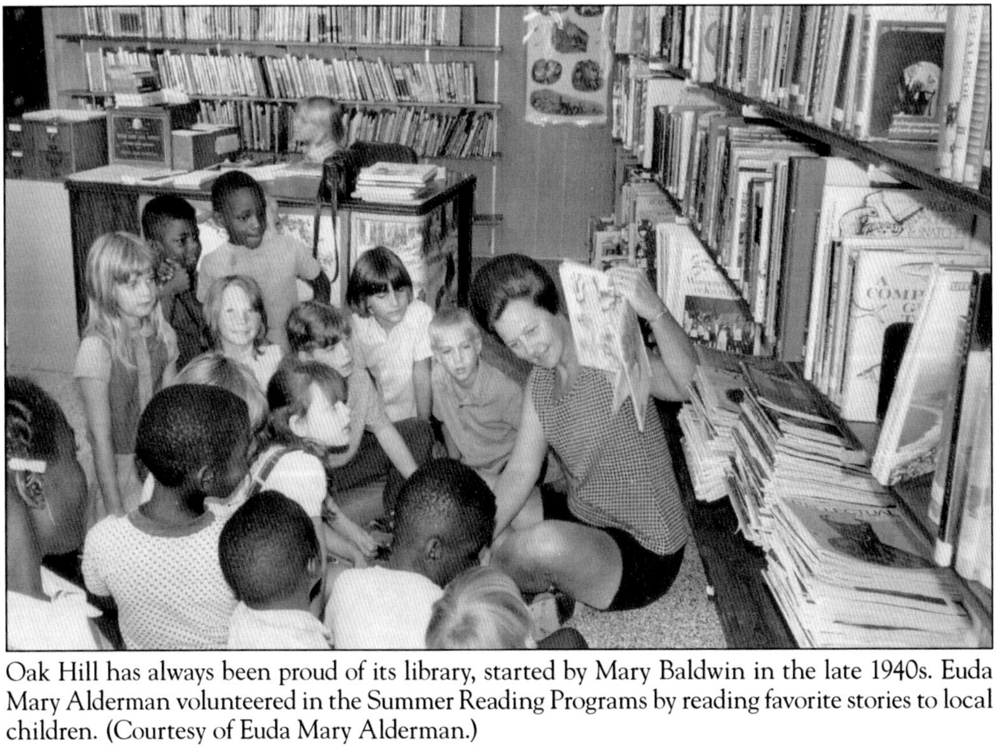

Oak Hill has always been proud of its library, started by Mary Baldwin in the late 1940s. Euda Mary Alderman volunteered in the Summer Reading Programs by reading favorite stories to local children. (Courtesy of Euda Mary Alderman.)

Mayor Clarence Goodrich Jr. and his wife, Ida Simmons Goodrich, celebrate their 25th wedding anniversary. Clarence worked at Patrick Air Force Base and Ida at NASA, entailing a long daily commute for both, but they enjoyed returning each evening to their Oak Hill home. (Courtesy of Ida Goodrich.)

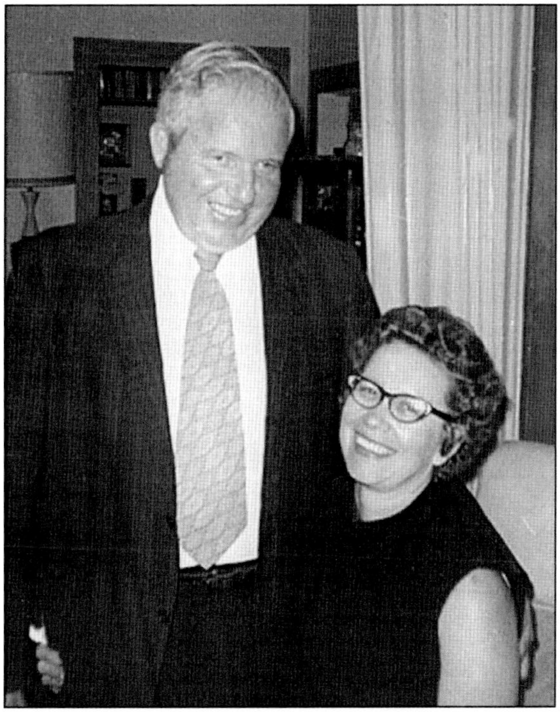

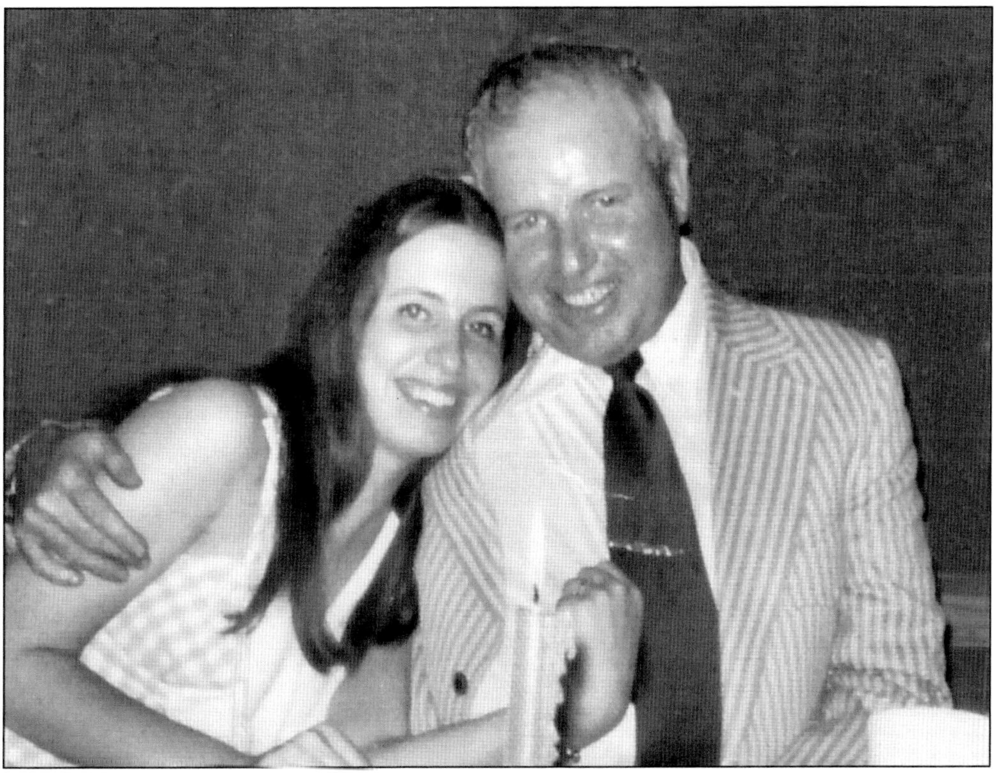

After taking the oath of office following an election win, Mayor Clarence Goodrich Jr. was congratulated by his daughter, Jennifer Bonamo. (Courtesy of Ida Goodrich.)

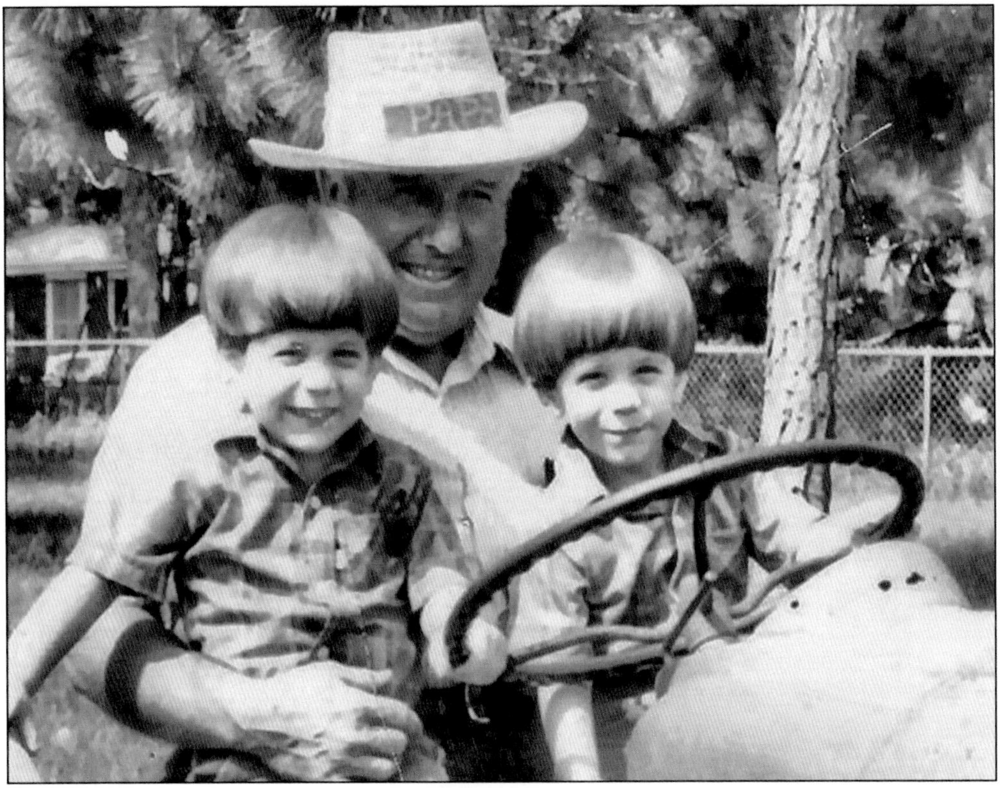

While working in his orange grove, Mayor Clarence Goodrich pauses to give his twin grandsons, Jon (left) and Jason Bonamo, a ride on his tractor. (Courtesy of Ida Goodrich.)

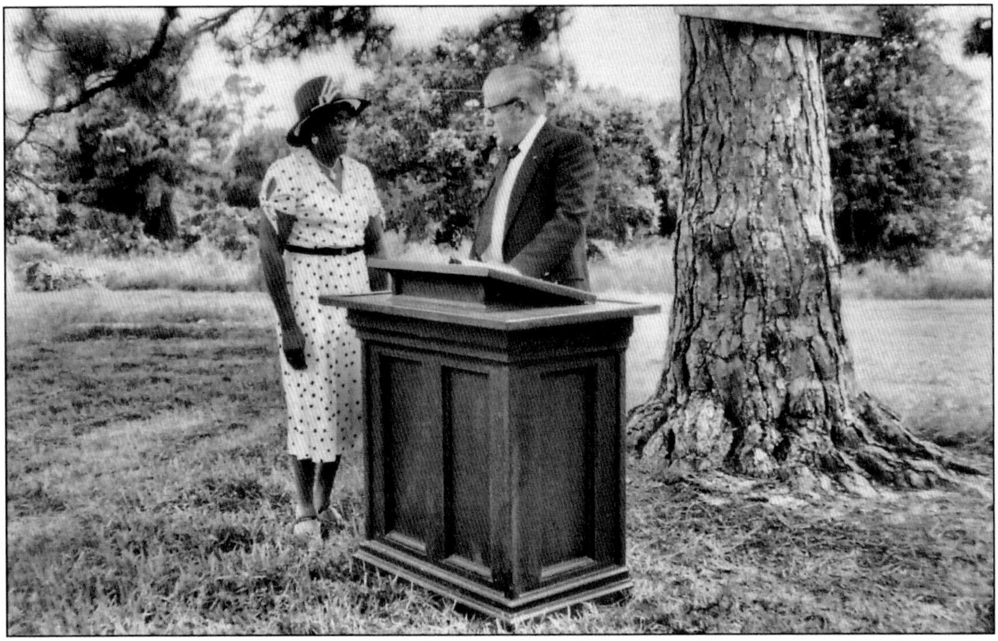

Nancy Cummings is honored by a proclamation read by Mayor Clarence Goodrich Jr. at the dedication ceremony of the new recreation park named for her. (Courtesy of Ida Goodrich.)

Millard Goodrich (at the wheel) hosts members of the London Symphony Orchestra (LSO) for an outing on Mosquito Lagoon. The LSO spent several weeks performing in Daytona Beach. (Courtesy of Ida Goodrich.)

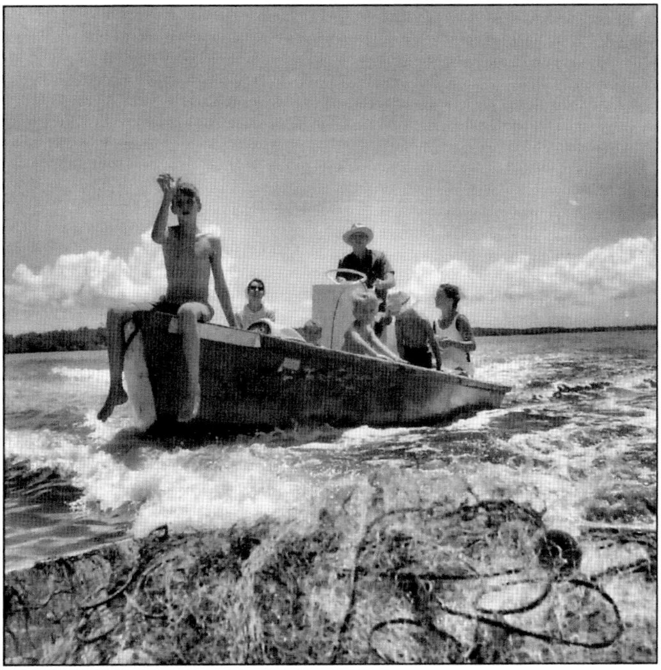

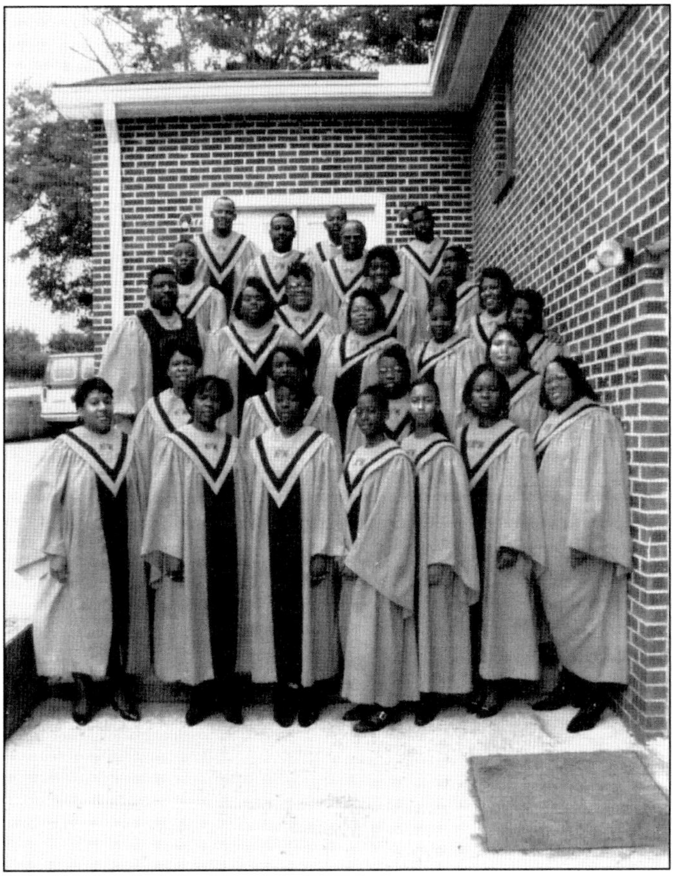

The Bible Way Church of God in Christ Choir shares its music with the community at the Christmas Tree Lighting Festival at Chung Park. (Courtesy of Johnnie Mae Golding.)

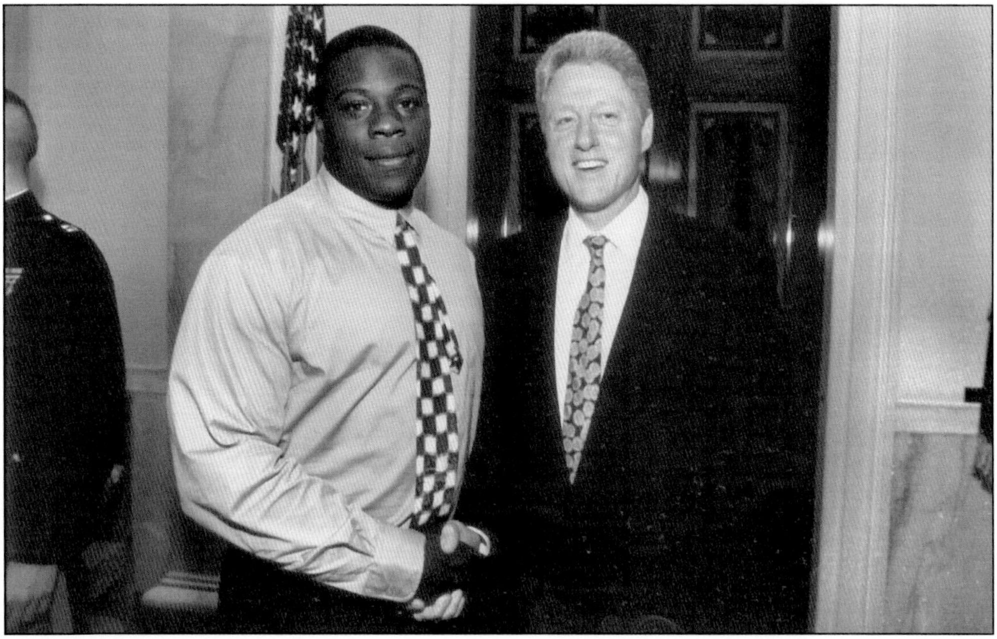

Oak Hill young people are excelling and accomplishing their dreams. Tim Beauchamp, son of Jose and Edith Beauchamp, represents this spirit. After winning the National College Championship as an outstanding Florida Gator football player, Beauchamp was invited to the White House and received personal congratulations from former U.S. president Bill Clinton. He went on to play for the Cleveland Browns, Green Bay Packers, and the Extreme Football League in Europe. (Courtesy of Edith Beauchamp.)

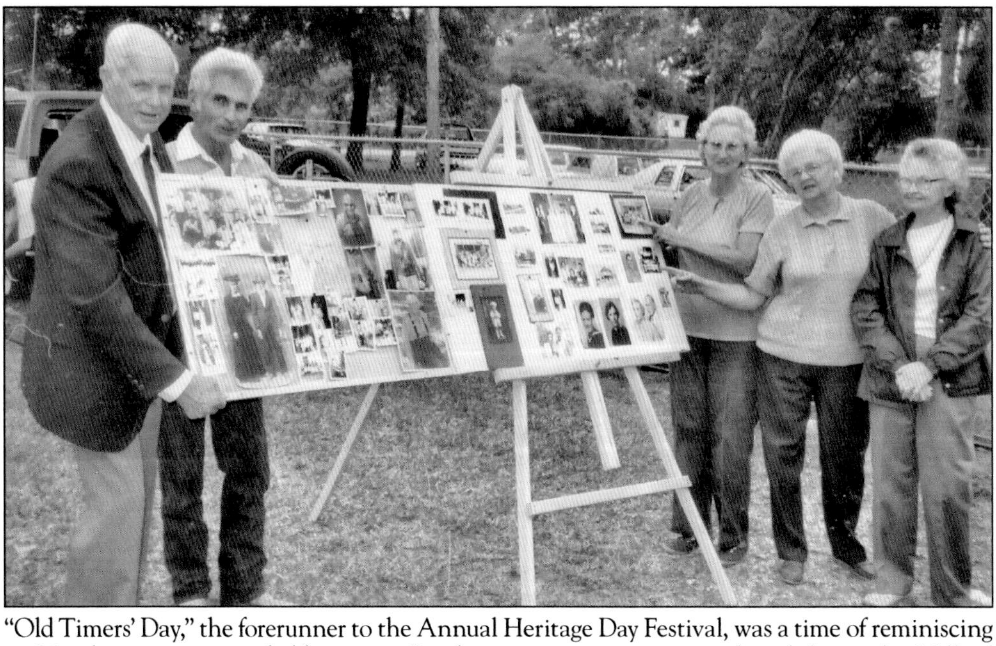

"Old Timers' Day," the forerunner to the Annual Heritage Day Festival, was a time of reminiscing and for sharing stories and old pictures. Displaying some memories are, from left to right, Millard Goodrich, Vance Jones, Evelyn Simmons, Jeanne Wheeler, and Lela Mae Avery. (Courtesy of Betty Bellamy.)

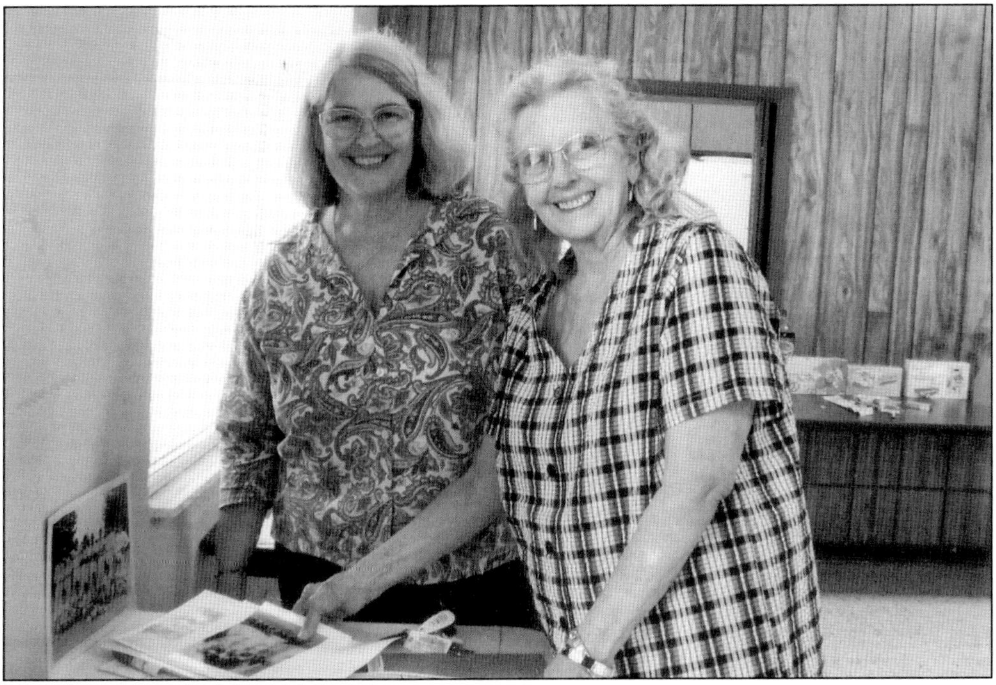

As Betty Bellamy (right), local community historian, and sister Bobbie Walker look through a display of pictures from the past, they recall their heritage in the community. Their mother, Lilly Burns, was a teacher here for many years, and their father became principal in 1939, retiring in 1957. He was an outstanding community leader, and the Volusia County School Board honored him by naming the local school after him: W. F. Burns Elementary.

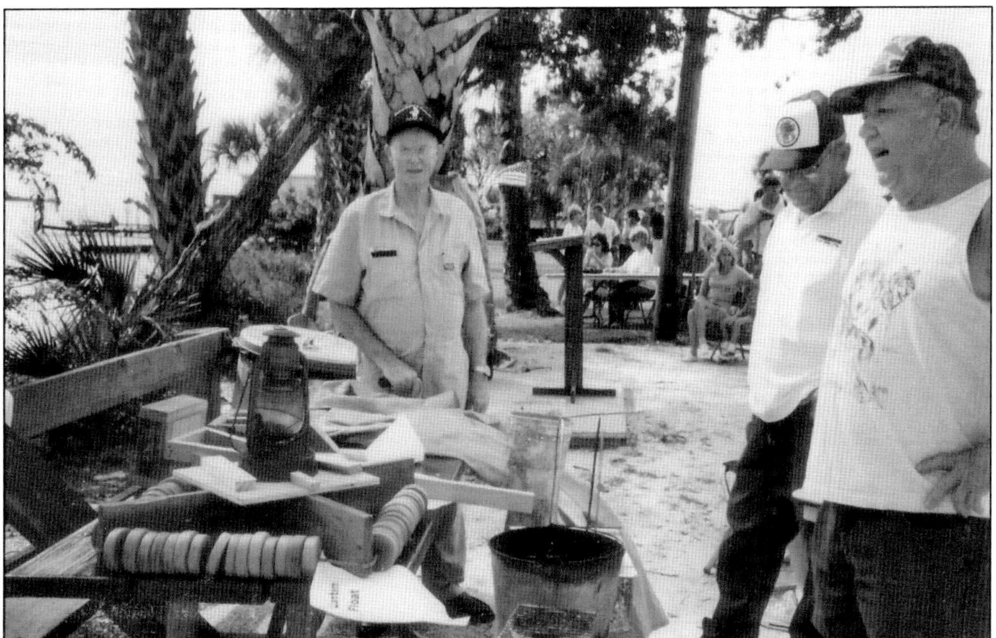

From left to right, Millard Goodrich, Jimmie Vann, and Curtis Vann teach about the old fishing days at Sunrise Park during the city's 70th anniversary celebration. (Courtesy of Betty Bellamy.)

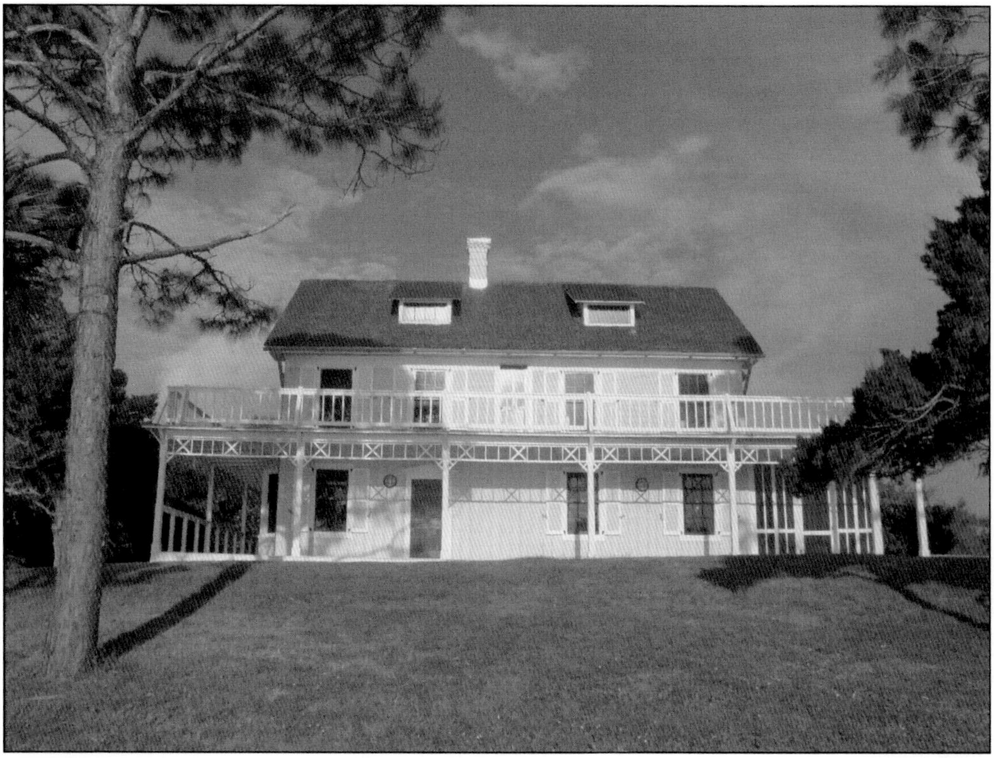

Seminole Rest, known to locals as "Snyder Hill," became part of the Canaveral National Seashore Park. The two houses on the Native American mounds were completely restored and remain open to the public as a historical site. (Courtesy of Ida Goodrich.)

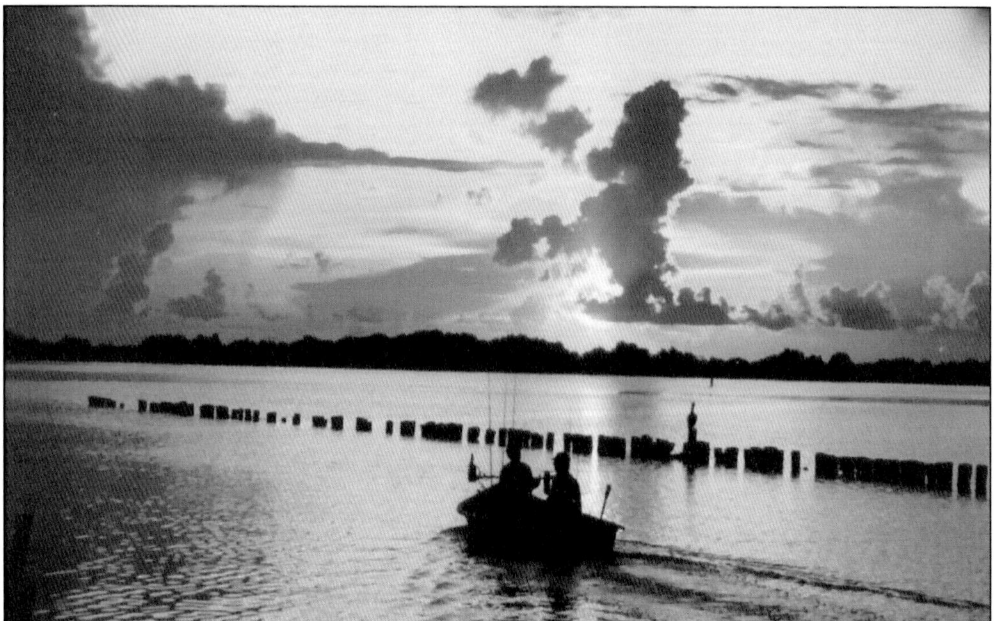

The waters of Mosquito Lagoon remain Oak Hill's treasure, and this familiar scene is a symbol of life in this unique community. (Courtesy of Ida Goodrich.)

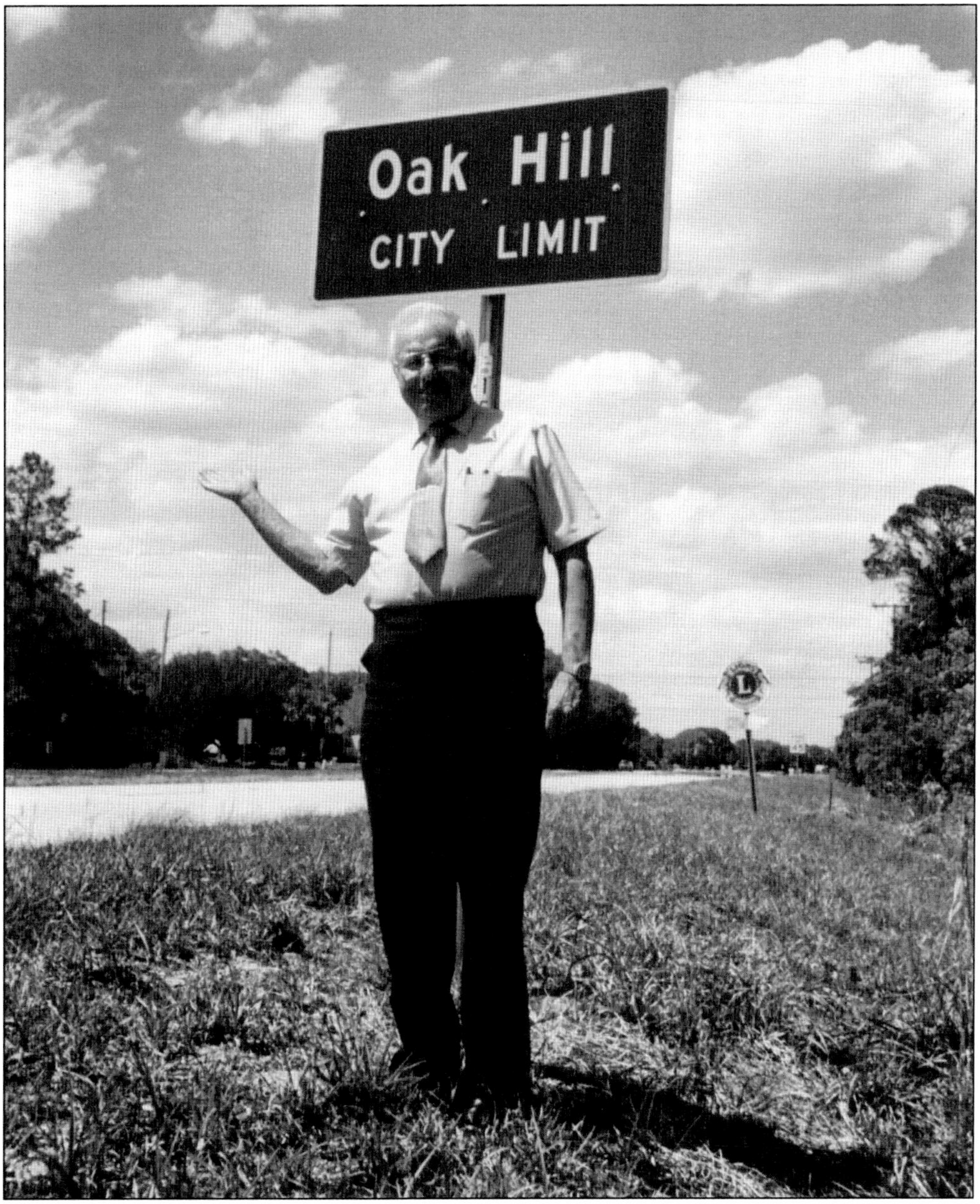

In the future, every time you see the city limit sign upon entering the community of Oak Hill, perhaps you will have a deeper respect and understanding for those who have chosen to call this place home. Present-day citizens should thank all those who have gone before them, demonstrating the values of sacrifice and hard work. Mayor Clarence Goodrich Jr. is just such a man. He chose to live in this community his entire life and served as mayor, without pay, for 27 years. Only his wife, Ida, and daughter, Jenny, know the personal sacrifice he made to lead this city forward from 1962 until 1989. He represented this city well and led it through difficult days, always fighting to preserve the heritage of a caring community spirit while continually moving the city forward. Whether you live here or just pass through, it is important to note that Oak Hill is a place in time where good people are friendly, still help their neighbors, and love to go fishing. (Courtesy of Ida Goodrich.)

Across America, People are Discovering Something Wonderful. *Their Heritage.*